Nick Duerden is a writer and freelan[...] has written widely on the arts, family [...] of two novels, a memoir on fatherhood[...]

Praise for Nick Duerden

'Incredibly moving.'
Guardian

'Entertaining.'
Telegraph

'Most books about pop stars focus on the way we turn average human beings into demi-gods. In writing a book about how they have to turn back into humans Nick Duerden has done both us and them a service.'
David Hepworth

'Funny, poignant and often inspirational.'
Mat Osman

'*Exit Stage Left* is the book I've long wanted to read about the PTSD-like after-effects of pop stardom – and Nick Duerden is the perfect writer for the job. The pop star's bittersweet lot is represented with flair and empathy.'
Pete Paphides, author of *Broken Greek*

'*Exit Stage Left* is a funny and poignant book, drawing on Duerden's considerable experience as a journalist and interviewer . . . he understands what motivates this strange bunch of people.'
Andy Miller, *Spectator*

'Fame is the brightest candle, but in this brilliant collection of interviews, Nick Duerden answers the question: what does a candle do after it's burned out?'
David Quantick

By Nick Duerden

Get Well Soon

A Life Less Lonely

Dishing the Dirt

The Smallest Things

NICK DUERDEN

EXIT STAGE LEFT

THE CURIOUS AFTERLIFE OF POP STARS

HEADLINE

First published in 2022 by
HEADLINE PUBLISHING GROUP

First published in paperback in 2022 by
HEADLINE PUBLISHING GROUP

3

Cataloguing in Publication Data is available from the British Library

ISBN 978 1 4722 7778 7

Designed and typeset by EM&EN
Printed and bound in Great Britain by Clays Ltd, Elcograf S.p.A.

HEADLINE PUBLISHING GROUP
An Hachette UK Company
Carmelite House
50 Victoria Embankment
London EC4Y 0DZ

www.headline.co.uk
www.hachette.co.uk

For those about to rock,

and who continue to do so,

over and over again

The pain I feel from The Slits ending is worse than splitting up with a boyfriend. This feels like the death of a huge part of myself, two whole thirds gone. I've got nowhere to go, nothing to do; I'm cast back into the world like a sycamore seed spinning into the wind.

Viv Albertine, *Clothes, Clothes, Clothes, Music, Music, Music, Boys, Boys, Boys*

I think nostalgia can be a real trap for an artist. When you reminisce about the good old days, you naturally see it all through rose-tinted spectacles. In my case in particular, I think that's forgivable, because I probably was literally wearing rose-tinted spectacles at the time, with flashing lights and ostrich feathers attached to them. But if you end up convincing yourself that everything in the past was better than it is now, you might as well give up writing music and retire.

Elton John, *Me*

In the world of rock, nobody ever gives up. Here, retirement is not an option.

David Hepworth, *A Fabulous Creation*

CONTENTS

INTRO 1

ONE – MARMALADE SKIES AND KALEIDOSCOPE EYES 19

TWO – THE DIFFICULT UMPTEENTH ALBUM 53

THREE – SCENESTERS 77

FOUR – TOP OF THE POPS 97

FIVE – INFAMY, INFAMY, THEY'VE ALL GOT IT IN FOR ME 133

SIX – THE PYRAMID STAGE 169

SEVEN – THE TROUBADOURS 205

EIGHT – ONE-HIT WONDERS 249

NINE – THE LEGENDS' SLOT 273

TEN – THE MAVERICKS 317

FADE OUT 363

ACKNOWLEDGEMENTS 367

INDEX 369

INTRO

About three weeks into my research for this book, as the world was closing its doors in an attempt to keep a pandemic at bay, I contacted Bill Drummond, arguably the wiliest pop provocateur of his era, and asked if he might like to talk to me on the subject of the curious afterlife of pop stars.

What happens, I wanted to know, to those women and men, whom we once so idolised, after their moment in the spotlight has been cursorily snuffed out, and they are replaced, with barely a pause, by the next big thing in an industry that has always fetishised the next big thing above all else? I was fascinated to learn how singers and musicians navigate the rest of their lives after that first flush of fame; how so many of them endure, and also why, occasionally, they don't; how they strive to reinvent themselves; and how they manage to keep life interesting for themselves when they've already had their crowning achievement. Is it really true that the muse can depart as quickly as it arrived, that there are only so many great songs any great pop star can churn out, after which . . . drivel? And is it true, as the American essayist Louis Menand had it in his 1997 *New Yorker* piece 'The Iron Law of Stardom', that stardom cannot last longer than three years? Stardom, Menand wrote, 'is the intersection of personality with history, a perfect congruence of the way the world happens to be and the way the star is. The world, however, moves on.' (If this is indeed true, somebody might want to inform Ed Sheeran.)

What's it like to be not just three years into your career, but thirteen, or thirty-three? Pop fans have elephant brains; we like reminders of halcyon days and the soundtracks of our youth. What this means is that while certain people will forever be Durannies, fanatical fans of the eighties group Duran Duran, they will remain far keener to hear 'Wild Boys' (1984) than, say, something off their disastrous 1995 covers album, *Thank You* – or, for that matter, anything the group have released this far into the twenty-first century, even if the new stuff merits attention.

And so, while the pop star may continue to live and breathe and function fairly cognitively, to draw their pensions *and* write new songs that crave a new audience, many in that audience would much rather they simply remained preserved in aspic, forever twenty-seven and pretty, treading water endlessly. If they are even permitted to still hang around today, it's only because their intermittent reappearances stir within us fond memories. Nostalgia is music's immutable side effect; best not mess with it. But is there dignity in this? More, is there creative satisfaction? Paul McCartney may be contentedly resigned to forever playing 'Hey Jude' in concert, safe in the knowledge that everything else he's ever done has also been mostly admired and dutifully indulged, but does, say, T'Pau's Carol Decker wish fans would stop clamouring for their 1987 number-one hit, 'China in Your Hand', and instead scream for something from their 2015 album, *Pleasure & Pain*, which reached number eighty-five in the charts?

So many questions. Perhaps too many. I didn't expect Bill Drummond to answer. He is, after all, the elusive type, the kind of man for whom *less is more* was always better than *too much*. I particularly wanted to speak to Drummond because he has, in a sense, done it all, but has done so in a way nobody else has, or could. If most other bands follow the same yellow brick road, Drummond was busy tearing up the tarmac with a pickaxe while dressed in a great long leather coat. He has been in bands (Liverpool's Big in Japan) and once shared a line-up with a pre-Frankie Goes to Hollywood Holly Johnson; he formed the record label Zoo Records with his friend David Balfe, the man who later signed Blur; and he has managed bands (Echo and the Bunnymen, the Teardrop Explodes) and produced their albums. He has worked within a major record label (WEA), where he attempted to launch the careers of new acts, including Brilliant and Strawberry Switchblade. And he was a foreboding frontman (but not singer) of the most unusual and unpredictable bands of the late 1980s and early nineties, beginning with the Justified Ancients of Mu Mu, the Timelords and the KLF, releasing a string of brilliantly inventive singles like 'Doctorin' the Tardis', 'What Time Is Love?', '3 a.m. Eternal' and 'Last Train to Trancentral' – bangers all, and several of which reached number one across the world. With his KLF co-conspirator Jimmy Cauty, he even wrote a book called *The Manual (How to Have a Number One the Easy Way)*.

He was a maverick, a Svengali, potentially crazy, and very likely Machiavellian. In that great leather trench coat of his, he looked like a henchman from a Hitchcock movie, and boasted a great slab of ominous face that, in another era, another calling, might just have been immortalised on Mount Rushmore. In 1992, the KLF were awarded Best British Group at the Brit Awards. The acknowledgement failed to flatter them but did titillate them. They agreed to perform at the ceremony, but only on the condition of doing so with grindcore act Extreme Noise Terror. Part of their performance utilised fake machine guns, which they turned on the first few rows – comprising record industry executives clad in bespoke suits, with the requisite cocaine residue about the nostrils – pretending to spray them with bullets in a display of mass execution.

During the same show, the British singer-songwriter Beverley Craven played a rendition of her hit 'Promise Me' on the piano, wearing an elegant silk purple blouse, and singing with a closed-eyed intensity that prompted fetching crows' feet to sprout at her temples. Craven didn't feel moved to deposit a dead sheep at the entrance of the aftershow party, but the KLF did.

If Drummond and Cauty were trying to convey the contempt with which they viewed the music industry they themselves were a part of, then they did an effective job of it. That same year, they announced their immediate retirement and deleted their entire back catalogue – an act which, from a financial standpoint, was like burning a million pounds.

A year later, now masquerading as the K Foundation, which celebrated the arts in a manner that required quotation marks around the word 'celebrated', they set up a £40,000 award – double the amount of the Turner Prize Award – to recognise the 'worst artist of the year'. Its inaugural recipient was Rachel Whiteread, who had also just won the Turner. She was not particularly amused. A year later, the K Foundation then *literally* burned a million pounds in a ceremony on the Scottish island of Jura. The ceremony was quite a to-do: they brought witnesses, the press. They waited until sundown. It was cold; they wore coats. And they filmed it, because of course they did. What else would one expect from art terrorists?

There were reasons for the burning of so much money, but the reasons changed depending on who you asked and when you asked, or else were never particularly clear in the first place, perhaps not even to Drummond and Cauty themselves. The watching world reacted just as they'd hoped: with horror, and the referencing of starving children in Africa.

Ever since, Bill Drummond has been circling the sidelines, anything but inactive. He has written more books, and continues to dabble in a kind of performance art, though he would no doubt loathe the description. He has shined shoes on the streets of Venice and given away daffodils to strangers in cities around the world. In 2017, he set up a choir; the same year, he and Cauty published a novel, *2023: A Trilogy*. It was difficult to follow.

If it's true that pop stars can struggle with what to do next in order to forge a sufficiently satisfying career after their commercial highpoint, then Bill Drummond – mischievously, impishly, gloriously – is surely the exception that proves the rule.

Anyway, the email.

I didn't expect him to engage with me, but in fact he responded with a gratifying swiftness. He thanked me for my invitation, then went on to explain that, as I may or may not know (I did not), he had recently gone through a period of answering all invitations to be interviewed by requesting from the interviewer four questions he had not been asked before, in writing. He then answered these four questions in writing, a transaction undertaken only on the understanding that he'd subsequently use the Q&A exchange in a book of his own, a kind of quid pro quo. (I was not aware of this book.) He did twenty-five interviews, answering 100 questions in total. The book was called *100*, and was published in a run of just 1,000 copies. 'They sold,' he explained to me, 'and that was that.'

His next interaction with the public was something called the 'Sixty Second Talks' project, a series of video performances in which he talks (in his pleasingly gruff Scottish accent, and full of droll enthusiasm) direct to camera on a series of topics – 'Pish on the Red Carpet', 'The Birth and Death of The Zoo (1978–1979)' – in one minute, more or less. There were sixty of these.

He was now responding to each new media request, the suggestion being that invariably there were *always* media requests, by offering up a 'Forty Second Play'.

In other words, if I understood correctly (and it was by no means certain at this point that I did), he was happy to engage with me, but only by his rules, on his terms. I would outline the sort of questions I'd have liked to ask him had we been speaking, and he would respond by writing me a Forty Second Play.

I found myself looking forward to receiving it, and woke each morning reaching for my phone with more purpose than I would normally muster at 7 a.m.

The play, however, was not forthcoming. Drummond was busy, distracted. We had recently gone into lockdown, this being the spring of 2020, and he was wrestling with the terrifying concept of homeschooling his young children. I left him to live his life, but several months on, I politely nudged him, and, very graciously, one day in early September that year, he went to his local café in north London, perhaps with a laptop – though I prefer to imagine him with a feathered ink pen and a scroll of parchment – to make good on his promise. I could use the play in my book, he said, so long as he could feature our exchange in a book of his own, too.

'Deal,' I said.

A minute later, my computer chimed with its arrival. At first, the screen went black, and I feared, for a queasy half-moment, that I was subject to a Drummond prank, a K Foundation virus, perhaps. I felt I could almost hear him cackling from his dank, windowless lair. But then the screen quickly came back to life. I unclenched, and read.

'At times, Bill Drummond is asked to pass comment,' the attachment began. 'At times, Bill Drummond responds to being asked to pass comment by instigating one of his other selves to write a Forty Second Play. One of these other selves takes the name of Tenzing Scott Brown. Three of these Forty Second Plays were written at the corner table of the ____Café N16. They were written over a period of three days in early September 2020. The titles of these three plays are:

The Glorified Walking Stick
There Is an Afterlife
and
The Public Execution of Popstars.'

The first two plays referenced, respectively, the BBC political correspondent Laura Kuenssberg and the band he'd once managed, Scottish one-hit wonder Strawberry Switchblade. The third play was, in effect, 'mine', but then there was an additional one, which had the tantalising title of *The Nik Kershaw Mini Fig*. It was included, Drummond wrote, 'just in case *The Public Execution of Pop Stars* is shite'.

I reproduce the latter two 'plays' here now, with permission.

THE PUBLIC EXECUTION OF POP STARS

The Public Execution of Pop Stars is a Forty Second Play by Tenzing Scott Brown.

The Public Execution of Pop Stars has been written in response to the writer Nick Duerden requesting an interview with Bill Drummond for a proposed book. A book about 'how singers and musicians navigate their life after the first flush of fame; how they endure, reinvent themselves, and keep life interesting for themselves.'

This request came in late April 2020, at the height of the first wave of the global pandemic. This request sparked off a brief flurry of emails between Nick Duerden and Bill Drummond.

It is now the early Autumn of the same year. The second wave is threatening.

What follows is the Forty Second Play written by Tenzing Scott Brown in response to this request. As a play it has been much informed by the previous Forty Second Play, *There Is An After Life*.

Two women, deep into their middle years, dressed in black and white, polka-dot dresses and red ribbons in their hair, enter the stage. They are carrying guitars. They face the audience – a worldwide audience. And in unison they recite the following lines:

We are Strawberry Switchblade.

We exist to confront the world with certain truths.

It has been brought to our attention that mankind is the
    only life form on earth that is hardwired to destroy each
    other. And in turn destroy themselves.

This hardwiring must be unwired, if mankind is to survive.

Or . . .

We propose a departure from the tried and tested forms
    of self-destruction. A departure that will celebrate Pop
    Music as the most vibrant and wonderful art form that
    has ever existed and ever will exist.

We propose that any future Pop Singer or Pop Group of
    any past, present or future genre, that has had a top
    forty record, and then follows it up with a record that
    fails to make the top forty will be taken to a designated
    public space and executed in front of the people. The
    failed Pop Singer or Pop Group will be given the choice
    of a noose hanging from a gallows or a razor sharp
    guillotine.

It is this course of action that will truly celebrate Pop Music
    as the most vibrant and wonderful art form that has
    ever existed and ever will exist.

Thank you.

The End

Strawberry Switchblade then pick up their guitars and start to sing their song Trees & Flowers.

And the audience will then compare and contrast the beauty of this song with the power of theatre to impact social change as opposed to merely entertain.

This is the second play.

THE NIK KERSHAW MINI FIG

The Nik Kershaw Mini Fig is a Forty Second Play by Tenzing Scott Brown.

The Nik Kershaw Mini Fig has been written as an alternative to *The Public Execution Of Pop Stars*. As in, in case *The Public Execution of Pop Stars* is shite.

The Nik Kershaw Mini Fig has only one character – a Lego mini fig of former pop star – Nik Kershaw. He addresses the audience directly.

Tenzing Scott Brown invited Prince to write a foreword to this Forty Second Play. What follows is the foreword:

Hi, my name is Prince. I used to be a famous pop star in the 1980s. What made me famous was that I was a genius. It's what got me noticed. But then I started doing stuff that made me look mad. I started to stop using my name and used a squiggle instead. And making records to annoy my record company, records that were indulgent. And although I was a genius, people stopped buying my records. So I changed my name back to Prince and did a world tour where I was a caricature of how I used to look in my purple patch in 1984. But this world tour was in 2007. It was as if the Beatles had reformed in 1987 and they went out touring as middle-aged men but wearing their collarless Beatles suits they wore in 1964. It was pathetic. But it is what the fans wanted. They loved me for it. So I took too many painkillers and died.

I am afraid I do not know who Nik Kershaw or Mini Figs are.

That was the foreword by Prince.

This is the Forty Second Play called *The Nik Kershaw Mini Fig*:

Hi my name is Nik Kershaw.
I used to be a famous pop star in the 1980s.
What made me famous was that I could write good pop
    songs and I was cute.
But then people stopped buying my records even though
    I could still write good pop songs and I was still cute.

It is now thirty something years later.
And I still make records.
But all my fans want to hear is my old hits from the 1980s.
So I have decided to become a Lego mini fig of myself.
And using a stop-motion app I have on my phone, remake
    all my old videos from the 1980s using Lego.
I think it is what all pop stars from the 80s should do.
Fans will love it.
And it keeps you busy.
And you never grow old.
If Prince were alive today, it is what he should be doing.
It is either that or the gardening.
I've got my own YouTube channel and everything.

The End

This was the end of our communication.

I read these plays twice, and then a third time, always with a certain glee. What Bill Drummond is getting at here, I think, is just how thankless a task it can be for the pop star – whether an unusually gifted one or a rather run-of-the-mill example – who dares try to endure beyond their Warholian fifteen minutes. By rights, they are supposed to be a flash in the pan, a pin-up who disappears before we have the chance to get bored of them, thus leaving in their wake slippery moments of throwaway bliss. Do we really want our favourite acts today to endure for a thousand tomorrows, to go on long after their commercial peak and release more albums still – personal albums, experimental ones, perhaps even concept albums – compelling us to bear witness as they continue to stretch themselves long after their creativity has waned? Don't those who do hang around have the good sense to simply stick to What People Really Want: a regurgitation of the old hits and nothing but, until the end of (their) time?

The fact that so many of them do not possess this notional good sense is why Bill Drummond, for one, wants to guillotine them – to stop, say, Rod Stewart from endlessly covering the Great American Songbook, to prevent Oasis making their cocaine record, and to block Paul McCartney from recording with frog choruses. Pop music is *supposed* to be fleeting; likewise, its players. It's good while it lasts, yes, but it's also yesterday's newspapers, to be replaced by today's edition. There is a certain thrill held for the band that lives fast and dies young, a thrill even to the one-hit wonder, to the act that manages to create something perfect, which goes out into the world and resonates wildly, and which is not then diminished and sullied when that same act later announces to the watching world: 'And now for my operatic concept album on the ravages of global warming, played mostly on the mandolin – please bear with me.'

Bill Drummond feels this way because this is precisely what Drummond did with the KLF. He pulled the plug while everybody was still wanting more. But then, this is deeply anomalous behaviour: we cannot reasonably expect the artists behind our favourite songs – clever, artistic people, with much to offer – to suddenly and politely disappear just in case we grow tired of them over time.

Can we?

In 1993, Billy Joel released his last album, *River of Dreams*, and aside from one further album of classical piano pieces, has felt no compulsion to write anything else. He still enjoys playing the hits catalogue live, he's sold hundreds of millions of records, and he's proved his worth. What else is there to say?

'I know some artists struggle with the idea of being relevant, [but] I stopped buying that a long time ago,' Joel told *Billboard* magazine in 2019.

This hints at someone entirely at peace with their identity, and as such marks Joel out as unusual. Most artists view things a little differently. They may have had their time in the sun, their three ironclad years, and they may have been forcefully shuffled to the margins by tastemakers wielding figurative brooms, but they don't really go away; they don't disappear and stop doing what they've always done. *Of course* they don't – they're *artists*, that breed of humans who were never cut out for the traditional nine-to-five, for the daily commute, for cookie-cutter conventionality. So even after they've reluctantly parted ways with the zeitgeist, the songs keep coming, they keep plugging away. This might actually be when their true mettle is revealed, when they can – and often do – come to seem genuinely inspirational. They've survived the sonic boom of youth and its attendant creative spurt, but they've ever since refocused and realigned their ambition and expectation. Still, they stride on.

And we, the fans, keep listening. In the age of streaming, it's never been cheaper, or easier, to do so. Bands and artists that have long since fallen off the radar continue to attract hundreds of thousands, often millions, of streams a month. Global pandemics permitting, they play live regularly. And they continue to make new music *all the bloody time*: the break-up album, the going-back-to-my-roots album. And if, occasionally, new music does run dry, no matter, because for heritage acts, the well is bottomless: there is always a new greatest hits selection to curate; a back catalogue to reimagine acoustically, or with orchestral accompaniment, or perhaps with added dance beats. The tenth anniversary of a number-one hit single; the twentieth anniversary of that seminal album, celebrations for which will see them comfortably back on the arena circuit again, fortunes revived.

Ostensibly, pop music exists within an industry obsessed with the idea of novelty. There is little more viscerally asphyxiating, or marketable, than an act that emerges seemingly out of nowhere as an instantaneous approximation of perfection. This prompts record companies to try and replicate that ungraspable magic with another singer, another band, whom they hope will follow in the trailblazer's wake, just as another singer, and another band, waits impatiently in the wings behind *them*, and so on and so on, like aeroplanes looming into Heathrow, one after the other, an endless line of blinking lights on the horizon. First there was Elvis Presley, who did things with his hips and lips and hair – *at the same time* – and who seemed to have about him more heat than dynamite, and who could, as Bob Dylan had it, 'take songs to other planets'; there was U2, who, if they didn't quite invent stadium rock, nevertheless made it their own, and without whom the stadium-rock industry of the twenty-first century wouldn't look the way it now does; and there was Adele, who could so capably articulate the bruises our hearts take in love that the power ballad is now the lingua franca of all truly effective pop.

And behind them: so many wannabe Elvises, so many half-powered U2s, so many anaemic Adeles. Thank you, next.

The best thing the Beatles ever did, in a career filled with best things, was to split in 1970. This way, they never tainted their canon, nor diluted it, but rather allowed time to ripen its individual notes like fine wine. (ABBA did likewise a decade or so later, before, a full 40 years later, they would inconveniently disprove this theory by releasing new music that sounded just like their old music, and seduced everyone all over again. There is only one ABBA.)

Janis Joplin, too much of a firework to be contained by the 1972 folk scene, died at the age of twenty-seven. So did Jimi Hendrix, Jim Morrison, Kurt Cobain, Amy Winehouse. Each gone before their time, with so much potential still to realise. But because they never got to scale their peaks, they never had to descend, either. They bailed out on top.

As for all the others, they survived. They're still here.

To be reckless enough to try and carve out an enduring career in pop, then, is not for the faint-hearted. By their very definition, pop stars tend to be exceptional people, not just gifted and talented, but preternaturally driven to be heard, to matter, to enthral. They are indulged and cosseted, cocooned from normality and inflated in ego. They lose their sense of perspective, and wear sunglasses indoors. Some of them are not nice people, not nice at all, but we remain mostly in thrall to them. Their experiences mark them out, and they are defined by them, sometimes ruinously.

In the many written accounts of what happened to the twelve men who have walked on the surface of the moon, the same two questions are repeated over and over, ad infinitum:

1) What was it like?

and

2) What did he do next?

Many of the thirteen were reported to have later succumbed to depression, others to alcoholism. Each were branded in some way by their achievement, by having blazed so brightly and left such a lingering, if steadily evaporating, trail; a group of people whose peak moment in life was already consigned to the past.

Achieving pop glory is, of course, in no way comparable to setting foot on the moon. It was always far easier, in decades past, for a bunch of hopefuls masquerading under some fanciful name to appear on *Top of the Pops* than it was to walk in zero gravity. But *pop stardom* and *astronaut* have always featured highly on people's dream ambition lists, and those who manage it remain, literally, *extra*ordinary.

And so relegation to civvy street isn't always easy, and the journey a former punk icon, say, is forced to take, from having terrified the nation's youth to endorsing a particular brand of butter, is long and winding and full of pathos. Or consider the tall bassist from one of the nineties' most strident bands who found himself driving a van for a living not six months after their final farewell tour. (When the offer of a reunion came a few years later, the tall bassist didn't have to consider his answer for long.) Life is a complicated business for all of us, and perhaps more so for those who still believe they are not entirely suited for the humdrum. It's not everyone who has the ability to walk out on a stage in front of thousands, possessed of the conviction that they command it. Those who do are never going to exit that stage entirely willingly – and nor do we tend to let them, either.

So they carry on, fighting – in the minds of their followers, at least – the good fight. They get older, and heavier, and more careful about their diet and the drugs they take. Their hair thins out; they become veterans of AA and NA. Some grow disillusioned and cynical; others feel nothing but gratitude that they still get to do the thing they love most, and still have an audience, irrespective of size, that appreciates their efforts. Correspondingly, their music becomes more demonstrably expressive, and more truthful, more capable of touching the heart.

Why do we remain so inexorably drawn to them, still fascinated by those whose posters we once so lovingly hung on our bedroom walls? What makes us so enduringly compelled by those who choose to sing songs for a living? And why do so many artists continue to do it, keep on putting down words that rhyme, and writing appropriately catchy melodies, over and over again? What's it like to still be at it at forty-five, at sixty, and how does it compare to the sensations it conjured two decades previously? Is it easy to redefine your goals, to come back down the mountain? And, ultimately, why is it so hard to walk away from it all?

ONE

MARMALADE SKIES AND KALEIDOSCOPE EYES

1

'I don't think I deserve anything because I rejected my art, the very worst thing an artist can do'

At the beginning, all was good and everything was swollen with promise.

The Only Ones, a cantankerous punk act from London that had formed in 1976 and then gigged relentlessly with the gritty purpose all half-decent punk acts had back then, were ready at last to announce themselves to the world. It was 1978. By this stage, the Sex Pistols had happened, so too the Clash, the Buzzcocks and Generation X, and so, the band figured, the ground was fertile and ready for them. Their single, 'Another Girl, Another Planet', was a freewheeling racket sung in the reediest of voices but packed with a snarling swagger typical of the time. It didn't break the Top 40, though great records rarely did back in the late 1970s. It didn't even make the Top 50, but this was fine: it allowed the music press to hail them as a great overlooked force whose day would soon come, like a reckoning.

The music press was wrong, as it turned out. The song itself would indeed be later hailed a classic, but the band never lived up to its promise. Instead, all that potential ultimately dashed against the rocks of their instinctive self-destruction. In other words: drugs.

By 1980, they still felt reasonably confident of a late break-through. Punk had died by then, but the Only Ones were now better than ever. That year they were in America, supporting the Who, playing huge arenas. But they were nervous. They needed fortification.

Peter Perrett, the singer, had always been prone to hedonism, but only, he points out, 'in my relaxation time. I tended to keep it – the drugs – to my downtime. So when we were working, when I was on tour, I wouldn't take drugs with me. Of course, if they happened to *appear*, then, okay, that wasn't my doing, that was fate. But I did try to keep them separate, because that's the way I felt I'd do my best work.

'But then, towards the end of the tour, they became a larger part, and they started to appear more often than not. I suppose I was already going in that direction,' he concedes, 'but I hadn't yet . . . *surrendered* to that way of life.'

He would in time, but right now, halfway through 1980, somewhere in California, Perrett, a sallow youth from Camberwell, south London, was enjoying the sunshine. He was four years into his career, and had come to realise that, while patience was a virtue, it wasn't always something he had ready access to. The band had released three albums, each to good reviews, but there was a creeping sense that their time had passed, that punk was already as old as the three-day week, and that the new decade was looking for something else.

He focused, for the time being, on what was in front of him: big shows each night supporting a stadium-rock act, good money, plenty of downtime, plenty of drugs. He couldn't want for anything else.

'When your life has suddenly taken off, and all your dreams come true, you want to explore those dreams, don't you? It's very tempting to do just that, to explore the entire universe. This wasn't really work, it's something you enjoy, and I think, maybe for me, I enjoyed being able to detach myself, I enjoyed the calmness, and the escape, from all responsibility. A lot of songwriters are sensitive human beings, aren't they? Perhaps that's where their passion comes from? But it is tempting, sometimes, to retreat from that.'

By obliterating himself each night, lying back, his eyes rolling to a point high above his eyelids, Perrett retreated.

When the tour reached California, however, there was an altercation that would conspire to colour the rest of his life. Parking his hire car outside that night's venue, he got into an argument with a man who wanted him to park elsewhere. When Perrett declined, the man became angry, and started to strangle him.

Perrett would later explain that he was used to having big people around to protect him, the Who's security guards mostly, but right now, here, he was alone and defenceless, and far too slight to fight back. Punks always were skin and bone. He could feel his windpipe being crushed.

'The only weapon I had,' he later explained in *Mojo* magazine, 'was the car.'

Managing to get free of the man's grip, he ran to the car, jumped in, started the engine and drove – not to an appropriate parking place, but rather, directly *at* his attacker.

'He had a smile on his face, and in slow motion, it changed to a look of total horror. The last I saw of him, he disappeared over some bins,' Perrett told *Mojo*. 'Then I drove off and felt really great, and then it dawned on me what I'd done.'

In the state of California, it isn't legal to run over someone with a car, even if provoked into doing so. It also isn't legal to flee the scene. Perrett, already paranoid from all the drugs he was ingesting daily, convinced himself, in those moments of clarity that panic sometimes allows, that he not only couldn't possibly hand himself in to the police, but that he had to get out of the country fast.

What happened next happened quickly. The Only Ones' part on the Who's US tour was cut short. The headliners were unimpressed, as were Perrett's own band.

A few days later, they were back on the East Coast, awaiting the flight home.

'Alan [Mair, bassist] came to me in our hotel in New York,' Perrett says, 'not happy. A lot of things had gone wrong, we'd had to cancel the last thirty gigs to get out of the country because of the trouble I'd got into, and he said that he wanted to leave. I got a sick feeling in my stomach. You know when you're thirteen and your girlfriend chucks you? It felt like that. But instead of saying to him, "Let's talk about it," *I* left. I quit. I regret that, I do. Ever since, I've kept thinking about what might have been.'

This may have been a sad development, but hardly an untypical one. Bands are not structured to remain harmonious: there is too much imbalance, too much stress, too much to fall out over. Nothing in Perrett's life had fully prepared him for this. Only experience teaches you, by which time it's too late. Singing had been his childhood ambition, and the ambition was realised, but then it was abruptly snuffed out. He was thirty-two years old.

Peter Perrett had been born into a working-class family in London, and until the age of eleven had briefly considered a career in football, because boys do, but he came to realise that it was music, not sport, that consumed his every thought.

'I got a guitar when I was seventeen, and learned how to play most things with the same three chords, and then how to fit those chords around tunes, and then I started writing my songs.'

He'd no idea what to do with those songs once they were finished. How was he supposed to get them out into the world, into the shops and on the radio? By the mid-seventies, still young, he was already in a relationship with the woman who would go on to become his wife, Zena, and it was Zena who encouraged him, insisting he should pursue it to the exclusion of everything else. Once he'd written an album's worth of songs, she told him, he should take them to record companies, whose addresses were in the phone book. That was how it was done.

'But I always thought that was beneath me,' he says, proving, in just eight words, that artists really aren't the best people to operate the heavy machinery of adulthood. 'I didn't want to be judged by lesser mortals.'

His genius, he suggests, wasn't recognised until he met some like-minded souls: Jon Perry, Mike Kellie and Alan Mair, the people with whom he would form the Only Ones. Here were people he could hide behind, who could bolster his confidence. Things started well enough, but Perrett soon started feeling the pressures of his role. The more he felt he couldn't cope with it, the more he couldn't cope, his feelings of panic a self-fulfilling prophecy. After America, he thought it best to hibernate.

His house in south London had a front door that was positioned at the top of several steep steps, a design, he would later say, that made it all but impossible for police to ram it open whenever they arrived with search warrants, looking for drugs. At first, Perrett was a mere user – smack, crack – but drugs cost money, and so, to fund his habit, he started to deal.

'It was like a fortress, our place. I felt very safe in my fortress.'

Here, he was removed from the complications of the world and his place in it, and life was reduced to its basic fundamentals: get high, come down, get high again, with occasional breaks for food, water, the toilet.

'You don't really live in the real world [when you're a dealer], do you?' he says. 'It's a black-market economy, and if you've got the right . . . the right contacts, if you can get something at the right price, then you can – well, you can imagine how the black-market economy works, can't you?'

Once, he was peddling songs; now it was drugs. Both can lift the spirits. 'The only time I wasn't surviving was when I got clean and started to do music again, in the early nineties, I think.'

If the eighties was mostly a lost decade, then by the nineties he'd decided to live again. To live meant a return to music, and penury. 'I'd be in the studio – which isn't cheap – and Zena would be asking me to see if there was any coffee or sugar I could bring back. That was hard.'

Despite the chaos of their lives, they did manage to eke out a kind of normality. They had children, two boys.

Perrett laughs. 'I think you'd better talk to them [his children, to ask] how normal they felt their life was. As they got older, they got better at looking after *us*, put it that way. But I think there were many times they wanted to put us up for adoption.'

Their sons would grow up to be in bands themselves, one in an iteration of Babyshambles (the act formed by Pete Doherty after the Libertines foundered for much the same reason the Only Ones had three decades previously). Both, now in their late thirties and early forties, have played in their father's live band.

If Perrett's tale is a horribly familiar one to anyone who may have battled with addiction, it's familiar in another way, too: once in a band, always in a band. Music never really gives up its possession of those it afflicts, and so artists invariably find themselves returning to it, so long as they are sentient enough to pursue it. But for the longest time, Perrett wasn't.

'Couldn't. Didn't pick up a guitar, didn't listen to music, not for years. I couldn't stop words coming into my head, lyrics and that, but I never wrote things down. I always thought that if things were worth remembering, I'd remember them. It's only as I got older that I realised I wasn't actually remembering the good stuff I'd come up with at all. It'd all gone.'

When we speak, Perrett is sixty-eight. 'I'm working hard just to maintain a sort of *old man* health these days.'

But he is clean, at last. He tried many times to stop drugs over the years, and occasionally managed, but never for very long. He first went to rehab in 1985, and his reaction to going cold turkey was to suddenly rediscover his appetite for music.

'If I was clean, I could write songs. It wasn't a conscious thing, it just happened, I suppose because, if I'm clean, then not every minute of my time is taken up with consuming drugs. I had to find other things to do with my hands. The plan was always to get clean and stay clean, and then to do music again, but, as you know, junkies have a habit of always putting things off. *I'll get clean next week; I'll leave London; go to rehab, get clean and start again. I'll do it next week, next month – soon.*'

A decade later, he found he had enough songs for an album, his first as a solo artist. But the sudden pressure he felt prompted a binge, which, he suggests, lasted all the way until 2008. 'That was my worst period, definitely.'

In the midst of his most enduring binge, the twelve most devastating years of his life, when he did nothing except take drugs and watch time pass, that single from 1978, 'Another Girl, Another Planet', was living its own life, growing steadily in stature and becoming regarded, in some quarters, as a classic. Contemporary bands began covering it: R.E.M., Billy Bragg, the Cure, the American pop-punk act Blink-182. Word of its buoyant afterlife would occasionally reach its author in his cave, and then, after he was taught how to use YouTube, he'd search for video evidence. It touched him deeply.

'It reminded people that we'd existed, and I suppose it opened the door for people to discover more of our music. I've always been incredibly grateful for that.'

It offered him a lifeline, and a crucially useful source of additional income, too, even if he'd ultimately squander it on more drugs. But if he squinted hard enough, and sometimes he did try, he could see light at the end of the tunnel. In 2007, Vodafone used the song for a TV ad campaign. 'Probably made a hundred grand from that.'

Around the same time, he sold his house in the hope that a change of postcode would encourage him to stop dealing. If he stopped dealing, maybe he and his wife could stop using. His neighbourhood was then becoming gentrified, and so what was once inescapably unappealing – the self-professed 'fortress' and drug den whose chief occupants were not always as house-proud as they might otherwise have been, and whose carpets needed changing – was suddenly viewed as a doer-upper, and worth a mint. He made about half a million pounds profit from its sale which, when combined with his Vodafone fee, made him properly flush for the first time in his life. Music had given him this, and he was duly humbled. Was this perhaps a second chance?

No, not quite.

'If we were sensible people, we'd have planned for the future, used it to buy a really nice house with, something like that. But instead, we just kept taking drugs until the money ran out.'

It takes quite a long time to smoke £600,000 worth of drugs. By the time he was penniless once more his health was poor, and so was his wife's. 'We were severely damaged by then, not just physically but mentally.'

Perrett talks about the ravages of long-term drug use by slipping into imagery. It's like being adrift at sea without a compass, he says. You're forever at the mercy of the winds, being pushed whichever way. 'No, wait – it's more like you're hurtling through space in a spaceship, controlled by the ship's computer, but the computer has a virus. Eventually, you find yourself crash-landing back to earth . . .

'It was when I crash-landed that I had my burst of creativity. But while I was up there – in space, at sea, wherever – everything just didn't exist.'

He blames his career choice for his narcotic tendencies. He might have felt less need to do vast quantities of drugs had he been, say, a plumber, for the simple reason that there is less performance anxiety in changing a toilet's U-bend than there is standing on stage in front of thousands. Music may have been a compulsion, but it was a nightmare for his anxiety.

After the Vodafone ad, interest in the Only Ones perked up. People learned of their story, and folk do love a cautionary tale. Perrett, who had no management, and little to no contact with anyone in the industry, was duly tracked down. His phone started ringing; occasionally, he felt moved to answer it. His fellow band members got in touch. They too were thrilled by the exposure, and wanted to reform, because there was money to be made, good money. Trouble was, the singer was still an addict. All he really wanted to do was stay at home and take drugs.

That same year, 2007, Warren Ellis, the bassist in Nick Cave and the Bad Seeds, was curating All Tomorrow's Parties, a music festival that took place at Butlin's Minehead in December. Ellis reached out, explaining he'd been a big fan. Could they come and play? Three quarters of the band said yes immediately, but their confirmation was contingent upon the lead singer. Would his skinny trousers still fit?

'They turned up at my door, perhaps the first time I'd seen them together, properly, in, what, twenty-seven years. So that was quite an emotional thing. I *knew* these people, I knew that I used to do good stuff with them. They wanted to get back together, and I suppose because I was the least disposable member, I had to say yes.'

But Perrett was nothing if not consistent. The moment he agreed, his stomach turned to liquid, and he reached for his stash.

'But I still said yes to the reunion. And so, all of a sudden, we were back on.'

It's not easy to marshal an addict into doing what needs to be done when they'd much rather be doing something else entirely. Perrett was fifty-five years old then, and hadn't played live in over

a quarter of a century. The more the date loomed in his diary –
and of course, the diary never existed; it's a metaphorical diary
– the more he quaked.

'I didn't let myself think about it,' he says.

Minehead is a two-hour journey by car from London. In the
weeks running up to the event, the band had managed to get
together for a couple of rehearsals, and these had gone well
enough – surprisingly so – to prompt them to attempt a small gig
in front of an audience, supporting the band Perrett's sons were in
at the time, Love Minus Zero. The show went well, the assembled
crowd clapped and cheered, and the occasion allowed Perrett to
remember who he'd once been, so very long ago.

At Butlin's – hardly Altamont, or Red Rocks, or Madison
Square Garden, but exciting enough – they were to open the festival. Stage time was 7 p.m. The band could have driven down on
the day, but didn't want to take any chances, and so had made the
journey the night before. This meant that any delays, any unforeseen issues, could be dealt with in sufficient time.

Perrett was prepared. 'I thought I'd brought enough . . . You
know, you always have enough smack with you because there's
only so much smack you can do, so that was okay.'

His plan: to do just enough to get him into the right headspace,
which would facilitate the Only Ones with their reincarnation.
'I also thought I'd brought enough crack for the whole weekend,
but then when we got there, the night before the show, I stayed
up all night, and when you stay up all night, you find you can do
so much more than you thought you were capable of. So there
I was, in my chalet, at the campsite, four o'clock in the morning,
all good, but then at five, I'd run out of crack, and so immediately
fell asleep.'

What happened next, the way he tells it, is a little confusing,
but it requires effort to climb out of a drug stupor, and Perrett was
out for the count. He slept through breakfast, through lunch. He

missed the soundcheck. Their stage time rapidly approaching, the band went to look for him, and found him still in his bed. They tried to rouse him, raising voices, slapping cheeks. 'They were trying to hit me, shake me, but I was out cold.' He laughs at the second-hand memory. 'Eventually, my son found someone who had some powdered coke, so they blew the powdered coke up my nose, and it worked: I woke up.'

By now, they should have been on stage already. They got him dressed, then led him, forcibly, to the venue. They made it on stage by 7.15 p.m. 'Only fifteen minutes late. Result!'

For one glorious, stolen night, the Only Ones were *back*, all their romantic ideas of recapturing some of that initial spirit and injecting it with something newly fresh and alive conjured up right there on stage in real time. The audience was appreciative, Warren Ellis admiring, relieved. A subsequent UK tour was hastily arranged off the back of it, and Perrett, importantly, seemed up for it. Being in front of an audience again had affected him profoundly.

'Some of them [at Butlin's] had tears streaming down their faces. They weren't reacting to the performance,' he adds, 'or the state of my voice, which is not what it was, but more because it was a celebration of what we'd done in the past, what we'd achieved, that immortality that musicians are so fortunate to have. Music is such an emotional release, isn't it? I mean, all art forms have pleasure, and I know I'm biased, but the buzz music gives you, you can't live without it really, can you?'

It made him wonder what life might have been like had he not become an addict. Drugs had been responsible for his undoing, for suffocating his creativity, and curdling his potential. He was adamant this time. When he and his wife tried to quit properly again, in 2011, Perrett was placed on methadone, which he stayed on for the next four years. After which: cured, junkie no more.

'You have all the normal mental health issues of every other junkie, of course,' he points out, 'and I know many people get depressed about it, a whole life wasted, things like that, but luckily me and Zena, we've got extreme gallows humour, so we've been able to laugh about it, we amuse each other that way. But the physical aspects? To be honest with you, they're not retrievable. We smoked our drugs, so our lungs are shot, severely damaged.'

Back in the early days, Perrett never really exerted much in the way of effort. What did come to him, in terms of talent and focus, came to him naturally; he never had the discipline of an athlete. Now he's old, he's more mindful. 'These days I work really hard at just being barely functional, because that's all I can manage. My lung consultant's amazed I can even sing at all.'

He thinks about all he's come through. 'When you stop taking drugs twenty-four hours a day, every day, you don't go cold turkey immediately. With crack, you don't get a physical withdrawal. If you stop smoking crack, you just sleep, which your body needs after not sleeping for such a long time. With heroin, you need something else, because otherwise you do get the physical with-drawals, so that's why I started on the methadone.'

He did go back on heroin once, a one-off, he insists, at the end of 2009, maybe 2010, but by 2011, he'd stopped smoking everything, including joints, which he'd been puffing on up to thirty times a day. And after that, he quit nicotine.

Sobriety, he says, allowed the songs back in.

'Music's something that's inside you. It takes you to a special place like nothing else. Nothing's better than writing a song, rehearsing it with your band, and it being everything you imagined in your head. The melody, the lyrics, the musical land-scape it exists within – when that does happen, you get such a buzz from it. It's like nothing else.'

Not even drugs?

'Not even drugs.'

And so for Perrett, a return to clarity meant a return to cre-ativity. He'd stopped dealing, thankful that it had never led to a conviction, or prison, and his band continued to tour. But magic is rarely rekindled for long. The Only Ones split up again, for all sorts of complicated reasons, but Perrett was determined to continue.

'You know, in some ways, I don't think I deserve anything any more because I rejected my art. That's the very worst thing an artist can do.'

He counted his blessings: a strong early start, an enduring single, and fans that wanted more. In 2017, he released a solo album, *How the West Was Won*, and followed it up two years later with another, *Humanworld*. If, as we shall see in future chapters, the public seem to have an aversion to musicians in their middle years, midlife being such a difficult period to navigate, then those that make it to the other side, and to *a certain age*, are treated quite differently. They're welcomed back with open arms, reappraised and lauded for their longevity. Perrett's pensionable comeback was a resounding success. The reviews were kind, the accompanying tours went well, and he was busy fostering his new addiction: songwriting.

'For me, there's no artistic pleasure to be found in playing old songs, so I knew I'd always need to do new ones. I mean, I know that I'm nowhere near as good as I used to be, and that I'm still stuck with my voice as it is today – I'm always going to sound like me – but I still like to push myself. And I'm enjoying it, I really am. And that, well, that's priceless.'

Over the last few years, he's become increasingly aware that his memory is unravelling, a ribbon flung to dark corners he can no longer quite see. 'I don't think I've got Alzheimer's or anything, but the extreme lucidity's gone. I'm working within parameters now.'

The titles of the new songs he's working on – 'Do Not Resuscitate', 'I Want to Go with Dignity' – suggest that his gallows humour, too, has remained intact.

'The physical and mental deterioration are the only real downsides these days, I think. But there is wisdom now, and a more measured outlook on this whole meaningless thing we call life. That's a plus. And the closer I approach mortality, the harder I find it not to face it. I'm a songwriter, so I write about it.'

2

'I wasn't just going to throw it all away'

With Shaun Ryder, it's difficult to know where to even begin. If ever there was a physical manifestation of the live fast/die young school of rock-star cliché, then surely it was to be found somewhere within the voluminous flapping flares of the Happy Mondays' frontman, a walking caricature of *dodgy geezer* writ so large that he practically came with his own sitcom laughter soundtrack. If Peter Perrett liked to do drugs in the privacy of his own home and found that they stifled his creativity and killed his passion, then for Ryder they were linked so closely to the creative process that one simply couldn't have existed without the other.

The cliché never wore thin, however, because Ryder has gone on to do something quietly remarkable with his career. For starters, he didn't die – at the time of writing, he remains a propulsive member of the gloriously undead – and though he may be somewhere close to the tail-end of his nine cats' lives, he has either shrewdly reinvented himself or unwittingly found himself unexpectedly reinvented multiple times to the point where, by now, the man is practically a national treasure. He's been in bands, indulged in some unusual collaborations, fronted television programmes, 'written' books, expounded on haunted houses in documentaries, done reality TV, and has even advertised nicotine patches on his Twitter page ('proper zingy!!'), never above product placement if it pays him a living wage.

At sixty-two, in competent command of most if not quite *all* his faculties, he still makes music, too. 'Still got things to say, innit,' he says.

No one could ever accuse him of being an inspiration, because Ryder's blueprint for how to carve out an enduring career in music is illegible to every single soul except himself, but his constant blinking wonder at the world around him – like a goldfish performing its circuit and seeing everything with new eyes as it comes around again – is somehow a marvellous thing to bear witness to. He grins more easily than most. While Keith Richards is falling out of coconut trees onto his head, and Shane MacGowan is increasingly cantankerous and lost, Shaun Ryder, the erstwhile dodgy geezer, is someone whose addled charisma could light up Regent Street at Christmas.

The son of a postman and a nurse, he grew up in Moss Side, Manchester, did not do well at school, and fancied he might deal drugs in adulthood, because dealing drugs meant cash transactions that would keep him in nice clobber, good drink and gear. He formed Happy Mondays in 1985, describing the five-man line-up – which featured his brother Paul, and his best mate Bez – as 'a bunch of scrotes'. They signed to Manchester's Factory label, surely the only record company willing to take the risk. At first, Ryder was going to play the drums, taken with the idea of hitting things, but he had little rhythm. He was no singer, either, his voice like a hyena coughing up a furball, but his way with words was erratic, nonsensical, streams-of-consciousness and entirely compelling – poetry by any other name. The band sounded like nobody else, an accusation you could level at precious few acts at any time in history. Their musical ability back then was small print they didn't bother to read, but they could make a noise, and it sounded great to their ears.

'If you're shit, you're shit,' he says, 'and you get found out pretty quick. But we were learning, and we were getting better.'

There has arguably never been a more work-in-progress debut album than the Mondays' 1987 effort, *Squirrel and G-Man Twenty Four Hour Party People Plastic Face Carnt Smile (White Out)*, with its careening songs like 'Kuff Dam', 'Tart Tart' and 'Cob 20', but there was a sonic chaos, too, that was intriguing. There was a lot going on here. Ryder says, 'that first album, to me, I was learning on the job, and by *Bummed* [the band's next album, in 1988], I was a bit better, and by *Pills 'n' Thrills and Bellyaches* [1990], I knew what I was doing.'

The band's ascent quickly became the stuff of fable and, sub-sequently, folklore. The Mondays' earlier underworld leanings didn't recede as their fame grew, but simply became a deeper part of their shtick. The chaos perpetuated, and clung to them. They became a spectator sport. You'd look and wonder: What next? What now? By 1990, Manchester was the epicentre of all that was exciting in music, and due to its reliance upon drugs, particularly ecstasy, was duly anointed *Madchester* for its decadence, its daring, its sheer rapacious appetite. While the Stone Roses headlined, the Happy Mondays *were* the aftershow party, their music thrilling and splenetic, a magnificent racket whose ramshackleness belied some serious talent. In Shaun Ryder, they had the poet laureate of the rave generation, and he and his sidekick, the perpetually gurning Bez, became counterculture heroes. They thousand-yard-stared from countless magazine covers and were the recipients of in-depth newspaper profiles because they had no filter, and a compulsion for the truth, or at least *their* truth, ugly as it often was. Today's cancel culture would have annihilated them in a heartbeat, but in 1990, battered on their own supply and having the time of their lives, they were icons.

But Ryder, deep down, away from the flash of the camera, was feeling far outside his comfort zone.

'I didn't want people looking at me, you know? Back then, I didn't even come alive when I was on stage, so when I did have to go up there, I just felt: *Fuck, I'm naked, everybody's looking at me*. Now, of course, now I love it. But back then? All I loved was getting back to our little den, our studio, making music and writing songs. It was going out on stage, that was the difficult bit. I was quite shy, you know?'

Their trajectory was bound to peak at some point, and they were surely due a fantastic implosion. And the implosion duly came – because how could it not?

By 1992, Happy Mondays were superstars, or at least Ryder and Bez were. There was big money now, bigger recording budgets, nicer keks. For their next album, *Yes Please!*, they wanted to record again with Paul Oakenfold, who'd produced *Bellyaches* to such winning effect. But Oakenfold was, by now, much in demand, and so the band was paired instead with Chris Frantz and Tina Weymouth, former members of Talking Heads, who would oversee the musical direction of the record that, Factory hoped, might just break them worldwide. The increase in budget allowed them to pick any studio that might help inspire their creativity: world, oyster.

Having grown up in Manchester, where the cliché of perpetual grey skies and low clouds was a cliché for good reason, they chose Eddy Grant's Blue Wave studio in Barbados. What could go wrong in a sun-kissed paradise at the height of their careers, with everything to play for and nothing to lose?

Everything, as it turned out.

The Mancunians found it difficult to concentrate on the island. The sun was shining; it felt like a holiday. Ryder, who was weaning himself off heroin at the time and therefore not in the best of spirits, was becoming increasingly aware that he and Bez had somehow splintered off and away from the rest of the band, who resented just how much attention and praise the two were getting. The duo received the star treatment; the others were all too often mistaken for roadies or, worse, their dealers. In the studio, the sessions soon stalled. They never turned up on time, and often didn't turn up at all. There were distractions, too. Ryder now found himself hooked on crack cocaine, and would smoke up to twenty-five rocks a day. This did not help him focus. Bez, meanwhile, who would always find himself at something of a loose end in the studio, where his good vibes and dancing skills weren't strictly needed, wanted to burn off some adrenaline. He hired a jeep, drove too fast and too carelessly, and crashed, badly breaking his arm. A few weeks later, while his arm was still recovering in a cast, he took a jet ski out to sea, and found it difficult to control. He flew off it, hit the waves, and broke his broken arm. The pain was like nothing he'd ever experienced, but Bez had ways of dealing with pain.

Eddy Grant's Blue Wave studios was state-of-the-art, and priced accordingly. Every day of delay was costing a fortune, and would end up bankrupting the band's label. When the album was finally finished, it transpired that what had gone into it was what came out: a mess. Whatever mojo they'd managed to voodoo up for *Pills 'n' Thrills and Bellyaches* had gone in a puff of smoke. Chris Frantz later said of the experience: 'You had to be there to really understand how dreadful things were. Tina and I went into that project completely unprepared for what the Happy Mondays were like.'

'Shaun is incorrigible,' added Tina Weymouth. 'But you still can't take away from the fact that he's an artist. Crazy, but there you go.'

The album limped to number fourteen in the charts, and if the premature end had always been in clear sight for the Mondays, now it swam aggressively into focus.

'Jealousy, that's why we split. It wasn't the drugs; we'd always done drugs. It was jealousy,' says Ryder now. 'You know, we'd walk into, say, *Top of the Pops*, and the door would be held open for me and Bez, but it would close in the face of the other guys. But that's because me and Bez did all the press; the other guys didn't want to spend their time doing things like that, or photo shoots. Ours were the faces on the front covers, not theirs. They didn't like that.'

He points out that success and stardom change a person, and that nobody is ever prepared for that. 'Everyone handles shit in different ways, don't they? So there was all this internal bullshit going on.'

Each member ended up dealing with their own personal bullshit not only differently, but separately. As far as Ryder was concerned, they would come back together in time, regroup, and start over. They'd survived worse, after all. Instead, the band informed him that, no, they were leaving to start over *without* him, and without Bez; Ryder's brother, Paul, would become the singer. But this didn't really work out. 'And then, for a while, the guy that did their security was going to become the singer. Didn't work out, either. I told them to come back, but they said they'd rather go on the dole than work with me again. I told them that that was where they were fucking heading . . .'

This was 1993, and Ryder was thirty-one years old. The presumption was that he would retreat to his local and prop up the bar, with enough tall tales in his arsenal to keep the drinks coming for the next several decades. But no, he insists.

'I wasn't just going to throw it all away. Me and Bez got into this business, the *entertainment* business, after years of really hard work, so we weren't going anywhere now. We'd worked hard to get where we were; last thing I was going to do was fucking throw it all away. People always thought the Mondays was just about getting off your head and partying. They forget just how hard we worked.'

With surprising swiftness, he formed another band, Black Grape, convinced that he'd learned a thing or two. There was wisdom at play now.

On *Yes Please!*, Ryder had collaborated with several singers and musicians, among them a rapper called Kermit from the British hip-hop act Ruthless Rap Assassins. He and Kermit had hit it off, and both were keen – and available – to work together again. Black Grape revolved mostly around the two of them, with Bez, loyal as a Labrador, as ongoing vibes master. By 1995, they'd come up with their debut album, *It's Great When You're Straight . . . Yeah*, which managed to do everything right in much the same way the last Mondays album had done everything wrong. It oozed funk grooves and a scattershot punk energy that was as goofy as it was improbably charming, Ryder presiding over its clatter with glee, and giving the drunken impression that its singles – 'In the Name of the Father' and 'Kelly's Heroes' – were dashed off in minutes, when they were, in fact, impeccably produced pop gems. The album went to number one, and the satisfaction this afforded its frontman was something he did little to hide. There was an added swagger to his walk now, and an increased awareness that everything he did to fuel his bad-boy image was grist to his mill. His afterlife would endure.

He dyed his hair peroxide blond, swore on teatime TV (and got banned for doing so), and used music journalists to perpetuate his reputation. In the late 1990s, for example, he was holding court at a five-star hotel in London on promotional duties, but was unexpectedly delayed up in his room, so his increasingly anxious record company representative explained, in order to indulge in a quick smoke. He eventually strode into the hotel bar two hours late, grinning impishly, his eyes pied, wearing a cricket jumper, and he proceeded to chat up the bar's waitress with the rarefied elegance of George Clooney. The smoke had made him loquacious, a court jester. The next day came reports that he had later been evicted from the hotel for defecating in his room's bathroom sink and leaving it for the cleaner to deal with. The cleaner was distraught. This story may or may not have been exaggerated, or even entirely false, but that didn't matter: it *could* have happened – this was Shaun Ryder, after all – and that was enough.

The next few years were all melee, trademarked calamity, increasingly tall tales. After another two albums, the band split. Ryder suggests this was because Kermit was becoming more singularly ambitious, fielding solo offers from other labels that thought he might flourish more easily without the hindrance of Ryder dragging him down and stifling him. In Ryder's estimation, 'he let [other] people get into his head. He landed the solo deal, yeah, but that just turned to shit.'

By 1998, Ryder's lifestyle finally caught up with him. Decades previously, he had signed a recording contract without reading it because he was 'stoned at the time'. By the time his second band had dissolved, he learned that he was now in hock to the tune of several hundred thousand pounds, which, after factoring in the accompanying legal fees, became several hundred thousand more. The way he tells it, for the next twelve years – 1998 until 2010 – everything he earned was taken away so that he could repay what he owed. He also had ex-partners, and several children, and he was trying to kick his multiple narcotic habits. This was not a good time in his life. He ballooned in weight, his teeth rotted, and he felt little point in even attempting to kickstart his career again if he wasn't going to gain personally from it.

Instead, he needed something else. Many rock stars have found themselves in similar positions, of course, but not all of them have had the sheer brazen cheek of Shaun Ryder, someone who knew, at a deeply instinctive level, that there were benefits to being a dodgy-geezer type who could exist quite fruitfully far outside the music industry.

He'd hustled before, and he would again now.

He landed a column in the *Daily Sport*, in which he wrote (or, point of fact, *didn't*; a ghostwriter did) about celebrities. 'I just put my name to it,' he said later. 'The writer was a scriptwriter who writes the sort of shows you get on BBC3. He sort of insulted everyone in Manchester, *Coronation Street* and *Emmerdale*, then put my name to it. I've spent the last fifteen years fucking apologising to people.'

He did the column, he explains, for the money: almost £40,000 a year. 'The lawyers took all that from me as well.' Later, he signed a book deal for £130,000, but didn't see much of that, either. 'I'm not bitter, I just see it as part of the process. Look, if you've not been ripped off or had problems in this game, then you've not even really been in the fucking business. It's all part of the fucking game.'

In 2005, he was a guest vocalist on the Gorillaz track 'Dare', which went to number one. He encouraged Damon Albarn, the band's creative leader, to keep Ryder's royalties, if only to frustrate his debtors, blissfully blind to the fact that the particular nose he was cutting off here was his own.

About a year earlier – he's not sure of the precise date, and it might have been a year earlier but certainly not a year later; time's relative, isn't it? – he was offered a predictable lifeline for one of his ilk: reality TV. *Celebrity Big Brother* wanted him in the house. Though he didn't know it then, he would have been in alongside the motliest of crews: Bridget Neilson, Sylvester Stallone's mother Jackie, the horseracing TV presenter John McCririck and Germaine Greer. The money was good, but then he knew where the money was going. A wiser head than his would have realised this was a quick and effective way to pay all his debts off at once, but Ryder said no. Instead, he told the producers that his faithful sidekick, Bez, who was also suffering from a dearth of paid employment (because if Shaun's not working, Bez isn't either) might be keen.

Bez was.

On paper, this wasn't a good idea at all. In his day, Bez's antics could make Ryder seem almost (if not quite) a choirboy, so to enter a house like that, with so many big characters and such a penetrating televisual gaze, was the ultimate lion's den. But Bez revealed hidden depths, surprising everybody, perhaps not least himself. He was clean by this stage, and had new teeth that almost fitted. He turned out to be an acquired taste, keeping his own counsel mostly, and exuded an errant, even humble, charm. The man who'd so often resembled a Strangeways inmate on the lam was actually a rather lovely fellow. Who knew?

And so while his fellow house celebrities combusted around him, much like the people he'd been in bands with, Bez kept his head down, and got on with things. He finished runner-up, and emerged blinking, squinting, and newly flush.

Ryder: 'I saw what it did to him, and it was good.'

Lesson learned. When reality TV came calling again – and reality TV, like bailiffs, always comes calling again – he would not be so quick to turn them down.

In 2010, Shaun Ryder, by now the beleaguered former frontman of Happy Mondays and Black Grape, an addiction survivor, and someone exhausted by successive legal cases and spiralling health issues, entered *I'm a Celebrity . . . Get Me Out of Here!* He was to some extent a changed man, newly married – to Joanne, a former childhood sweetheart, who was keeping him on what he called the 'straight and narrow'. ITV, then, were getting a reformed character. The show would go on to reinvent him entirely.

He was, by now, finally free from debt, and his fee for the show – somewhere in the region of £100,000 – was his to keep. He was also by this stage well on the way to cultural icon status. He'd been immortalised on the big screen in *24 Hour Party People*, the brilliant Michael Winterbottom film depicting Tony Wilson's Factory Records label, and though Ryder wasn't particularly happy with the on-screen depiction of him ('a caricature', in his estimation), it nevertheless struck many as a largely accurate picture, and painted him as the ultimate rock 'n' roll hedonist.

Ryder thought that *I'm a Celebrity* might allow him to present to the watching public another side of himself: a more gentle, humane side.

'Cos at the end of the day, I'm a nice guy. Just because I used to get off my head on drugs doesn't mean I'm a total arsehole, you know?'

On the show, he did what all celebrities must – the pointless tasks, the consumption of the genitals from various marsupials – and did so with the equanimity (the blissed-out serenity, even) of one who has lived through far worse in life. Like Bez, he finished runner-up, and, also like Bez, stepped into a newly three-dimensional personality.

The offers came rolling in now, one after the other, and he said yes to most of them. There have been more books: various instalments of his life story, alongside those which focus on his obsession with UFOs. (As a child, Ryder would regularly see unidentified flying objects; he has more than once suggested that he's been kidnapped by aliens.) He has appeared, with Bez, on *Celebrity Gogglebox*, reformed both the Happy Mondays and Black Grape, having made peace with his former bandmates, both acts realising that they are stronger together than apart and that, like him or not, they need him. He has recorded songs with Robbie Williams and Lee 'Scratch' Perry. He has published a book of lyrics, confirming his status as the poet laureate of, well, something: a chaotic Manchester upbringing, a lifetime of 'scrote' shenanigans, and his unerring ability to put down on the page precisely what it is to be alive with the most pugnacious, drunken spirit, via rhyming couplets. He's had a hip replacement, new teeth, and endured a thyroid gland condition that made all his hair fall out. 'I look like Uncle Fester,' he says.

But he's still clean, very happily married, and life, he suggests, has found an equilibrium no one could have seen coming.

'If I didn't have my wife, I'd probably still be running around like the twenty-year-old Shaun Ryder. Joanne'd binned me shortly after we were seventeen, when we first met and the band was first taking off, because she wasn't going to put up with all the bullshit she knew was coming. She reeled me in again when I was forty years old, got me grounded, and so I've got a very stable home now.' They have two daughters together, adding to Ryder's previous four with other partners. 'First time I had kids, I was basically a kid myself. This time around, I'm an adult.'

This is said with pride, with relief, and a kind of awed amazement. If Shaun Ryder has spent much of his life surprising all those around him, then he has surprised himself even more.

Like Frank Sinatra, he did things his way.

3

'The nerve endings are much more receptive there'

While it's not a matter of public record whether or not Shaun Ryder, at the height of his drug intake, liked to either blow cocaine up the bottom of his associates or have it blown up his, it has become common knowledge that his Madchester peer Tim Burgess of The Charlatans *did*.

America is a big country – endless conurbations, vast plains, and freeways that stretch on for ever – and this is never more evident than when being driven across it at a steady fifty-five miles per hour in a tour bus from city to city, and venue to venue, from one Taco Bell to the next. Even those executive tour buses of the 1990s that were kitted out with TVs and video players and boasted mini fridges palled after a while, and became filled with the most eye-watering tedium. To let off steam, one had to be imaginative.

'Drugs were always a part of my life, and I had a great time on them, to be honest,' Tim Burgess once said. 'One time in America, we discovered the process of blowing cocaine up each other's arses. The nerve endings are much more receptive there.'

Previously, the sharing of needles in such situations seemed an intimate activity, but this act, dubbed 'cocainus', took the whole notion of intimacy to new levels. The Charlatans always did seem a particularly close-knit gang, and would become even more so after this particular twenty-eight-date US tour. 'It seemed like the right thing to do at the time,' Burgess added, in both mitigation and defence.

As a teenager, Burgess, born in Salford and raised in Cheshire, would often seek a chemically-induced escape. He sniffed petrol and glue remover. He dabbled in magic mushrooms and ecstasy. At twenty-one, he joined the Charlatans, who were influenced by psychedelia and early Pink Floyd, and they rode to prominence in Madchester's slipstream, perpetually third on that particular bill, a kind of Small Faces to the Stone Roses' Beatles and the Happy Mondays' Rolling Stones. Though they boasted many of the same predilections as their counterparts, they were not merely understudies, but rather brilliant musicians in their own right whose totemic sound was built around the Hammond organ. Burgess was puppyishly cute, and, in an era of voluble frontmen whose next move you could never quite predict, he was an altogether more chilled presence, his chocolate-drop eyes peeking out from behind a curtain of hair, wide but meek and always just a little wary.

As if to perpetuate the enduring myth/inalienable fact that bands are never more potent than in their first flush, the Charlatans are still chiefly remembered for their first hit, 1990's 'The Only One I Know', though they would go on to endure for three decades and record thirteen studio albums. 'We're still here because of that song,' Burgess says, 'and I'm grateful for it.'

Their endurance has been no mean feat. If luck often plays an intrinsic part in the careers of many acts, then for the Charlatans, it has often seemed conspicuous by its absence. In 1996, keyboardist Rob Collins, recently released from prison for his part in an armed robbery (the very presence of a successful pop star at an armed robbery in the first place was never satisfactorily explained), was killed in a car crash. His replacement, Tony Rogers, suffered testicular cancer. Bassist Martin Blunt has battled depression, while drummer Jon Brookes had a brain tumour. When the band's accountant absconded with their money – a stroke of bad luck by no means restricted to the Charlatans – they were plunged into bankruptcy.

Little wonder they sought chemical oblivion with such reckless abandon. Eventually, something has to give.

They survived, and continued sporadically to thrive, because they were friends, a band of brothers; they'd seen each other's bumholes, for goodness' sake. Nothing could come between them – until it did: wedded bliss. Marriage, a union between two people that can often unwittingly sever the respective earlier friendships of both bride and groom, can have seismic impacts on a band's dynamic (cf. Yoko Ono). Once a member marries, with its promise of intimacy, domesticity and a sudden interest in the colour pallets of Farrow & Ball, the tunnel vision that had allowed the band to exist in the first place is compromised. Many rounded human beings can weather this storm, but not everyone can.

In the late 1990s, Tim Burgess fell in love with an American woman, married her, and moved with her to Los Angeles. This presented an immediate geographical problem. Zoom had not yet been invented, and Burgess, punch-drunk on romance, didn't always readily return phone messages from the others. He was busy, distracted. His argument that there was more to life than music didn't hit home as smoothly as he might have liked.

But the time was right for Burgess. The Charlatans had been chart regulars for almost ten years by this point, and in one sense had already peaked. This was their midlife crisis, then, the point at which they were no longer writing songs out of an overwhelming creative urge, but more because it was their job; it was what they did, clocking in and out every day. Things had become a little stale. A change of scenery was needed for them all.

The singer was also increasingly aware that his own narcotic proclivities were only ever going to lead to one destination. He may well have enjoyed his drugs – one chapter in his 2012 memoir, *Telling Stories,* is entitled 'My Drug Heaven' – but now, newly married, he wanted, not unreasonably, to *live.*

He found Los Angeles pretty much as advertised: smog in the morning, bright sunshine every afternoon. Nobody owned a coat. There was traffic everywhere, everyone was in the film business, and if you knew people who knew people, the *right* people, its social life offered more colour than anything he might have encountered in Salford. California quickly came to feel like his spiritual home. There had always been something psychedelic and West Coast about Burgess's demeanour, and so here, now, in the newly dyed blond hair that made him resemble a magic mushroom in human form, and with the permanent presence of climate-appropriate sunglasses, the crumpled smile that spread across his face like warm butter fitted snugly. In a sense, he'd stepped into himself, fully, at last. He set about the process of getting clean. A doctor prescribed a course of pills for twenty-one days to help him stay off the drugs. He took them for three years.

'I wanted to become ultra-clean,' he says.

A few years later, a friend introduced him to transcendental meditation, the practice of meditating for twenty minutes twice a day to your own personal mantra in pursuit of long-term peace and holistic well-being. He took to it better than he might have expected, and soon it became part of his physiology. 'When you come out of the meditation, for some reason, the world seems brighter.'

He continues to practise it every day, and through it, he met and became friendly with the film director David Lynch, who has spent decades extolling the virtues of the practice. Together, they've appeared at festivals around the world, talking about the power of TM and how everybody can harness it for a better life: the eccentric film-maker and the rock star who pulled himself back from the edge.

A happy ending? Not quite, for bad luck wasn't entirely eradicated from Burgess's life. His marriage ended and, with it, his extended American sojourn. He returned to the UK, settled at its eastern perimeter, the county of Norfolk, fell in love again, and had a child. The opportunity to write his memoir coincided, he says, with post-marriage poverty – his divorce had been a costly one. 'I needed the money.'

Its success prompted several more books, each revolving around music and his abiding love for it. He wrote and recorded the occasional solo album, set up his own record label, and, in an attempt to satiate enduring Charlatans fans, established a series of 'Listening Parties', in which he would revisit their back catalogue and post his memories of those times on social media. It was a nice way, he says, to interact with the faithful. Every act that wants to endure must interact with the faithful.

And then something interesting happened. In 2020, with the world in lockdown, Burgess felt as much at a loose end as everyone else. He thought he might extend his Listening Parties, inviting the main players behind his favourite albums – the band members themselves, sundry producers – to hold their own Listening Parties using his Twitter platform. If people were no longer able to go and see music live, why not bring a classic album back to life on everybody's phone? You could have a venue's worth of fans, alone but together online.

Early on, he hosted Dexys Midnight Runners, Joy Division and New Order, and members of each band, along with a smattering of superfans and celebrity fans, joined in. It proved a curiously emotional experiment, everybody listening online in real time, reading the posts, adding memories of their own – a tightly bound community for the album's duration. The idea was a hit.

'Did I have any idea that would happen?' he says. 'No, no idea. I knew that they'd been really popular within the Charlatans' community, but when people like Franz Ferdinand's Alex Kapranos joined in, and Dave Rowntree from Blur, Bonehead from Oasis and Wendy Smith from Prefab Sprout, it just kind of took on a life of its own.'

One of its unforeseen consequences was bringing previously warring band members back together. After airing the Dexys album *Don't Stand Me Down*, the band's singer Kevin Rowland and guitarist Al Archer began talking again; when it was the turn of Joy Division's *Unknown Pleasures*, bassist Peter Hook and drummer Stephen Morris attended and exchanged pleasantries in 140 characters when, in real life, they hadn't exchanged anything resembling pleasantries in years.

'That was a thrilling side effect, to be honest with you,' Burgess says. 'They appreciated the work they'd done together, and could see eye to eye at least on those records. It felt incredibly fulfilling, and it goes to show, I suppose, the unifying power of music.'

Burgess spent most of 2020 as a new kind of record industry supremo, helping to breathe fresh life into old songs and bring people back together. CBEs have been awarded for less. Acts continue to contact him all the time, requesting a Listening Party of their own: Bonnie Tyler, Spandau Ballet, Barry Gibb, Daphne & Celeste, Shirley Bassey. The ongoing success has boosted his own profile, and he now finds himself busier than he has ever been.

'Music is still the huge love of my life,' he says, as he coasts towards his mid-fifties, still with a head full of hair, still with the same puppyish demeanour. 'It sustains me, it absolutely does, and I never want it to stop. I've been through phases where I did want it to stop – I once wrote a song called "Inspired Again", and that inspired me to make an album because of it – and sometimes, you feel like you might deserve a rest, but then the more you do, the more it comes. Creativity begets creativity, right? That's why I write the books, and make albums, and host Listening Parties and . . . well, whatever else it is that I'm doing. Sometimes I can barely remember *what* I'm doing, because there's just so much.'

This is the optimum state, of course: the fruits of his labour in perpetual season.

TWO

THE DIFFICULT UMPTEENTH ALBUM

4

'Why make music if it's just something that wears you down?'

It is routinely said that an act has a lifetime to make a first album, and then just twelve months to produce its follow-up. A debut is, or at least can be, the glorious summation of a band's early pent-up energy and vision, an outpouring of everything they always wanted to say given voice at last. The debut album is not always the *best* album, if only because everyone develops, gets better with age, learns their craft and, in an ideal world, has a bigger budget to enact grander aural concepts, but it is very often the benchmark, a distillation of what just might make the band unique, offering an indication of what could come next. Bill Drummond (him again) wrote on this subject in his book *17*: 'It is a well-known fact that most artists produce their best work early in their career. They may refine what they do, but you usually get the measure of what they are about on their first outing.'

The follow-up, meanwhile, is often by necessity a rushed affair, conceived at a time when the act's world has changed sometimes beyond all comprehension, and when the record company is keen to offer an audience more as soon as is feasibly possible. The Adele who made *21*, for example, was an entirely different woman to the one who had made *19* just three years previously. Selling six and a half million copies of your debut album changes you at a fundamental level, although in her case she was somehow not hampered by expectation: the next one sold thirty-one million copies. Nevertheless, a follow-up can often sound ill-conceived, a facsimile of its predecessor, and leave its creators feeling uncomfortably naked in public. Not for nothing is it all too frequently referred to as the 'difficult second album'.

Difficult second albums don't always have to follow a debut. If a band is lucky enough to grow with stealth rather than haste, then they may not break through until their third album, or their fifth, but the maths is otherwise the same: to follow up a successful record with another exacts a pressure on an act that they don't always recover from.

Stereo MC's difficult second album was actually their fourth. A British hip-hop act originating from Nottingham, they'd spent much of the second half of the 1980s making music that borrowed from rap, electronic and funk, much of it often gloriously out of sync with the trend of the day. But by the turn of the next decade, the band, complete with its errant apostrophe, suddenly seemed like a natural culmination of dance and indie that now possessed much urchin appeal; a Midlands take on the Happy Mondays' raffish charm. They were fronted by Rob Birch, someone who never rose to his full height but rather hovered in a perpetual half crouch, as if his bones were made from elastic bands. If the Mondays could look like drug dealers, there could be a case to make suggesting that Birch looked like a regular customer, with his sunken cheekbones and Steptoe whiskers, a Rizla perpetually clutched between the skeletal fingers of his right hand. Lost in oversized denim, he was all exaggerated hand shapes and headphones, another Artful Dodger on the take. In 1992, this had somehow come to resemble everything that was cool.

Connected, the band's third album, was filled with the kind of loose-limbed grooves that every band of the era craved: music that sounded like it was recorded in a hammock tied between two palm trees on a Jamaican beach. Alongside Primal Scream, they were perhaps the best live act of the ecstasy era, and *Connected* became that year's unofficial soundtrack: it set the collective mood *and* helped temper it after a big night out.

There was something about their organic rise that felt right-
eous and good, but the general sense of *chill* emitted was actually
a smokescreen, deliberately built to conceal what they were really
feeling: fear.

'For us, it was like: *Oh shit, we've achieved our childhood dream.
Where do we go now?*'

They couldn't go home because the fear was even more keenly
felt there, so they stayed on the road, on tour, for months on end.
For a time, it all seemed like a victory lap, belated acceptance
and welcome elevation. But even worldwide tours have a habit
of ending, at which point there really is no more avoiding the
requirement to go back to the drawing board, and start again.

Writer's block is a more common phenomenon amongst
novelists than it is musicians, but it exists in music and is just as
daunting. There is good reason many second albums sound like a
re-tread of the first: an act has nothing new to say, and so simply
says it again until inspiration strikes. Stereo MC's didn't want
to repeat themselves. Birch says that they wanted to get out of
the 'public domain' and 'get back to our roots'. To do this, they
couldn't use a conventional studio, because they'd always made
music in their front room. Making music from nothing was how
they did it; opulent studios where Pink Floyd might once have
recorded intimidated them.

'What we needed to do,' he says, 'was to make our *own* studio.'

A worthwhile project, then. They started looking, convincing
themselves that once they'd found the right location, the magic
would come flooding back. It doesn't take a psychologist to
suggest that the four years it took them to find it had little to do
with the ineptitude of estate agents but more the band's own
procrastinating. They'd bottled it, in short, and by delaying the
process of starting over, they could delay the inevitable: confirmation that there was nothing else. They'd said all they needed
to say.

'Success made us feel naked, I suppose,' says Birch. 'A bit of you wants to be who you were before, because that at least was real. But we'd lost touch with that. Couldn't find it again.'

They'd lost touch with their private lives, too. 'That ends up in tatters, because you just spent eighteen months away from home on tour. So your girlfriend's gone bananas, everything's gone down the pan, you just want to go home, or down the supermarket and do some shopping, have a normal life . . . but it's not there any more because when you *are* back home again, that normal life is . . . it's gone. People look at you when you're successful, but you've become separated from a part of yourself. Some people deal well with that, but we just burned out.

'Success,' he concludes, 'doesn't always pan out the way you might expect.'

They did eventually find their own personal Valhalla in Brixton, south London, their collective relief still edged with worry. No pressure, they told themselves. They wouldn't push it. The songs would come when they were good and ready; they were not things to order at the press of a button.

They waited another five years.

'Why make music if it's just something that wears you down? Music,' says Birch, 'should be a joyful process, you should feel the vibe of it. But to be worn down by it? What's the point of that?'

In the thirty years since the Stereo MC's managed to produce something so sublimely right and of its time, Rob Birch has remained more or less true to his craft. He quit Brixton a long time ago, and now lives by the sea in Margate, where he shares custody of his children with his former partner, and is on a sustained health kick. The band never did recreate the magic of *Connected*, and, indeed, there have only been two more albums since.

Birch long struggled to acclimatise to 'normal' life, and still does. 'But maybe that's just part of the fact of being a musician, that it's difficult to fit in?' he muses. 'I don't really do things like holidays, and I'm a bit antisocial. I just want to be in my home studio all the time. It's only when I hit the stage, that's when life feels like a matter of life and death, and I love that, but away from that, I'm a quiet guy. All I can tell you is that whatever it is that drives me to still do this is a very intense feeling. It's the only way I can live my life.'

In recent years, his band have set up their own label again, and are now working with younger acts, in pursuit, perhaps, of keeping young themselves. 'It helps you rejuvenate. I'll find myself in the studio with people who could be my children – let's face it, my *grand*children,' says the sixty-three-year-old, 'but I'm not even really aware of that, mostly. Maybe that's the beauty of this job. Music sort of keeps you young, and I've been incredibly fortunate to be able to spend my life doing what I wanted. Yeah, it's had its ups and downs, its struggles, but then every walk of life has its struggles, so I can't be negative about it. I still get nice vibes from people about what we've done. I like the nice vibes.'

In 2010, David Gray, to all intents and purposes a 'sensitive' singer-songwriter whose stock-in-trade was a pronounced lyrical vulnerability shackled to songs that easily bled, was prowling around the celebrated London recording studio he then owned like a boxer before a fight. He was full of what Americans call spunk, the bit between his teeth, his eyes so wide open you imagined their lids were feeling the strain, and raring to *go*.

There was good reason for this. He was about to release his new album, *Foundling*, which he believed would be the one to establish him as an artist for the ages. It would build further on the huge global success he'd achieved a decade previously with *White Ladder* and its lead single 'Babylon', a song so ubiquitous and inescapable that when it was later revealed that US inter-rogators in Iraq were using 'Babylon' as a form of torture, not everyone was surprised. (Gray himself was, understandably, not flattered.)

Anyway, *Foundling* would confirm him as a twenty-first-century Van Morrison, and an arena act for life. He'd earned it.

White Ladder was still fresh in the collective memory, one of those comparatively rare records that occasionally exist within music's sphere that *everybody* seemed to like, whether they usually favoured that sort of music or not. Previous records in this category include Bob Marley and the Wailers' *Legend*, Sade's *Diamond Life* and Portishead's *Dummy*, albums played everywhere, by everyone, all the time, the obligatory soundtrack to pizza restaurants and chain cafés and shopping centres. *White Ladder* was a quiet, ruminative record, feeling generally lovelorn, as so many records of similar ilk do, but without once giving over to cliché. Much of its strength could be found in Gray's voice, a gravel gargle that hinted at a curmudgeon who could spin poetry from broken hearts.

Its success had not come overnight. There had been three albums before it that no one had bought. Having exhausted the patience, and limited funds, of his independent record label, Gray made *White Ladder* on his own, a kind of last gasp as he approached, forebodingly, his thirtieth birthday.

'Everything I had, I put into that record,' he says. 'It was full of my heart and my soul.'

Expecting nothing, he released it in 1998, and was pleasantly surprised when it became a tangible hit in Ireland. It kept selling there, slowly but steadily, causing enough ripples that he was able to tour across the UK off the back of it. A major label in England thought him worth a punt, and released it with a bit of a marketing push, because if it was good enough for Ireland, why not elsewhere? They put out 'Babylon' as a single, and suddenly everything Gray had worked for came belatedly good. The single was a hit, the album too. Both then rapidly became something of a sensation. Good news, no?

'It was, but fame turned me into a bit of a twat, to be honest,' he admits.

Rushing towards him as it did, like a train arriving too fast into the station, he was blinded by its light. Gray had never grown up craving this kind of fame, had never wanted to be Freddie Mercury. Sold-out gigs were a novelty, likewise fans crowding outside the venue afterwards, hoping to claim an autograph. He found that if he didn't sign every scrap of paper proffered, he'd later receive letters of complaint, which cut him to the quick. One time, he was invited to a party by Elton John, John having declared himself a fan. Gray didn't go, on account of being too shy.

'I did get to meet him years later, and I thought he was very nice, actually. I can't think why I made such a big deal of meeting him the first time, but then I suppose I'm much more relaxed and at ease with myself now. I wasn't then.'

And so he chose mostly to stay at home, and hide. Married with two daughters, he felt safer there, in greater command of his sanity; it was where, too, he was able to lose himself in the music in the purest way. It was with the profits from *White Ladder* that he was able to buy the Church, Dave Stewart's north London recording studios, where My Bloody Valentine had recorded and, later, Beyoncé and Adele. Here, he indulged himself in his art, never quite believing his luck, but also wallowing in it.

But success had reawakened his competitive streak. A fanatical football fan, he began to think in sporting terms, couldn't help himself. With *White Ladder*, he'd beaten others, was at the top of the table. He wanted to keep winning, and so he threw himself into his work vigorously. He was keen to tap into the rich vein he'd opened up with 'Babylon', convinced he was only just beginning. There was more to come.

He was right. His two subsequent albums, *A New Day at Midnight* (2002) and *Life in Slow Motion* (2005), were eloquent, affecting records that seemed to reach deeper, and offer much more than the usual platitudes. They were big hits, too. But they cost him. World tours were leaving him 'pretty shredded', and he'd grown no more accustomed to, or fond of, the world one must exist within at this altitude. And so he faltered. There would be four years until his next album – years in pop music are like dog years – and 2009's *Draw the Line* seemed almost prophetically titled, in that it merely offered both more of the same, but in a more underwhelming fashion: the sound of an artist going off the boil.

By now, the singer-songwriter *du jour* selling millions, as Gray had once done, was James Blunt, a former reconnaissance officer in the Life Guards regiment of the British Army, who had served time in Kosovo and now sang love songs that revealed *his* sensitive side. Blunt's promotional video for 'You're Beautiful', which was filmed on the precipice of a cliff, with a roiling sea below, showed off what army training had done for his biceps and abs, which he proudly displayed by appearing topless, even though it was clearly cold and windy enough to warrant a coat and scarf – also mittens.

The message conveyed here, with great unsubtlety, was that singing soldiers are SexyTough™. David Gray had never been SexyTough™ – not like this.

Duly spooked, Gray returned to the studio immediately and, in a fit of creative competitiveness, whipped up *Foundling*, an album into which he poured the kind of focus that had so benefitted *White Ladder*. This would reclaim him his crown, surely.

'I've always wanted to see the nuance in the work that I did, and to see where it would take me creatively,' he says. 'What I do has to come from the heart; I have to be proud of it. Of course, when I listen to something I've written that I particularly like, I do dream of it – and me, I suppose – becoming massive again, but I know I'm not in control of that.'

Foundling felt like another last throw of the dice, but he was confident and pumped, full of conviction. How much conviction? *Foundling* was a *double* album, twenty songs. In an era of streaming, where nobody was really listening to albums any more, because they could instead pick and choose tracks, David Gray was offering up his magnum opus. But as its release date loomed, he began to question his bravado. 'This record is going to disappear off the face of the earth, bar some freak occurrence,' he decided perilously late, a pronouncement that probably gave his manager a migraine. He was proved right. Critical reaction was iffy, a collective shrugging of shoulders. One review suggested that the lyrics were 'so swaddled in poetic obfuscation, it's hard to summon enough interest to decode them'. The reviews failed to spark industry excitement, which meant that the record never fully engaged its intended audience, and it expired quietly.

A few months later, James Blunt released his third album, *Some Kind of Trouble*, which would sell over 100,000 copies in its first week. Blunt sat robustly pretty for another full year until a ginger-haired man with a battered acoustic guitar arrived on the scene singing plaintive ballads in a plaintive voice. But Ed Sheeran may as well have been touting a machine gun, so deftly did he ultimately dispose of his opposition.

It can be a cruel game, pop music.

David Gray nods his head and clears his throat. 'It's how it happens,' he says.

Now in his fifties, there is still fire in him, but these days it burns mostly off-camera. He's given a lot of thought to the fire of late, why it dominates his life so much and, to an extent, controls it. Increasingly, he considers himself 'vaguely on the spectrum', convinced that he must be 'slightly autistic'.

'Creativity, I think, is a vaguely autistic process, an obsessional thing where you go down a rabbit hole and get pleasure in it, in music, this abstraction in your own mind that is as beautiful as anything else in the world.'

A sensitive, sickly child, he'd been born with a condition called pyloric stenosis, where the stomach muscles neither open nor close properly. Eventually, if untreated, the stomach seizes up completely. As a baby, he couldn't articulate this discomfort, 'and so for the first few weeks [of my life], I was basically starving'. He underwent an operation, from which he still has the scar. 'They say that the first part of your life is the most formative, and so here I was, with this experience where I was wailing a lot, and nobody could comfort me, because nobody knew what was wrong.'

Following the operation, he was placed in an incubator for weeks. His parents couldn't pick him up or hold him; no flesh-on-flesh contact. He believes that this early trauma gave him a certain outlook, that the world was dangerous and he needed to inoculate himself against it. When he started making music at around eleven or twelve, it very quickly became one of the most important parts of his life. Unlike school, which was full of people and noise and potential threat, much like the rest of the outside world, music was something he could have a certain control over, and he could pursue it as he pleased. He derived a sense of protection from it, but also escape. 'Creating a world within a world, that's what music is. It's its own thing, and it allows you to live within your imagination.'

He continued to grow up tightly wound. He didn't like crowds, felt awkward in class. The more the world pressed in on him, the more he retreated inside. The fact that he was capable of writing songs, and that the songs didn't sound terrible, immediately afforded him a sense of achievement and identity that he wanted to build on. He could live here, like this, quite comfortably. It soon became an imperative, then a requirement, a need. Increasingly, if he wasn't actively engaged in writing music, then he didn't feel fully alive.

The same is true today. 'If I don't create music regularly, I feel incomplete, of very low worth. It's like, I almost feel that *this* is what I'm here for.' He laughs self-consciously. 'It's a deranged way to think, obviously, and of course it never ends, because of course there's always more. You write a song, and then you want to write another song; you get to the top of one hill, and then you're back down with this little nugget, but you have to climb back up again and do it all over.'

Achieving recognition became part of the process, and this is what led him, in the mid-nineties, to put his music out into the hostile world. When the hostile world lived up to the billing he'd afforded it by ignoring him, he retreated more. *White Ladder* proved the schism, requiring him to spend more time outside his head, to sign autographs, to field invitations to Elton John parties.

The subsequent dwindling of his public profile, then, has offered mixed blessings. He has already proved himself, so does he really need to do so again? For someone as competitive as he is, the answer is an infuriating 'yes': yes, he does need to prove himself again, over and over. But increasingly, he's come to accept the perameters within which he exists. He talks about acts like Coldplay, U2, Foo Fighters and Ed Sheeran, and how it strikes him that, for them, maintaining a consistent level of success is paramount.

'They want the arena shows, the stadiums, all the bells and whistles; they want to talk to presidents, to fix the world. I can't do that. I found all that a drain on my resources, and I didn't enjoy it. If I was to have that all again now, I would definitely enjoy it more, but you need something special to be part of that world, and I don't think I want that. Look at Beyoncé: she's like this super-person, but I can't help but think of the other side of her, the human being. She's got twins, a famous husband; her life must be fucking madness, and a lot of shit must have gone down to make that [her ascendancy to – and maintenance of – superstardom] work.'

In 2020, Gray put out a twentieth-anniversary edition of *White Ladder*, figuratively allowing himself to stand back and admire the work that went into that make-or-break album, and he's still proud of what it went on to do, and grateful for the artistic freedom it gave him. These days, he's stepped back from the limelight somewhat, just as the limelight has swung inexorably away from him. He lives in London and has a bolthole in Norfolk to which he routinely departs to work. He still can't relax, because relaxation is not a part of his make-up. His family do not always follow him to the bolthole, and when he is alone, he paints – a hobby he has recently taken up – and continues to feel the same compulsion to write songs that he first felt at the age of eleven.

It's when talking about new music that he fully comes to life. His voice raises, and he doesn't quite shout, but rather barks his enthusiasm for the task at hand, like a Jack Russell that has just stumbled upon the biggest branch in the park and is going to drag it back with him, however cumbersome.

'I make music all the time. It's a job, *my* job, but it's also a process, and I love that process, it's what I do and who I am. When I write a good song, I still feel like a bird soaring on the thermals, it's this overpowering feeling, and I love it. It feels like a risk, somehow, because every time you put another record out, it's harrowing. You want it to be loved, you want people to love it, to say it's special.'

Which is not always the outcome he gets. 'Exactly! But then I like that risk, to be honest. If you're not risking something, then you're not fully in the game. Every time a record I finish goes out into the world, I'm scared. Any knives that come my way' – bad reviews, he means – 'they hurt. My family, they hate to see the pain that gives me. They feel it vicariously, but perhaps even more acutely than I do. I know for a fact that my wife can't stand it. For her, the whole process is agony.'

For David Gray, it's agony too.

He offers up the most enormous grin. 'It is. But it's who I am. No changing now.'

5

'Because I'm Billy Bragg, mate. What's your excuse?'

The worst thing that ever happened to Billy Bragg, of course, was Margaret Thatcher. Not the historic election of 1979 that saw her confirmed as the UK's first female Prime Minister, but rather the moment in 1990 when she was coldly and deliberately ousted by her party, thus forcing her to leave Number Ten, and public life, for good.

Bragg had long been a political activist who'd used songwriting as a way to vent his mounting frustration with Tory rule. Its leader was a perpetual source of material, the gift that kept on giving. When Thatcher wanted to reduce the power of trade unions, and pointedly ignored the demands of miners in 1984, which led to them striking for a full year, Bragg responded with the *Between the Wars* EP, a clarion cry of support whose title track somehow became a hit. A year earlier, his 1983 debut album, *Life's a Riot With Spy Vs Spy*, had been full of politically charged songs that addressed rising unemployment, and issued a plea for unity and a New England, all to the accompaniment of a clanging electric guitar. Not much else sounded like this in 1983, the charts otherwise full of Dionne Warwick, Cliff Richard and Kajagoogoo, while Duran Duran were chasing supermodels on superyachts in the Caribbean and grinning about it.

Bragg, who looked like he would sunburn easily and so was best kept far from exotic beaches, co-founded the Red Wedge movement alongside fellow musicians Paul Weller and Jerry Dammers. Their aim was to help promote the Labour Party among younger voters. They staged concerts in the belief that by raising political awareness amongst their fans, they would inspire corresponding action at the ballot box.

'In the 1980s,' Bragg says, 'music was our social media. If you wanted to comment about the world, you had to buy a guitar and write songs. I received some good advice from an American once: don't sing about politics, *be* politics. I thought that was very interesting. I wanted to find out how music could make a difference.'

Though many would hitch a ride on the same bandwagon, motivated by the same honest impulses, Bragg always stood out. Where Paul Weller, the Communards' Jimmy Somerville and the Blow Monkeys' Dr Robert were perhaps easier on the eye and could carry a tune – in other words, behaved like pop stars – one could never really forget that Bragg was, at least in the early days, first and foremost a protest singer. He looked like he sold the *Socialist Worker* newspaper, and he boasted a singing voice that had the same impact on the ears as a pair of Doc Marten boots being dropped into a dustbin from a great height. He played his guitar in an abrasive manner. Whenever his songs made it on to Radio 1, no mean feat for such a progressive patriot, their sense of agitated purpose was palpable. The Labour leader Neil Kinnock loved him.

'I knew I'd never be able to sing like Boy George, and I'd never have hair like Tony Hadley,' Bragg says. 'I'd never wear make-up like Adam Ant, or slap a bass guitar like [Level 42's] Mark King. So I just thought to myself: *Okay, when everybody else is zigging, I'll zag.*'

He'd grown up in Barking, Essex, a fan of Bob Dylan and then, later, punk. Punk had given him the permission to pursue music as he wanted to pursue it. He craved seeing singers of intent, artists with something to say, but there was a dearth of those within the New Romantic movement, and so, he says, 'I just thought to myself: *For fuck's sake, I'm just going to have to do this myself, because I'm not going to get the music that reflects my experience otherwise.* I was just going to have to steel myself, and learn how to write songs that would be able to punch a hole in mainstream culture like a stiletto.'

The fact that Bragg would go on to do just that would have been thrilling in any era, but all the more so in a decade where music was predominantly flashy, sparkly and so full of Simon Le Bon. In his earnest jeans, his earnest boots and with that jut of his lip that flared to unleash such strident passion, he became one of the era's more interesting stars. Though routinely labelled a politically motivated protest singer, he wrote love songs, too – good ones. Over the years, his voice softened around the edges, became warmer, a croon, less hectoring. He began writing more unambiguously emotional tunes, one of which, 'A New England', was covered by Kirsty MacColl and made the Top 10. Ever more keening examples followed: 'Must I Paint You a Picture?', 'The Price I Pay'. The man was a romantic.

Nevertheless, 1990's historic political scalping of a famously divisive Prime Minister served largely to douse Bragg's still-fervent political flame. He may not have been particularly enamoured with Thatcher's replacement, John Major, but in one sense, his work here was done. By this point, Bragg had been making music for a decade. He'd established himself, very firmly, within the public's consciousness. The miners' strike was long over, and now its chief antagonist was gone, too.

'It was time for a break, then. A bit of a rethink.'

In 1991, he returned, a kind of Billy Bragg 2.0. Having spent the last decade flirting with the charts and writing actual pop songs that other people had hits with, he now attempted to reinvent himself as a fully rounded pop star. Not someone to start swilling

Dom Perignon with *Top of the Pops* regulars, perhaps, and never a champagne socialist, but still: a pop star nonetheless.

Two years previously, he'd written a song entitled 'Sexuality' that, to his ears at least, boasted his most ringing melody yet. He subsequently handed it over to Johnny Marr, formerly of the Smiths, who 'went away and worked on it', and delivered back something that sounded like a hit: bold and declarative, with a chorus to die for. Duly encouraged, Bragg and his producer Grant Showbiz realised they were now going to have to make an album that 'Sexuality' could sit comfortably in, 'a huge pop album, in other words, and so that's precisely what we did'.

Don't Try This at Home was the result. It included contributions from Kirsty MacColl and R.E.M.'s Michael Stipe and Peter Buck, and featured some of Bragg's least political, and most personal, songs to date. This was not the Billy Bragg of 1983, or of 1986, when his album *Talking to the Taxman About Poetry* had made him one of the most lauded British singer-songwriters. (Bragg himself considers that album to be his most important, 'the one that defines me; the core perception people have of me is based around that record'.) It was by now 1991, a new decade, and he was trying something new: to become a mainstream commodity, not just amenable to the masses but appealing, too, a left-leaning singer who could grin with the best of them. The guitars no longer jarred, and the voice was now a thing of mellifluous wonder.

Don't Try This at Home proved itself a fine home for its ebullient lead single, and it received the kind of reviews many artists spend their careers dreaming of.

'But here's the rub. We sold exactly the same amount of records, about a hundred thousand copies. It did not,' Bragg says, 'go gangbusters.'

Even 'Sexuality', a song made for heavy rotation on daytime radio, only made it to number twenty-six. The project, valiant as it was, had failed.

Bragg was philosophical. 'The point is, I wanted to see if I could do that thing, to be a pop star, and I could, but only to a point. And in many ways, it was a cul-de-sac for me. It didn't lead me anywhere after that, either up, or next. So after almost ten years of making music, where the fucking hell *do* you go? I mean, I'm Billy Bragg, for fuck's sake. I'm Mr Miners' Strike, remember? So even if certain people at certain record companies do get excited by me, I always have to remind them who I am: I'm Billy Bragg, I'm *this* guy.'

This was less glass ceiling than brick wall. People's attention spans were evaporating, and that was not solely the fault of Margaret Thatcher. He couldn't hold her responsible any more.

Fair enough, of course. Eras pass. Nobody ever suggested that pop stardom offered a lifetime career, and precious few get tenure.

Woody Guthrie was a fabled American folk artist, who was born in 1912 and died in 1967. He grew up in a wealthy family who lost their fortune in the Depression, and went on to become, briefly, a faith healer and a comedic hillbilly act before settling on something that felt more *him*: folk music. He was a politicised folk artist, and wanted to rouse crowds. 'A folk song is what's wrong and how to fix it,' he once wrote.

According to a 2004 essay in the *New Yorker*, Guthrie was 'aesthetically less a socialist than an anarchist, contemptuous of the prevailing rules and standards'. A young Bob Dylan would look up to him, as would, many decades later, and an ocean away, an emergent Billy Bragg. The latter was once part of a tribute concert for Guthrie in New York, but could have had little idea, then, that Guthrie was to prove his salvation, of sorts, and would offer him the kind of second life few could have seen coming.

In 1992, just as the ramifications of having made a not particularly well-performing album were beginning to make themselves plain to Bragg – he had a lot of time on his hands – Woody

Guthrie's daughter Nora contacted him. Her late father, she told him, had left behind countless lyrics for which he'd never got around to writing music. Would Bragg be interested?

By this stage in his life, Bragg had set down roots. He was in a relationship with a woman, Juliet Wills, who'd previously worked at his record label and had been the wife of his former record-label boss. Together, they had a child, allowing the singer a glimpse of a steadier life. He warmed instantly to it, having long been aware that he needed to step back and disengage. He was also suffering from a swollen appendix, which had left him bedbound for months.

'It was almost like my body said: "You've done your bit, mate. Just chill out now."'

While parenthood doesn't generally allow for anything that might be described as 'chilling out', remaining in one place *did*. For the next five years, he was husband and father. He didn't write a single song.

The Guthrie offer intrigued him as much as it daunted him. His first thought was that this was a project for Bob Dylan, not him. He didn't say no to Nora Guthrie, but he didn't automatically agree to it, either. Instead, he let it percolate. Once his son was safely ensconced in primary school, he became increasingly aware of just how empty life had become. How to fill it? He did so initially by quickly reverting to type, with a solo album called *William Bloke*, which was more *Taxman* than *Don't Try This at Home*. It sold to the faithful, which pleased him, but post-album satisfaction was now a case of diminishing returns. He'd reached the stage of his career where he was repeating himself. He needed to stretch more.

And so he returned to the Guthrie project. Bragg was keenly aware that, though there may have been an implicit connective tissue between him and his subject, he was still a little too *Barking, Essex*, to fully do justice to an American icon – alone.

He approached the US band Wilco, closer in spirit, and closer geographically, to Guthrie, to ask if they might like to collaborate. There were over 1,000 sets of lyrics, but this didn't necessarily translate – to Bragg – to 1,000 songs. Even legends have filler. His idea was to pick and choose, and to record one album.

The project eventually extended to *three*. The first, *Mermaid Avenue*, came out in 1998. It was a big success, far bigger than Bragg had ever achieved before, the combination of his musical chops, Wilco's melody, and the impeccable source material proving formidable. It reinvented him amongst his supporters and introduced him to an entirely new fanbase. The political singer was now a folk artist. It might have seemed odd, but instead felt like a natural continuation for him, an evolving. Gone was the clenched fist; in came a ruminative beard of salt-and-pepper streaks, with flecks of auburn. Now he looked the part. People complemented him on the beard, and his wife approved. He kept it.

'You know, I always thought it would remain a side project, but when it connected me to a new audience – specifically, Wilco's audience, which was much younger than my own – it allowed me to pursue Americana, which I've always loved. I have always loved American roots music.'

Not many artists are comparably fortunate, but then it wasn't only luck on Bragg's side. He's always been a shrewd player: he owns his entire back catalogue, for example, so while many of his peers were, as we shall see, done over by either unscrupulous record company contracts or accountants with the morals of Ronnie Biggs, all the profits from Billy Bragg's old records go directly to their author. When he put his Chesil Beach house up for sale in 2019, the *Daily Mail* noted that the 'staunchly socialist music star who railed against bankers' bonuses and promotes equality and anti-globalisation' was set to make a 'whopping' £2.4 million profit on the 'mansion' he'd bought two decades previously for £630,000.

Alongside his deep delve into Americana, Bragg, like Shaun Ryder and Tim Burgess and many other singers, has written books, his on the themes of memoir, roots music and a Brexit-inspired analysis of Britishness. He has mostly avoided the nostalgia circuit, but even he isn't immune to a little looking back. In 2019, he revisited his first three albums on a UK tour, which not only brought him more satisfaction than he'd expected, but also reminded him why he sang in the first place, and why he continues to do so.

He says that he has always remained engaged with his career, has never taken it for granted, and that he and his wife, who is his manager, are constantly coming up with new ideas to perpetuate it further still. 'So if I'm going to write a book about, say, skiffle [which he did in 2017], Juliet will work out how that will fit into what else we're doing, I suppose because it's all just another thing for people to help keep them engaged.'

Things are now not as linear as they used to be – album, tour, album, repeat to fade – but rather more varied, unpredictable and, occasionally, surprising. 'It keeps the audience interested, but us interested, too.'

He calls himself a journeyman, someone who likes to turn up to work every morning at ten o'clock 'and see what there is to do. And then I ask Juliet what to do, because Juliet always did have a much better idea about "Billy Bragg", about what he's doing, what he should be wearing, and where he should be going next, than I ever did.'

And the way he remains Billy Bragg is to remember who Billy Bragg is, and was, and to remind the rest of us, too. To this end, he will occasionally write op-ed pieces for the *Guardian*, appear on *Question Time* defending, say, Jeremy Corbyn, and will routinely upset, or at least mildly rile, people on Twitter.

A short while back, he arrived on the picket line for some or other political issue, one of many he feels almost instinctively strongly about. It was early in the morning, midweek, and pouring with rain. Inclement weather can often diminish the collective ire of a picket line, and there weren't very many people there. But those present stood firm, held their banners proudly aloft, and occasionally chanted their protest aloud.

Presently, one of his fellow picketers made glancing eye contact, then promptly did the double-take that all famous people are routinely the recipients of. The man sidled up to him, and the following conversation took place.

'Hey, aren't you Billy Bragg?'

The singer confirmed that he was.

'Why are *you* here?'

He smiled his response, teeth flashing behind his gradually greying beard. 'Because I'm Billy Bragg, mate. What's your excuse?'

THREE

SCENESTERS

6

'You've got to be ruthless, and stay ruthless'

Herein lies a cautionary tale of the most rudimentary, textbook kind.

At the very end of 1999, while many of their former peers were counting down to Y2K at parties whose highpoints would be recounted in the tabloids the following day – if, that is, Y2K did not herald either the abrupt end of the world or else a frustrating computer malfunction – three members of a once briefly popular act went trekking in Nepal. This represented for them not so much a fun holiday as a necessary respite from the perpetual shitstorm of everyday life in the kind of group that only ever ascends to *almost-famous*, in part because they'd been slung onto the bandwagon of a short-lived scene. When the short-lived scene then dies, as they surely must, the bands tend to die with them.

The three members of Echobelly were, in a general sense, miserable and morose. They took this ominous mood with them, packed tight into their rucksacks and mindsets, convinced that fate had dealt with them cruelly. They'd been overlooked, lumped in, never given the chance to breathe. While in Nepal, sufficiently far from the madding crowd, the small plane that had taken them high into the mountains from their base in Kathmandu then crashed on its return flight, killing everyone on board. Perhaps this was fate offering them a second chance? But if so, how to interpret it? They'd narrowly escaped with their lives, and as their thoughts went out to the dead, they could not have felt any more despondent.

Just a few short years before, Echobelly had been on the rise. Things were looking good. They were a so-called 'female-fronted' band about whom much was written, and much correspondingly expected. They'd been referred to by the music press of the day as 'female-fronted' in order to alert readers to some kind of USP: Britpop was mostly men in ankle-revealing skinny denim, and so those that weren't – namely Echobelly, Elastica, Sleeper and, a little later, Catatonia – tended to stand out rather, and Echobelly all the more so because their singer had been born in Delhi. (This was exotic; the singer from Sleeper was from Gants Hill.)

In the time of Britpop, when so many of the bands that came through in the wake of Blur, Oasis and Pulp, excelled only in their ability to underwhelm, these particular female-fronted acts stood out, not simply because of their singers' gender but because they were more erudite than their male counterparts: smarter, more wily. If Elastica's Justine Frischmann, within whom a sultry beauty melted into existential ennui and a pout tailor-made for cigarettes to dangle from, was the coolest rock star of the era, then Sleeper's Louise Wener was a Machiavellian marvel in interview situations in ways that Damon Albarn, and certainly Liam Gallagher, could only dream of.

Echobelly's Sonya Madan may have been the quieter proposition, but she was no less articulate. Her band's touchstones were Blondie and the Smiths, and they rose to prominence just as the British music scene was reasserting its dominance after a long period of being overshadowed by American acts whose collective sense of drama – musical and otherwise – had been far more thrilling. Echobelly reached their height in 1994 with the winningly upfront single 'I Can't Imagine the World Without Me', a song whose melody was as memorable as its title, and which so tickled Morrissey – still, back then, a venerable God before whom all alternative musicians genuflected – that he claimed he wished he'd written it himself. Madonna was similarly impressed, and wanted to sign the band to her label in America, while Michael Stipe of R.E.M. personally invited Echobelly to support his band on tour.

If all acts have career highlights, Echobelly's were ones to dine out on. But a counterbalancing was on its way. Madan came to hate the implicit hierarchy of Britpop, its masses converging beneath a couple of monobrowed kings, everyone trading off everyone else, everyone bullish to cartoonish extremes, often strung out on cocaine, sleeping with one another and generously exchanging STDs. She grew increasingly uncomfortable over the combative manner of promotional duties, how she'd invite the press into her inner sanctum with politeness only to then read vicious takedown pieces about her band's purported failings. She grew exasperated over their ineffectual management team, a battle that went all the way to the courts and that cost them £60,000, after which their accountant, not someone troubled by conscience, absconded with what remained of their bank balance. (The accountant was caught and imprisoned, but the money never recovered.)

Kathmandu, then, was a kind of running away, a chance to consider: what now? When they returned, they resolved to limp on. Madan took out an extension on her mortgage in order to fund two further albums, but when they failed to catch the public's attention, one member left, then another, leaving just its core two, Madan and guitarist Glenn Johansson. They routinely discussed what the continued point of all this was. Shouldn't they just quit? Too late.

'It was the industry that quit me,' Madan says now. 'I only stopped making music at times because it was utterly depressing to carry on, to create something you love but have no outlet for.' They wanted a new deal, new opportunities, and to remain relevant. But, she says, 'all doors were shut to us, people wouldn't take our calls.'

There were two options: either survive on dwindling royalties, and persist with the occasional performance, a rolling-out of all the old hits (and in doing so, live like a hermit), 'or let go of the creative urge and live a secure life in the "real world".'

Perhaps precisely because so many musicians find it hard to contemplate existing in whatever this 'real world' might look like, Madan chose the former. Echobelly elected to go on. When a small UK tour of 2015 included several sold-out dates, Madan considered it 'a turning point, and a lifeline'. It meant that there *was* a living they could eke out here, reliant as it was upon a clutch of increasingly old songs that defined them and that, in the minds of many, were enough. Nobody really needed anything else from them.

This is not a healthy way to live, of course, and doesn't take in the reality of their situation. To keep themselves sane, they continued to write new songs, sometimes as Echobelly, other times as a side project called Calm of Zero. Back in the mid-nineties, they were writing big, ebullient pieces like 'I Can't Imagine the World Without Me' and 'Great Things'; nowadays, they sing songs called 'Dying' and 'I Don't Belong Here'.

Madan says: 'With us, it's always the same few songs that are still played on the radio. I understand that; I just don't want to be remembered for nostalgia's sake alone. I'm still making music.' But whatever for? 'Ultimately, because of a desire to know myself.'

Back in 2001, during an interview, Sonya Madan was asked what was her greatest fear. Her answer: 'Dying unfulfilled.' When asked what her motto was, she said: 'What doesn't kill you makes you stronger.'

Echobelly's story is, to an extent, *everybody's* story. It's music's overriding narrative, a script unavoidably followed by most, if not quite *all*, acts. Successful businesses tend to be the most ruthless, and the music business is very successful indeed. And so while it was Echobelly's unwittingly poor timing that saw them harnessed to the runaway train that was Britpop, they benefitted from it too, enjoying an exposure they might not otherwise have had. They landed a sizeable deal, a marketing budget, ample studio time. The doors were thrown open to them, and they were encouraged to run before they slammed shut again.

Nothing quite energises the industry like the arrival of a new scene. Each boasts its leading lights, and each the lower wattage variations thereof. It happened in the 1960s with the Beatles and the Stones, and the countless copyists that followed in their wake, and it happened again in the seventies with punk. During Madchester in the early nineties, labels fought to throw lighted matches on its careless petrol spill, and signed up anyone with a bowl cut and flares in the hope that they too might spark: there was Northside, the High, Paris Angels and so very many more. But by the time the spill reached the capital, it was promptly snuffed out by Flowered Up, a London equivalent straight out of central casting – bad dentistry, chemical dependencies – whose enthusiasm may have matched that of Happy Mondays, but whose talent was ultimately found wanting.

Britpop's holy trinity were not directly responsible for the Supernaturals or My Life Story, and certainly not for Gay Dad and Menswear, but their success did allow such acolytes to follow gleefully through on the logic and the hope that something might stick. Many of them hoped to be scooped up by Blur's label, Food Records, which ensured that its co-proprietor Dave Balfe spent much of his time in the mid-1990s separating what might have been wheat from chaff. Balfe had previous. In the 1970s, he'd played keyboards with the Teardrop Explodes, and in the early eighties founded the record label Zoo with Bill Drummond. By the end of that decade, he'd co-founded Food, signing acts like Voice of the Beehive, Crazyhead and Zodiac Mindwarp, before finding breakthrough success in the early nineties, first with Jesus Jones, and then, paydirt at last, with Blur. In the wake of the latter's popularity in particular, his mission was to sign more and more bright young things with international appeal. Easier said than done: by 1994, he was burned out and announced his semi-retirement, leaving the capital and moving to a house in the country, in the process inspiring his most gifted charge, Damon Albarn, to write what would become Blur's first number-one hit, 'Country House'.

Many people in previous positions of power are happy to talk up their achievements, and to underline their impact and influence. Balfe, though, is good on clarity. 'I think there's a lot of bollocks talked about A&R [artists and repertoire],' he says, 'because all you're really trying to do is find anybody good. But even then you've got no idea how they're going to turn out. It's pot luck.'

For Balfe, it's easier to look for another Mariah Carey than it is, say, a Blur, a position which probably explains why he never went on to become Simon Cowell. Mariah Carey has an identifiable talent, an octave-ranging voice, a natural sense of rhythm, and the deportment of someone cut out for the finer things in life. 'But when you're in the alternative thing, you don't really have a clue. You're putting out some wacky, weird thing that's good for the first alternative record, but then have no idea whether they'll learn how to write good pop songs, or just remain wacky and weird. You sign a band who might just go on to become another U2, but who might never get bigger than, say, Crazyhead.

'It's like poker,' he says. 'You keep taking a series of punts.'

Balfe had felt moved to take a punt on Blur because 'three of them were good-looking'. Cheekbones, it seems, matter in the alternative world, too. Food once came close to signing an act Balfe believed was full of promise, 'but the singer was dreadful-looking, so we didn't.'

A few years earlier, he'd seen Pulp live. By this stage, Jarvis Cocker's band of Sheffield misfits had been around for a long time, but nothing was happening. Cocker was fascinating: he'd once spent several months in a wheelchair after falling out of a window while trying to impress a girl, a story he perpetuated that probably has only a loose attachment to the actual truth. Either way, the wheelchair became a stage prop for a while. Balfe had been intrigued by the band, and thought there was something particularly compelling about the singer. But doubts lingered. 'It's about instinct versus analysis,' he says, perhaps ruefully wishing that on that particular occasion, instinct had trumped analysis. Back then, in the late eighties, almost a decade before Jarvis Cocker would find his long-legged stride, Balfe rightly knew that Pulp would take work, and that such work was a costly business. 'Too many record companies go bankrupt that way,' he notes. 'You've got to be ruthless, and stay ruthless.'

And so while there were a lot of freshly minted popstars made at the dawning of Britpop, excited for their prospects, enjoying being on the brink, not all of them made it to sundown.

7

An average day for Martin Carr today comprises getting out of bed, readying the children for school, seeing them off with a packed lunch and a wave, and then retreating upstairs to the spare bedroom (his home studio), where he considers his recent diagnosis of ADHD and the consequences thereof, listens to music, and maybe writes a song, but not always.

Like an entomologist who mounts and privately displays their butterfly collection with great attention to detail but doesn't necessarily show anyone else the fruits of their intricate labours, submerging himself in music is simply something Martin Carr *does*.

'I don't have any hobbies; my hobby is music. It's what I do when I'm working, and what I do when I'm not working. It's what I think about pretty much all the time,' he says.

His studio is small and compact, but studios can be these days: in it, he has everything he needs. He has written *a lot* of music in this room, and the vast majority of it has never been given fresh air to breathe. But then, such exposure to oxygen is something his songs no longer really need; nor, by extension, does he, or at least not as much as he used to. Once, the music he created had been head-spinningly ambitious, often astutely commercial, and, for him, pleasingly celebrated. He was no U2, and his band would never fill out stadiums, but the people who liked him loved him, and the critics who wrote about him did so in purple ink.

Perhaps the most vibrant song of his commercial peak was also the most unlike him. 'Wake Up Boo!', composed in 1995 and released by his band, the Boo Radleys, was the kind of hit single that made much more impact, and had a greater endurance, than its number-nine chart position might suggest. The song was an exclamation mark in aural form, a burst of effervescent joy so acute it could have been read as a parody of fizzy, disposable pop. Either way, it was quickly adopted by morning DJs and, subsequently, TV programmers whenever their shows required an injection of pep. A quarter of a century on, and it can still be heard frequently (perhaps too frequently) in the unlikeliest of places – most recently, at the time of writing, for a Venetian blinds company.

For Carr, 'Wake Up Boo!' had been an experiment. The song-writer, who'd been born in Scotland and raised in the Wirral, and whose natural bent was the kind of sonic experimentalism Brian Wilson would have appreciated in 1966, also had main-stream dreams. A child of *Top of the Pops*, he wanted to be on it. The music he'd made before then had been left-field and avant-garde – 'alternative', as Dave Balfe would have described it – and sufficiently alternative at a time when such music rarely graced the Top 40. But 'Wake Up Boo!' was a pocket rocket, and perfect for the times. It couldn't fail, and didn't.

They got to play on *Top of the Pops*. Carr found it as thrilling as he did disappointing, not an unusual reaction for dreams coming true. The studio was so small, he says, and the audience aggressively stage-managed. The band's singer, Simon Rowbottom, was forced to mime.

Nevertheless, job done. He could move on now. 'It turned into a leviathan, that song. But then it's also been such a relief to me in so many ways. I think I'm probably here at all, these days, thanks to "Wake Up Boo!"' He may wish he'd written better lyrics for it, and he may occasionally cringe when he hears it, but its continued existence allows him to pay the bills, and he is grateful for that.

'My daughter shows me YouTube videos of people playing it to wake themselves up in dorm rooms in America, things like that, and that's just amazing to me, but I can't really connect with the song, not on a personal level. It's just so long ago, and no longer really anything to do with me.'

Licensing requests for the track came flooding in almost the moment it made the Top 10, but Carr, an artist with a moral core, always turned them down. Music was art, not the soundtrack to complicated curtains. But then life happened to him: the band broke up, he broke down, his earning power became anorexic, and he needed help. When the requests kept coming, he taught himself to say yes.

He says, 'It's been my lifeline, that song.'

It takes a while for Martin Carr to agree to talk. He admits he's unsure about the benefits of discussing his halcyon days, fearful he'll have nothing much to contribute, or else won't be able to remember them. He explains in an email that his story post-Boo Radleys is a 'long, sorry tale of frustration and failure. [But] of course if that's what you're after, then I'm your man. Looking forward,' he signs off, 'to letting you down.'

In person, however, Carr turns out to be a delightful proposition: warm and friendly, a little uncertain of himself but deeply thoughtful; he answers questions as if each word possesses a physical weight. The spectre of ADHD had been hanging over him for some time – he'd seen doctors, had tests – and when the diagnosis finally came through, 'it explained a lot'. Quite *what* it explained, and the extent of it, is something he is still trying to process by himself, privately.

Twenty-five years previously, Carr was an unusually focused musician and occasional singer who wanted to express himself on a canvas far larger and broader than that of the average band that came of age in the early nineties. He wanted to push boundaries, and delve deep into his unconscious, unsettled by the thought of what he might find there, but compulsively fascinated by the prospect nevertheless. As a twenty-year-old, he was impossibly fresh-faced, like a page of A4 not yet coloured in. He had flyaway curly hair, and wore an expression of perpetual curiosity, as if thoughts were constantly falling into his head from a great height and taking him by surprise.

He formed his band with his childhood friend, Simon Rowbottom, aka Sice, who became singer to his guitarist. Inspired by American guitar bands of the late 1980s, their first couple of albums were exercises in foot-shuffling and woozy throat-clearing, easy to underestimate, easier still to overlook. It was with their third album, 1993's *Giant Steps*, that everything abruptly changed for them. Britpop hadn't yet thrown its Union Jack over everything, and the British music scene that wasn't busy revolving around Suede and an early incarnation of the Verve was generally unexciting and plodding, and smelled a little too much like cider. *Giant Steps* was a deliberately ambitious album, a haunted house filled with endless rooms, each concealing different colours, different styles, and frozen in different eras. Carr's touchstones were Lennon and McCartney, the Beach Boys, free-form jazz, and the sonic scares of horror-movie soundtracks that coincide with the precise moment the protagonist tiptoes down into the dark cellar.

'Previously, I'd been listening to dub music, to Aphex Twin, and gorging on the Flaming Lips, the Beach Boys, the Beatles and the Clash, but then I suddenly stopped.'

Giant Steps was the result of that cessation. 'For me, it was like someone had unscrewed a lid on a bottle of Coke, or something. I was listening to all these records, I didn't have a day job for the first time, I was living in London with no money, and trying to make music. I didn't really care what I was doing as long as I didn't have to work in an office, and so all this music just poured out of me, and it felt really easy. But then I was on my game back then, and able to communicate what I wanted, which I wasn't necessarily able to do later on.'

Though the album was sufficiently strange to keep its singles at a safe distance from the charts – which were busy at the time hosting Bitty McLean, Culture Beat and Ace of Base – the Boo Radleys were critically lauded and thus elevated to a position from which they could gaze loftily down at their peer group. If music can so often seem like an elaborate game of one-upmanship, the Boo Radleys had just registered the highest score.

Carr's reaction to this was unexpected: he tumbled headlong into depression. 'I had problems. I was letting myself get led into . . . *situations*,' he says. 'I didn't really stand up for myself, and went through phases of just feeling completely isolated. That year, 1993 and into 1994, I just had an awful time. We didn't make any records, we just toured.'

To outsiders looking in, this makes scant sense. You start a band to make music. To be able to go on tour in order to play that music is the natural endpoint, the highlight. For Carr, it just piled on pressure he wasn't able to shoulder. Everyone around him was made to feel it, too. He did not suffer in silence. One newspaper review at the time suggested that the guitarist was 'fatally attracted to being a tortured artist'.

He believes today that even if he'd never been in a band, if he was working in an office job, 'I would still have felt like a tortured artist. I remember going through a brief period during the making of that album where we were going to be – in my head, anyway – like free-form jazz. I'd really got into a John Coltrane album, *A Love Supreme*, a beautiful record, but I wasn't a good enough musician, and was too embarrassed to play the guitar in front of people. So all I could really do was make a noise, but I was trying to be more complex, and make complex music – jazz music. But I think I only really managed it for one B-side, and it didn't work out.'

This brought him to a certain realisation: he didn't want to be in an indie band any more, and you could keep your critical plaudits. 'I wasn't patient enough to build up a following, so I decided that what I wanted to do next was to become a pop star, to be on *Top of the Pops.*'

Shortly after their tour finally ended, in 1994, he set himself the task of writing their next album, *Wake Up!* The title, with its strident punctuation, was a directive to himself as much as to anyone else. He wrote the song that would go on to become their defining hit single – thereby halving their previously loyal audience – and waited for *this* to make him happy.

But it didn't, at least not really. Now that he'd proved he could do whatever he wanted, a musician who could elicit a response in whichever genre he chose, he launched another about-face, adamant that it was time to reassert those avant-garde tastes, and extend them. He learned more about John Coltrane, and retreated further into himself, behaving in a manner that would once have had people referring to him as a 'mad genius'. Meanwhile, his band's label, Creation, had been partly bought out by Sony, a move inspired chiefly because Sony wanted Creation's most important asset, Oasis, but could only have them if they took the rest of the roster, too.

Creation had never been run like a normal record label, but rather like Factory in Manchester: on a whim, on gut instinct – often on drugs, too – and always with a tangible passion. The vast majority of Creation's acts were not commercially successful, and didn't much want to be, but now, under the umbrella of corporate Sony, they had to earn their keep or else find themselves increasingly pushed out towards the nearest gutter.

Martin Carr was not designed to work well in such circumstances.

'All of a sudden, our promotions guy wasn't a drug dealer but rather a guy who'd previously worked at Virgin, and had all these "ideas", and stuff. He wore a suit. He wanted us to have another Top 40 hit, not more of *Giant Steps.*'

Two albums followed, quietly and cursorily, each another nail in the coffin Carr was steadfastly, and deliberately, creating for himself, as his own Grim Reaper.

It was singer Simon Rowbottom who left first. Carr's first instinct was to ask him to reconsider, but, he says, 'I've always been one for the grand gesture. I could have asked him to carry on, or perhaps suggest we have a year off and go off and do our own things separately, then reconvene later and see what happens then . . . But, no, it had to be the big split.' He laughs sourly. 'Nobody seemed to notice, anyway.'

In his converted warehouse in east London, which he shared with his then-wife, he assiduously tuned out of daily life. He woke up, stayed in bed, got drunk. Occasionally, because he had money, he booked out some expensive rehearsal rooms in which to dabble and experiment, keep his hand in, articulate his talent. If he'd already produced one grand opus, who was to say he couldn't produce a second? But there were pubs on the way to the studio, and so he frequented those instead. He drank more and more, and made for a bitter drunk.

'Definitely bitter, kind of angry, and very confused,' he confirms. 'My wife, who was French, had come into a load of money from a family member, and so we'd bought this really stupid place in Shoreditch. This was the late nineties, before Shoreditch became Shoreditch, and so we had this whole floor of a factory building, and in it I just took drugs, drank, didn't do any work, couldn't concentrate, couldn't stay in, couldn't focus – just *couldn't*, really. My head was all over the place.'

Did he seek help, therapy perhaps? 'I did, yes, but . . . I don't know. It just didn't really happen, didn't really work.'

In time, he stopped even bothering trying to write songs. Why force what wouldn't come? Instead, he simply listened to the music others were making, specifically electronica and Northern soul.

Sometimes this inspired him, a crackle in the brain, an itch to the fingertips, but he didn't know what to do with that inspiration, or where to let it lead him. His marriage ended, he left London knowing he could never return, and headed west – not to America, the land of opportunity and foolish romantic hope, but rather to what he calls a 'dodgy part' of Cardiff, where he continued to drink, 'for years and years; *so* boring'.

If this were fiction, then this is the part that would describe a phoenix rising from its flames, Martin Carr an artist reborn. But this isn't a novel. Eventually, he did start writing songs again, and came to realise that Cardiff might be good for him: a new situation, an opportunity to look at things differently. He wrote a bunch of songs, which became a double album, then wrote instrumental music heavily influenced by the electronica he'd been listening to, 'but nothing,' he points out, 'that would end up on the radio'. For a time, he tried to offer his services as a songwriter for hire, often the default setting for erstwhile pop stars who turn their talents to producing hits for others when they themselves are no longer the appealing prospect, but that didn't work out. He found it a soulless enterprise, and the effort it required upset him.

'To do that, to write a hit single for the sake of it, you have to be a businessman, and my kind of skill – whatever skill that might be – simply wasn't enough.'

Around this time, he, like so many artists of his era, lost a lot of money due to what we might call, for legal reasons, *imprudent accountancy practices*, and the wealth he'd built up vanished.

Requests came in to license his one big hit single, but for now he kept saying no.

'It's a vestige of punk, I suppose: never sell out.'

Some good things *did* happen. It wasn't all grey clouds and Ken Loach. He met someone in Cardiff, fell in love, settled down, had children. Suddenly, there was responsibility, and so when the requests kept coming for 'Wake Up Boo!', he over-rode punk's imperative, and gratefully cashed the cheques. He enrolled onto an Open University course in humanities, 'just to see if I could do it.' He bought himself an exercise book, his first since school. On the title page, he wrote, 'Oh, the humanity . . .', and that was as far as he got, this inability of his to stick at anything for very long convincing him, and not for the first time in his life, that he might have an attention deficit.

He resurrected a solo career, of sorts, under the name bravecaptain, the man who had once put exclamation marks on seven-inch singles now whispering in lowercase to better highlight his new timidity. In 2005, as bravecaptain, he released an album entitled *A Sublime Number*. It comprised twelve songs, each named after a month of the year, beginning with January and ending with December. Aside from three tracks, 'January', 'November' and 'December', whose respective running times were 3:40, 3:24 and 1:43, they all had the same very precise duration of three minutes and six seconds, proof perhaps that the muse can sometimes make very exacting, and arguably pointless, demands on a creative individual.

Gradually, he started doing electronic gigs, playing live while standing in front of a couple of laptops, before progressing on to keyboards. He'd occasionally support local Cardiff bands, and enjoyed the fleeting thrill it afforded. But in terms of resurrecting things properly: nothing.

Taking stock, he knew that he'd lost a lot: his former identity, old friends, a certain lifestyle. If he continued to make music at all, then it was for the simple pleasure – and need – of it, nothing more. 'But I don't actually earn any money, much as I may try.' He lives simply, and the money he earns from his back catalogue, combined with his wife's work earnings, suffices. 'You don't need much money to lead a contented life,' he says.

'The other day, I was thinking about Paul McCartney's album,

Tug of War. On the inside, there's a photograph of him, and he's sitting at a low table in a big, beautiful room, with sunlight falling in; he's half in shadow, and deep in thought, pen in hand, writing. That's exactly what I want to do, how I want to be, always making something, writing, creating something, expressing myself – and not being on the clock.'

In the weeks and months following his ADHD diagnosis, Carr felt he had much to ponder on. It helped frame for him a life that, for too long, had been bleeding over the edges. At the age of fifty-one, he learned that there was a reason for the way he behaved, the way his mind ran. It gave him clarity, and it also gave him strength. He decided to start writing, not just music this time, but also words, cautiously working on a memoir. 'I've been here, writing away, making fun of myself, and it all seems really easy, I suppose, because I've now got all this [behaviour] to hang it on.'

He knows he wants to record music again. In 2017, Carr's last solo album, *Shapes of Life*, brought him a level of satisfaction he hadn't felt in twenty years. But as well as reviving him, it left him exhausted.

'It really did a number on me, but it was a good album, and I'd want anything I do next to be as good as that. So I'm going to wait and see what happens with this whole ADHD thing. If I get some medication that works, then, yes, I'll definitely record again. I like making music, but I like people hearing it, too. I like them telling me it's great, because that, of course, is definitely part of it. I'm always happy simply to make music, but feedback is – it's nice.'

He is silent for a moment. Then he says: 'Feedback makes it all worthwhile, really.'

FOUR

TOP OF THE POPS

8

'. . . And then it's gone, and that can be hard'

While Martin Carr was lost in limbo after the demise of the Boo Radleys, the band's singer, Simon Rowbottom – who'd been the first to quit – found himself similarly adrift. He'd known for a while it was time to stop, but how many of us ever manage to walk away from what has become the wrong thing, at the right time? *His* breaking point came around 1998. He was thirty years old, married, and just starting a family. The band's most recent album, *Kingsize*, had managed to articulate every doubt he'd long harboured about their continued existence. Remaining in situ was no longer an option.

'Being in a band is a major part of your identity, and for us, in our case, that was for a full twenty years. It defines you, defines everything around you – your friendships, your lifestyle – and then it's gone, and that can be hard.'

Due to his personal circumstances, he had a focus that his erstwhile bandmate didn't. For the next few years, all he wanted to do was be at home and be a parent. He loved the sudden tangible solidity of it, its routines and, especially, the lack of ego it required from him. He felt that this was where he was meant to be.

It was only once his children came of school-age that he tried to write songs again. He began, and completed, a 500-page novel. But these were stopgaps, projects to fill the time, not redefine who he now was. He needed something else, and he thought perhaps he might return to studying. He remembered just how much he'd enjoyed psychology at school, and so decided to revive that interest now. It felt like a fittingly grown-up pursuit, and his wife concurred, happy to support him while he did so. He bought himself a wardrobe of nice shirts, the kind that required ironing after washing, and retrained as a chartered psychologist. Today, he has a practice in Oxfordshire. He plays golf at the weekends.

'I think a lot of someone's self-worth is very tied up in being a successful musician,' he says, 'but the more I've thought about it, the more I've realised it's not about being a musician; it's about being famous. That's the thing, I think. When I look back on it, and try to analyse its appeal, then what was it? I love music, and I loved the songs, but when I really think about it, it was *Top of the Pops*, it was about having people scream, adore you, love you. That's the huge pull, especially when you don't have a strong sense of self-worth. And when I look back now, I think: *Yeah. That's what I wanted to experience.* It's like the Stone Roses said: "I wanna be adored . . ." That's why people are drawn to make music, I think.'

No matter how long it takes an act to become successful, how slow it can seem, when it finally happens, it does so with a speed that can take your breath away and leave you forever changed. In other walks of life, nobody gets promoted from the mailroom to CEO overnight, but this is often the case in music. You can be playing the Dog & Duck in November, and by the summer be appearing high on the bill at festivals. All it takes is a smash hit for that turnaround to occur. It can be as thrilling a thing to bear witness to as it must be to personally experience.

When Robbie Williams played Glastonbury's Pyramid Stage in 1998, for example, he was two years free from Take That, and his debut solo album *Life Thru a Lens* had singularly failed to capitalise on either his boy-band success or his cheeky charm. Rumours circulated that his record company were preparing to drop him – rumours that had reached, and duly affected, him – but they decided upon one last-ditch attempt to see if his music still had the ability to connect with the masses. They released the album's big ballad, 'Angels', and waited to see if it would take flight. It did. Suddenly, the same people who had barely paid it any attention when it was simply the fourth track on a lacklustre album now decided it was not only a song of surprising maturity for a twenty-three-year-old, but that Williams actually had talent to burn, and was worth watching closely. His middle-of-the-afternoon slot on the Saturday had been a punt about which he'd been rightly terrified; a Glastonbury audience, the majority of whom had arrived thirty-six hours earlier and been lashed with near-perpetual rain while waiting for Blur to headline, was a long way from an enthusiastic *Smash Hits* crowd.

But when Williams went on, the rain stopped. The sun came out; briefly, there was a rainbow. The singer was nervous but deadpan, funny, with everything to gain – and also everything to lose. He made fun of himself and the incongruity of his presence here, then put on the kind of performance he would later become internationally renowned for. He left the stage forty-five minutes later to screams of appreciation that were almost entirely sincere. By the end of the year, he would be well on his way to becoming the biggest pop star on the planet, when just a few short months previously he'd been all washed up. Soon, he would sign a deal with EMI reported to be worth £80 million.

Immediately after his appearance at the world's most celebrated music festival on that Saturday afternoon, he was ushered towards a people-carrier where his then-girlfriend, All Saints' Nicole Appleton, was awaiting him. He spoke briefly to a journalist en route, his eyes glazed, a disbelieving grin on his face.

'I won, didn't I?' he said.

According to his long-term producer, Guy Chambers, Robbie Williams then entered into his 'imperial phase'. This part of a career, for those lucky enough to achieve it, is the time in which an artist's sales keep rising and rising, when everything they touch is certified gold by the audience that buys it. (The Beatles' entire career, truncated as it was, was an imperial phase, while the Rolling Stones' lasted, approximately, from 1965 until 1972, before solo projects, successive divorces, and general ennui fatally disrupted their flow, relegating them to heritage status, in which they could continue to play the world's stadiums as long as they focused on those hits made between 1965 and 1972.

'Rob had his imperial phase from 1997 until about 2003, 2004,' says Chambers, who was Williams' producer and co-songwriter during that time, and then again from 2011 to the present day. 'So that's about nine years, which, by the way . . . well, normally most artists, if they're lucky, get about five, so for Rob, that was pretty incredible, a time when sales just kept going up, and it just kept getting bigger and bigger.'

Williams' first album, *Life Thru a Lens*, sold four million copies, his next, *I've Been Expecting You*, seven million, 2000's *Sing When You're Winning* eight million, and 2001's *Swing When You're Winning* nine million. In 2002, he experienced a dip when *Escapology* went back down to eight million.

After splitting with Guy Chambers, not entirely amicably, Williams began collaborating with other writers and producers. The subsequent album sales figures, still spectacularly robust, nevertheless continued their southern trajectory. Williams grew a beard, developed an interest in the existence of UFOs, unexpectedly married and had children, became a TV talent show judge and, in a general sense, no longer wanted to 'win' quite so determinedly any more because, as he'd pointed out himself, he already had. Imperial phases like his are self-sustaining. He could relax now. In 2021, he bought a house in Switzerland, near one of its lakes, the view majestic. He started skiing.

Guy Chambers, meanwhile, was a marked man. Now a proven hit-maker, he was promptly employed to make hit-makers out of other pop hopefuls, the assumption being that his Midas touch wasn't fussy; he'd anoint anyone. As it transpired, working relationships like the one Chambers and Williams had shared aren't always easily replicated, and lightning didn't strike twice, but this didn't stymie his work rate much, and Chambers remained in demand. He wrote with, and for, Annie Lennox, Melanie C, Kylie Minogue, Chaka Khan, Rufus Wainwright, Guy Chadwick (from eighties indie veterans House of Love), and Lana Del Rey, 'who kept looking at her phone during our session, so that was frustrating'.

A huge inspiration for pop songwriters, he says, 'is the knowledge that you're still on an upward trajectory yourself. I really felt that with Rob in our first five years, and knowing that there are millions of people waiting to hear your songs is an unbelievable source of inspiration. But I find it very hard these days to write with another writer who isn't an artist like that. I've tried it many times, and it just doesn't work.'

It's when it *does* work that Chambers is reminded why he continues. He never really wanted to be a pop star himself – although he did try. His pleasure was, instead, vicarious: he was the studio boffin, the latter-day George Martin, sprinkling stardust onto those who seemed most cut out for it, for fame. He'd find it endlessly fascinating watching fame from up close, but at one remove: what it did to an individual, how it exposed them, how they benefitted from it, and how it often gobbled them up and spat them out.

The Boo Radleys' Simon Rowbottom, speaking not just as someone who had a fleeting taste himself, but as a psychologist keen to analyse it, says: 'It's a fascinating thing, fame. I think everybody goes into it thinking that they're going to be the artist with longevity, the artist that carries on, and it becomes their whole life. But the reality is not always like that. When the realisation hits that, for most of us, that doesn't last, it's a tough process. And for the Boo Radleys, that's what split us up. When you do go from that CEO boardroom back down to the mailroom, you know that you've done all that before, and it's like, oh, we're back here. It becomes boring, there's no excitement to the journey any more, and it can prompt a very rapid decline.'

If such a decline can be swift and merciless in all areas of music – in rap and in folk, in rock and in alternative – then nowhere does it seem more merciless, more needlessly cruel, or more shamingly public, than in the world of pop, the genre that feeds on fresh meat like a Pac-Man feeds on the monsters, before the monsters eventually begin turning on you, and then, just like that, it's Game Over.

Then what?

The International Powered Access Federation (IPAF), which has offices across the world, promotes the safe and effective use of powered access equipment. It does this by providing technical advice and information through influencing and interpreting legislation and safety initiatives, and by running training pro-grammes. It's associated with the parallel industries of Elevating Work Platforms (EWP), Aerial Work Platforms (AWP) and Mobile Elevating Work Platforms (MEWP), each of which offer mechan-ical devices used to provide temporary access for people who need to reach inaccessible areas and to work, 'usually', says Wikipedia, 'at height'. They can be found mostly in maintenance and on construction sites, where work at high altitude is both common and dangerous, but necessary. You need training before being allowed onto an EWP or a MEWP. If you happen to live in, or around, the Birmingham area, then one Dennis Seaton could well be your trainer.

Dennis Seaton is fifty-five years old. He has a friendly face, a ready smile, and the kind of resonant voice suggestive of an innate confidence. A safe pair of hands. If you are nervous about aerial work before meeting with him, it's likely you won't be afterwards. Seaton has been in this role for a number of years now. These days, only a few of his clients look at him with a kind of far-off recognition, as if his features trigger a deeply recessed memory muscle. Those that do tend to be of a similar vintage to him, children of the late seventies and early eighties, who might see, somewhere about the eyes or perhaps the width of the grin, a visual déjà vu, and with it a particular soundtrack, a melody that sounds suspiciously like 'Pass the Dutchie'.

All the way back in 1982, the British music scene was in the midst of one of its vigorous reinventions, and almost all pop music seemed to be made specifically to put smiles on faces. (Pop would never be this straightforwardly accommodating again.) And that year, nothing put smiles on faces with more determination than Musical Youth, a five-piece from Birmingham who came to be dubbed the British equivalent of the Jackson 5, due chiefly to their age. Their single 'Pass the Dutchie', a cover of the reggae standard by the Mighty Diamonds, and originally titled 'Pass the Kouchie', a reference to marijuana, was reworked for a family audience, 'dutchie' being a West Indian cooking pot. Bottling pure sunshine into its chorus, the song didn't connect as widely as it did because it was slick and sophisticated, but rather because it oozed an almost playground cheek, and a patois that didn't so much alienate its mostly white audience as helplessly charm them.

Its universal appeal became apparent when it sold five million copies worldwide, in the process wrenching its performers from school and out into the watching world. They would be the first Black artists to be played on MTV in America, visited Stevie Wonder in the studio, and were invited for dinner at Michael Jackson's house – safety in numbers, hopefully – where the emergent King of Pop introduced them to his snake, Muscles. They would duet with Donna Summer, and cosy up to Paul and Linda McCartney, Prince and James Brown. Because they were minors, they could only work for forty-two days a year, but school became increasingly difficult to concentrate on when demand for them was still so high, like the time they played before a star-studded audience in Washington DC, to which they'd been flown first class, and were put up in hotel suites far more opulent, and roomier, than the houses they'd grown up in.

Seaton, then fifteen, who was the band's main singer, had been brought into the fold comparatively late when the original singer, Freddie Waite, formerly a vocalist in the Jamaican trio the Techniques, had it explained to him precisely why it so jarred that *he* was fronting Musical Youth: he was thirty-five, the other members barely pubescent. There was nothing *youth* about him. He'd initially formed the band with a friend and two of their sons in the hope of revitalising his Jamaican success, but record companies saw more marketability in teenagers than thirty-somethings. Seaton was drafted in, and the band suddenly made sense.

Reggae was not a commercial proposition in the UK in the early 1980s, but then Musical Youth were never sold on their musical chops so much as the dimples that appeared in their cheeks whenever they smiled, which was often. It was during an early gig at London's gay venue Heaven, supporting a young Culture Club, that they realised what they were sitting on with 'Pass the Dutchie'. The 3,000-strong crowd 'just went crazy,' Seaton says.

The single went to number one in twelve countries, and was a Top 10 hit in America. While they were busy taking in its success, pressure mounted for a follow-up. The band, and several of their respective parents, wanted to delve deeper into their reggae roots, while the label wanted them to keep going with a steady supply of radio-friendly pop songs. In the internationally recognised shorthand for serious conflict, they *deliberated* until a compromise was struck: the band could write their own B-sides, but the A-sides would be taken care of by the professionals.

A second single, 'Different Style', flopped, and though they did manage a couple of further hits, notably their collaboration with Donna Summer in 1983 on 'Unconditional Love', they were becoming increasingly unappealing, virulent adolescents far less sellable than cherubic tweens. What would happen next would pass into folklore, and Musical Youth would be held up as a prime example of the fate of child stars: a cautionary tale all future child stars would be wise to take note of.

Forty years later, Dennis Seaton is a father of four. He holds a master's degree in music, trains people how to use ladders for the IPAF, and though for a short time, decades ago, he had grown to call Los Angeles home, he's back on his native turf now, Birmingham.

'You can have a long career in music, but not always,' he says. 'Either way, you've got to learn to survive it. I did.'

The five members of Musical Youth did not handle their moment particularly well, but then how could they? They'd had their lives changed irrevocably, were used up, and then cursorily returned to sender, forever marked. One member, Patrick Waite, became increasingly paranoid in response to a world he now considered hostile. He turned to petty crime, and was jailed for reckless driving, credit-card fraud and assaulting the police. In 1990, he robbed a pregnant woman at knifepoint, and was later arrested for marijuana possession. In 1993, at the age of twenty-four, and struggling with a virus, he died. Another member, Kelvin Grant, became a virtual recluse.

Dennis Seaton became a born-again Christian. 'It saved me,' he says. By twenty, he was a father, and needed grounding. 'Even when I had money in the bank, I thought to myself: *There's got to be more than this*. At that age, you ask yourself questions, questions like, "What's the meaning of life?" My mother, my brothers and sisters had brought me up, and I was very close to my older brother, and he would tell me things, educate me. I think that's

why I left the band, because I wanted more from life than all that
. . . frustration.'

Convincing himself that 'Dennis Seaton from Musical Youth'
must have at least some mileage left, he booked gigs in unlikely
places: the south of Ireland, and Ghana, where, to his surprise, he
found himself playing stadiums. In 1989, he secured a solo album
deal, and recorded it in Los Angeles, with two of its tracks produced by Stevie Wonder. In his downtime, he'd go to Rod Stewart's
house to play five-a-side football.

His album would be nominated for a Grammy Award, but it
did not chart highly, and didn't sell. His contract was not renewed.

'So I went back home, and did my own thing.' He took work
in a car rental firm, and in time became the assistant manager
of another. Occasionally, people would ask him if he used to be
Dennis Seaton, and he learned how to fashion his smile in such a
way to deflect further questions. He had more children, bought his
own car hire firm and, years later, sold his shares. Today, as part
of his work for the IPAF, he is Chairman of the Ladder Association
Training Committee (LATC).

'Which is funny, I know,' he says. Of course, it isn't really
funny at all – he's a father, he has a job – but he feels it necessary
to suggest otherwise, because people don't expect former pop
stars to sink to the depths of becoming an ordinary civilian doing
ordinary, honest work. 'But you know what, I love it. I'm happily
married, I've got four kids, a nice house, and things are good.'

At the age of thirty-seven, he decided to study for a Masters
in music, because 'by that age, I finally wanted to learn the craft
properly, and because I knew that at some later stage in my life
I would want to pass that knowledge on to others.

'When you've made a lot of money, I suppose you can just sit
back and – what? – just enjoy yourself. Perhaps. But if you haven't
made a lot of money, and we never did, not really, then you have

to diversify your skills.' After his solo deal came to an end, he says, 'I didn't have any record companies knocking at my door, didn't have music managers approaching me, didn't have anyone to advise me on what I should be doing next, or where, or how. So I've had to do everything myself, had to figure out for myself what I was going to do.'

He focused on the tangibles, the achievables: family, home, church, job. As the years passed, and the eighties began to hang forever suspended in the minds of those that had lived through them, he learned to enjoy his small place in musical history, and to enjoy, too, the public acknowledgement that came his way, first via letters and then emails, each essentially saying: 'Thank you, big fan, that song *was* my childhood.'

'To have touched so many lives,' he says, 'let me tell you, is humbling.'

He liked hearing his song on the radio. It would give him a sense of pride, and a sense of ownership: *I made that*. And he knew that at some point he'd resurrect his former self again, for the simple reason that he could. When he's not playing gigs around the country (mostly to backing tracks and with fellow Musical Youth survivor Michael Grant by his side, where they play a short selection of songs but mostly *that* song, over and over again to an audience that want from them nothing more), he is quietly helping to save lives. In July 2019, a railway maintenance worker suffered significant injuries – a broken collarbone, eleven broken ribs, a punctured lung – after falling four metres from a ladder while cutting back vegetation. The man spent thirteen days in intensive care, and was put back together using metal plates to pin his clavicle and ribs. Subsequent investigations into the accident found that the maintenance contractor was guilty of an offence under the Work at Height Regulations 2005, and the contractor was fined £500,000.

'There are many situations where a ladder can be the right solution, but they shouldn't automatically be your first choice,' Dennis Seaton, Chair of the Ladder Association Training Committee, was quoted as saying at the time. 'It's one of the main reasons we launched our Get a Grip on Ladder Safety campaign, with the clear message: *When it's right to use a ladder, use the ladder, and get trained to use it safely.*'

Ladder Safety Awareness training courses start from £15; see online for details.

9

'As soon as fame turned up, he thought he was David Bowie'

Brian Nash, 'Nasher' to those who know him well enough to consider him a friend, likes to walk many miles a day along his native Liverpudlian pavements, some vigorous pre-prandial exercise to keep up his daily step count and to help blow the cobwebs from his mind. He prefers to walk as he talks, and he talks in torrents, all verbal uppercuts and split lips, more opinions than the average taxi driver, and unwavering convictions about how to put the world to rights. If he is a fully paid-up member of pop's walking wounded with the scars to prove it, someone who holds a grudge and forever remembers those that did him wrong, he is also entirely aware of the good fortune that came his way in the first place – as an eighteen-year-old electrician in the early 1980s, who just happened to play a bit of guitar on the side – and will be eternally grateful for it. Sometimes being in the right place at the right time helps. And even if that right-time, right-place combination was all too painfully fleeting, you can still trade off it, and still make it work for you.

The internet will tell you that a funeral celebrant is someone who officiates in a non-religious manner at funerals and cremations, performing sermons. The role requires a certain flair for public speaking, and a level of confidence not just to successfully manage the mood in the unavoidably sombre room, but also to steer it away from suffocating misery. The death of a loved one is always a sad business, but a good funeral celebrant can remind extended family members and friends of a life lived well and memorably, and can render the proceedings a celebration of sorts. In Liverpool, Brian Nash – Nasher – is a *very* good funeral celebrant.

'I tell you, doing funerals is better than doing an acoustic gig any day,' he says, 'because at least every cunt shuts up while you're talking, and there's no one standing at the bar with beer bottles chatting shit cos they're full of coke.'

It's hard now to fully convey the impact Frankie Goes to Hollywood had in the midpoint of the 1980s, but put it this way: Kajagoogoo were never going to get very far printing up T-shirts suggesting LIMAHL SAYS RELAX. While people were listening to Frankie Goes to Hollywood, they were wearing them too, their cultural significance spilling over into sartorial requirement, the ultimate marker of impact.

The five members of FGTH came together out of various other Liverpudlian bands. Singer Holly Johnson had been in Big in Japan, while the moustachioed co-frontman Paul Rutherford came from Hambi and the Dance. The three remaining members, the so-called 'Lads', thus termed perhaps to highlight their difference from the two men upfront (and to highlight that they were straight), had served time in Sons of Egypt.

Combined, they were a pair of 'ferocious homosexuals' backed by, as the *Guardian* would later have it, 'three prototype Liam Gallaghers'. Brian Nash was one of the Liam Gallaghers. The gulf between the two camps seemed unnavigable, but together they clicked, a unit of raw material that just needed polishing.

In 1983, they signed to ZTT, a new label created by record producer Trevor Horn, Horn's wife Jill Sinclair, and the former NME writer Paul Morley. This was to be no ordinary record label but rather one that played with form, style and, thanks to Morley's esoteric leanings, content. ZTT gathered up FGTH in their raw material state – which, in various other tellings from the era, was a little like trying to scoop up mincemeat in a teaspoon – and transformed them into an assault on both the ears and the senses, all energy and pomp and ridiculous posturing, to offend wherever possible, to titillate and to thrill. The eighties were full of big, attention-arresting bands, but Frankie Goes to Hollywood were, simply, the *most*.

By 1984, they were the single biggest event to happen in British music since punk, whipping up orchestrated controversy and delivering it on a platter to a mostly adolescent, *Top of the Pops*-watching audience who may not hitherto have had much of a cogent grasp on precisely *what* the controversy was, but did enjoy the accompanying hubbub nevertheless.

Their debut single, 'Relax', released in October 1983, didn't become a hit until the following January. A juggernaut of sexual posturing – *gay* sexual posturing – it took a while to upset the mainstream, but when it eventually did, as, of course, it was designed to do, it took off and became the only firework in the box. It had enjoyed plenty of daytime radio play before the Radio 1 DJ Mike Read decided to ban it, on-air, appalled to be required to play a song quite so grubby and nefarious. He deemed it 'obscene' and insisted that hell would freeze over before he slipped it on the deck again. (Read would later suggest that his 'banning' of the song was a myth, claiming that the BBC had already decided to ban it; he'd stopped playing it simply because he'd found himself playing the twelve-inch version, which went on far too long.)

There could not have been a more effective way of encouraging a nation that had previously enjoyed 'Relax' for the thrillingly pro-pulsive pop song it was to suddenly lean in closer and pay greater attention to its lyrics. In the chorus, it encourages you to 'relax, don't do it, when you want to come'. This directive wasn't entirely clear to everyone (don't do *what*, exactly?), though the manner in which Holly Johnson – a lascivious-sounding singer at the best of times, and never more so than here – sang the word 'come', in a way that made it sound like he was spelling it 'cum', was . . . *interesting*. Thrills came cheap in the pre-internet era. In order to now give the song the full attention it clearly demanded, everybody, it seemed, needed to buy a copy. It stayed at number one for six weeks.

A few months later, with 'Relax' still high in the Top 10, Frankie's next single was released. 'Two Tribes', which didn't benefit from a ban, went straight to number one, and was accompanied by the decade's most visually arresting video: US President Ronald Reagan and Russian leader Konstantin Chernenko taking great chunks out of one another in a wrestling ring. It dominated the charts for nine weeks, and by the end of that year, they had the Christmas number one too, with the unexpectedly straightforward ballad, 'The Power of Love'. By the time their debut album arrived, a double entitled *Welcome to the Pleasuredome*, they'd covered 1984 like wallpaper. If there were other songs recorded that year, nobody can remember them.

Welcome to the Pleasuredome was one of the strangest and most over-produced albums of its time. It sounded more like the work of Trevor Horn than it did Frankie Goes to Hollywood, its canvas big enough to fill galaxies. It was wilfully schizophrenic, replete with cinema trailer-style voiceovers, tectonic gay anthems and political treaties, alongside determinedly cheesy covers of Dionne Warwick's 'Do You Know the Way to San Jose' and Bruce Springsteen's blue-collar holler, 'Born to Run'. Such was Horn's overarching vision, it ran to four sides, and it was only by Side 4, so the rumour went, that the band were permitted to highlight some of their own compositions, among them 'Krisco Kisses', which did not have the same impact as those rollercoaster singles.

But Holly Johnson was nevertheless the perfect focal point, the kind of man who behaved as if he'd spent a lifetime waiting for adulation and wasn't a bit thrown by it. His voice sounded like a cheeky wink of the eye, and his wink was filthy. He'd often perform on TV holding a walking stick, not to keep him upright, but to make him more lordly, more commanding. It worked: you couldn't take your eyes off him. If by direct consequence 'the Lads' fell into soft focus behind him, then this probably wasn't by accident. In Simon Reynolds' book on the music of the early eighties, *Rip it Up and Start Again*, Trevor Horn asserted that much of the band's contribution was minimal, not just because Horn had so many ideas himself, but because they weren't up to the task of making music that sounded as sonically big as Frankie Goes to Hollywood required. They were a visual aid, part of the overall package but not the present itself.

The upshot was this: 'the Lads' were ultimately dispensable. And so it came to be.

'Look,' says Brian Nash, 'I was born lucky.' Becoming part of the band in the first place, he adds, 'was like going to a party in 1984, and coming back home in 1987. Travel broadens the mind, they say, and you grow up very quickly when you travel. It was incredible, so what's not to like?'

Nevertheless, he and the other Lads, Mark O'Toole and Peter Gill, were quickly made to feel superfluous, a factor that few people around them bothered to hide.

For Nash, watching the impact fame had on his lead singer was telling. Pretty soon, he says, 'it was like having to deal with someone who was not on the same wavelength as the rest of you. As soon as fame turned up, [Holly Johnson] thought he was fucking David Bowie, and that was the end of that. You know, you think this is going to be for life, you think you're going to be Mick Jagger: *I'll be doing this when I'm seventy, me.* That's the arrogance, I guess, the invincibility of youth. That's what it gives you. But then the reality of the situation is that you can so quickly become yesterday's news, and that's what happened, and when it does happen, you have to learn to fucking deal with it and just get on with it.'

Welcome to the Pleasuredome sold millions around the world. When they came to record their second album, 1986's *Liverpool*, the band insisted on greater creative control. ZTT must have known where this was heading, but they gave them licence to express themselves anyway. They'd earned it. What their songs lacked, Horn could make up for in the production. *Liverpool* cost an entirely unnecessary £760,000 to record, silly money. The band's joy at gaining creative control was therefore short-lived, and proved a hollow victory; ZTT were preparing to euthanise.

'Yeah, but the writing was on the wall long before then,' Nash says, explaining that Johnson was already eyeing a future that had little to do with the rest of them. When the five of them decided to form individual limited companies, thereby taking greater financial control of their collective enterprise, they learned that their singer had already attempted to register the name 'Frankie Goes to Hollywood' for himself. This came as a surprise. 'We all looked at each other, like: *What?* Everybody in the room, we just looked at him and said, "What sort of cunt are you?" He told us he was just trying to protect the name, [but] it was just like, "Fuck off, man, you're just a snide little cunt."'

(Legal wrangles over the band name would drag on for decades. In 2004, Johnson would again apply to register the name, and once again did so without notifying his former colleagues. His attempt proved unsuccessful, partly because Johnson's efforts were seen as an attempt to 'monopolise the name to [the rest of the band's] exclusion merely to interfere with their rights'. Among the case's conclusions were that, 'bands should register trademarks sooner rather than later.')

Hurt but not yet down, not quite, Frankie Goes to Hollywood trudged on until 1987, bickering their way through a tour of North America that no one much enjoyed. The moment they returned home, each knew that was it; it was over. There was relief in that.

But, 'I was twenty-four years old, had no job, was signing on, housing benefit, all that shit. But then you don't really have time to think about it, to sit on your arse and think *woe is me*. It's just how it is. Besides, I'd just had a baby, so I had to get my arse in gear and do something about it.'

It would take Nash a good while to realise that the abrupt cessation of his music career, and the stability of his home life when he'd grown so accustomed to action and incident, was sending him into a depression. At home alone while his wife was out at work, the baby asleep, he'd burst into tears. 'What the fuck was all that about?' he'd ask himself. He consulted a doctor. 'I went to the doctor, and I said, "Something's not right here, Doc." And I'll tell you, my GP was fucking brilliant, a lovely woman, she recommended me on to someone – shrink, psychotherapist – who asked me to tell her what had happened in my life in the last ten years, and when I did, she said that I was suffering from the echo of a crisis, because when this crisis happened to me, I didn't have the opportunity, or the time, the presence of mind, to really absorb it, "because you are still wound up in the whirlwind", she said. And it was only afterwards, now that it'd all gone pear-shaped, that I could do that. "And now," she said, "because you have this enforced period of solitude, these thoughts are resurfacing." And I was like: "That sounds perfect, Doc, makes me feel a whole lot better, cos it means I'm not going crackers."'

In this way, he was able to contextualise his mood as posttraumatic stress. He'd been, to borrow the popular idiom, three feet from stardom, not quite a star himself, but the guitarist, and the guitarist was important, too – not as much as he would have been in an indie act, the Smiths, say, but, still, he was there, he'd been part of it, one of the five.

And now he wasn't.

'If you can take a positive from something that comes from something negative, then you should,' he says, 'And I have. Even talking to you now is me doing that. You don't want to sit on your arse with your own dark thoughts, do you? There's a lot of that about, you know, a lot of cannabis psychosis, people suffering depression cos of skunk and all that shit. You've just got to go and see someone, talk about it.'

For a time, he tried to extend his pop life. He and his fellow 'Lads' became the Three Lads, a name whose lack of forethought and impetus gave every indication of where his head was at back then. They briefly considered roping in another singer, the antithesis of Holly Johnson perhaps, but nothing happened. Nash was philosophical. 'There's a saying about fame, when it passes: *you've had your go on the swings*. I mean, who gets to have two goes? Not many.'

Nor, he points out, did Holly Johnson, not properly. 'Musically, he can strum a guitar, but he's a collaborator who needs someone helping him.' Johnson did actually go on to have a solo career after extricating himself from the inevitable legal battle with ZTT, and in 1989 he scored a couple of hits, 'Love Train' and 'Americanos'. He didn't seem to show much interest in being David Bowie thereafter. In 1993, he announced that he was HIV positive, and for the past three decades has focused on his work as a painter.

Brian Nash, meanwhile, went back to his old job, and spent twenty years working as an electrician. He lived in north London with his wife, a nurse, and they raised a family. For the first few years, money was tight. 'We never made any money at the time, because of our exorbitant recording costs. When your second album costs almost £800,000 it takes a long time to pay that back.'

It was only in 1992, when the record company put out a greatest hits compilation, that the debts were finally paid off and money started to come in. 'At the time, I was living on the dole, in a rented house, still trying to get a record deal with my mates, and going down fucking Tesco's with my milk tokens. So to suddenly get a cheque for, like, fifty grand, that was nice.' He used the money to buy a house, and to revive his career as an electrician. 'And I was a good electrician,' he says.

After his children had grown up, he sold his business, and he and his wife moved back to Liverpool, where he reinvented himself as a funeral celebrant, and found himself inevitably dwelling more on the past.

'I've reached the age where I want to pass my musical skills on.' At the time of writing, he is fifty-seven. 'I want to collaborate with people.' He always liked the idea of making film music, 'but nobody ever gave me the opportunity, so I thought: *Fuck it, I'll make my own film, I've got a lot to offer, I've got things to give back.*' Not as a solo artist, he emphasises, because at fifty-seven, there is the age barrier to consider, and the temperament that comes with it. He has already written, recorded and self-released five solo albums, but no more. 'Can't be arsed. Without wanting to blow my own trumpet, I'm very good at what I do. I know how to write songs, I know what my strengths are, and though it hasn't been a career so much as an unpaid hobby for a long time now, I've enjoyed it. But now's the time to collaborate with other people, to write for other people, to help *them* out, cos you've got to give something back, haven't you?'

Besides, he adds, 'younger people are eminently more marketable than a fifty-seven-year-old fucking angry cunt, which is what I am these days.'

10

After a while, Andrez Harriott found it more fulfilling to go to prison than to attend any more meetings with record company executives. If one institution is full of people with shivs, the other is riven with sharks. He came to prefer the former.

By the early 2000s, Harriott felt he'd served enough time under their guidance. He'd been in an act called Damage, a boy band whose main selling point – at least briefly – was not that they were good, but that they happened to be Black in a genre that was almost exclusively white. Damage sounded more American than British, their vocal harmonies reminiscent of Motown groups. They were an alluring prospect to UK labels when it became clear that Boyz II Men, a modern vocal harmony group, were taking 1990s America by storm. In the UK, there was no serious equivalent to Boyz II Men. Until Damage.

The five Londoners had been singing since their mid-teens, and boasted the uniform good looks required of all pop stars who sing with maximum teeth while dressed in expensive cashmere. Soon, they were paired with the most efficient pop songwriters of the day, several of whom were within the employ of Simon Cowell.

Things happened quickly from this point. There were hits that not only slavishly followed the recipe of their American counterparts but also offered subtle typographic suggestion, just in case potential listeners needed further nudging: the 'II' in their single 'Love II Love' was a barely subliminal nod to Boyz II Men. Clever.

Damage looked as good as they sounded, and sounded as good as they looked.

But, Harriott says now, 'the bandwidth for us was always limited. Why? Because we were five Black boys. We'd come from a lineage of bands like the Temptations, but we'd also always positioned ourselves as a boy band. Everything was a fight.'

There were issues with marketing and radio play; the problem never the quality of the music, but rather the colour of their skin. Commercial pop entities were largely, if not quite universally, white. Boy bands were white. Damage's colour was somehow viewed as uncharted territory, and uncharted territory is rarely a sure thing in an industry desperate for sure things.

Their early success had bolstered the fortunes of their songwriters, who were subsequently employed to write more songs in the same style, but now for other acts. One of the bands that ended up with songs that might otherwise have been Damage's also looked good in cashmere, and boasted a similar ability to sing while sitting on tall stools. They were an all-white Irish act called Westlife, who would face few of the marketing or radio-play issues Damage did. Westlife quickly became huge, thus rendering any competitors redundant.

'I think we were always pragmatic about what was happening,' Harriott says. 'When the music business itself gets involved, when the *system* gets involved, things that have nothing to do with creativity start to happen.'

Damage split. Some left to pursue solo careers, another married a Spice Girl. And Andrez Harriott went to prison, repeatedly – but *not* as an inmate.

Harriott had grown up in south-east London. While he was occupied with singing, many of his childhood friends got jobs, settled down, had children. Others turned to crime. 'Several,' he says, 'have been murdered.' In comparison, he felt lucky, blessed even:

why had things turned out so well for him and not them? He decided that the best way to show his appreciation was to give something back, and so after his pop career came to an end, he trained as a mentor for those who'd fallen victim, as he saw it, to the system. DJing at night, both to keep his love of music alive and to support his young family, he began volunteering as a prison visitor, then studied social work and took a degree in Criminology and Sociology. After a decade working with youth offending services, with gangs across London (the victims of violence *and* the perpetrators), and with those entering witness protection, he set up his own company, the Liminality Group, to be of more direct help.

As a result, he spends most of his days within the prison system. Many who have come under his care, once released, do not reoffend. In schools, the Liminality Group have worked with thousands of children who had been facing expulsion but who now continue with school, with many considering further education.

'This isn't just work for me, it's a calling,' he says. 'It feels like a calling.'

Harriott was never particularly lucky. He made his own good fortune. When one world came to an end, he stepped into another. It was finding another identity, a worthwhile one, that saved him from a life pondering, *What if?* Those who don't find that tangible *something else*, or who at least haven't found it yet, can find reinvention after pop life a bit of a struggle.

In 2018, a vaguely familiar face to twenty-something television viewers popped up on the ITV lunchtime show *Loose Women*, the magazine programme featuring real-life stories that strive to reach out through the screen and touch its audience. The face belonged to Paul Cattermole, former member of nineties pop act S Club 7, a group that had been manufactured by the man behind the Spice Girls, Simon Fuller, and which enjoyed enormous success amongst its primary target audience of tweens and the unselfconscious. If

Cattermole's face was only vaguely familiar, that's because it was fuller than its earlier incarnation, the hair around the temples greying, and he now had a sculpted beard that ran the parameters of his jawline before meeting around the mouth and chin. He had put on weight, as people tend to do over time, and exuded an air of wary acceptance that this was now his fate: to discuss his fall from grace on daytime TV.

The reasons for inviting him to appear were entirely unambiguous, and not music-related: he'd recently hit the headlines for being broke, having grown so desperate for cash that he was attempting to sell his Brit Award on eBay. Bankruptcy loomed. Since his pop-star heyday, work had been thin on the ground, he'd been stung by a colossal tax bill, and a recent injury, which he appeared reluctant to expand upon, meant that he sometimes found it hard to leave the house. As all of this was read out by a presenter, Cattermole's resigned expression deepened. It was difficult not to feel incredibly sorry for him.

Daytime TV thrives on stories like this, and so did the Loose Women. Ostensibly a show with its heart in the right place, the four female panellists gathered around him in a maternal huddle as they teased out his tale of woe. As a tickertape banner at the bottom of the screen read 'I'm broke', one of the hosts revealed that the show's producers had bought Cattermole the shirt he was wearing because he couldn't afford a new one himself, and that he had, by all accounts, been surviving on a diet of packet noodles. 'But I love them,' he pointed out, an attempt perhaps to save face.

'They were definitely playing games,' Cattermole says now, 'and when I'm put in a situation like that, I'll say whatever comes out of my mouth first.'

The panel wanted to help him, to cajole and encourage him. He could find some kind of work, they said, couldn't he? And if not in music, then surely elsewhere? They suggested he might take a sales assistant position, for the simple reason that there are always

sales assistant jobs. When, at the end of his segment, fifteen minutes that stretched on for hours, he revealed that he would like to
fall in love, settle down and have children, the panel encouraged
anyone watching who might be interested to get in touch. As
they did this, the camera panned to the studio audience comprising women old enough to be his grandmother. The smile on
Cattermole's face was by now the rictus grin of one who had just
tried valiantly to negotiate the mapless stretch between having
had it all and being left with nothing.

A producer from the Channel 4 dating show *First Dates* subsequently made contact, keen to fill their 'Aw, bless' quota, and
asked if he'd like to take part. A few months later, Cattermole had
his first televised *First Date* with a sweet and sympathetic woman
over glasses of wine, good food and low lighting. His date didn't
recognise him, had no idea who he was. At one point during the
evening, when she told him that music was important in her life,
he felt required to enthusiastically concur.

'Performing in bands,' he told her earnestly at one point, 'that's
my main thing.'

Now she leaned forward, interest piqued, and asked him to
tell her more. He prevaricated, and began to sweat. 'S Club 7,' he
eventually revealed.

The loud noise that immediately followed was her jaw hitting
the floor. In this way, television gold is made.

Paul Cattermole had always wanted to be a performer. His
grandfather had worked at Abbey Road, and this was enough
to convince his grandson that music must run in the blood. At
fifteen, he entered the National Youth Music Theatre, thinking
perhaps his destiny lay in stage musicals; his ambition was to be
in *Bugsy Malone* or *West Side Story* – never the lead, but simply
part of the cast. Then, a year later, he formed his own band, which
dealt in an entirely different kind of theatrics: heavy metal. They

played Rage Against the Machine covers, and he thought they were great, that there was a future here. He'd have to grow his hair out, and invest in tattoos, but all artists suffer for their art. He would, too.

So when, shortly after, an opportunity came to him unbidden to join a pop band – and not just that, but a pop band with its own television show, The Monkees for a new generation – he felt conflicted. Art or commerce? Niche or mainstream? Credibility or, from certain quarters at least, eternal ridicule?

S Club 7 was the sound of an expanding pink bubblegum bubble a heartbeat before it burst. As their name suggested with an admirable lack of ambiguity, there were seven of them, and they were a club: four girls, three boys, all teenage, all cute. The collective avatar for Simon Fuller, a man with a proven track record in pop confection, the band were positioned at the end of a conveyor belt into which all the key ingredients were duly poured. Pop fluff of the most effervescent kind came out from this Willy Wonka-like process, its appeal as infectious as it was undeniable. Easily malleable and easily confused, its individual members could hardly be blamed for finding it difficult, over time, to work out real life from their on-screen narrative. S Club 7's TV show, *Miami 7*, which aired on CBBC, was a sitcom that charted the lives of the members of a pop group called S Club 7 who move to Florida in search of fame. Each member played their own character, based not so loosely on themselves, and were given colours that represented their pep and spirit. (One member, Hannah Spearritt, was yellow because yellow was bright and happy, as was Hannah Spearritt.) Over time, a soap-opera element was developed to keep viewers watching – ninety million viewers across 100 countries – and Cattermole's character began a relationship with Spearritt's. Filming days were long and intense, the band were barely into their twenties, and so of course were entirely caught up in the momentum of it all. Cattermole and Spearritt's on-screen relationship spilled over into whatever passed, in their frenetic existence, for reality, and that was fun – for a while. When they were not recording the show, they were recording hit singles, and there were plenty of these: 'Bring It All Back', 'S Club Party', 'Reach', 'Don't Stop Movin''. They made personal appearances up and down the country, across the world, forever on TV, all over the radio. Pep and spirit, those blazing characteristics of Spearritt's, became professional necessities for them all. They were overworked and always tired, but exhaustion hardly matters when you're nineteen, twenty, twenty-one. The smiles never faded, not in public. But the more successful S Club 7 became, the more the media focused on whomever they deemed to be the group's leading light, or lights. Single or plural, Paul Cattermole increasingly felt that he wasn't among either, and that he wasn't getting his due. He wanted to sing more, to be on the front line, not the back. By airing his dissatisfaction, though, he'd broken ranks, torn the fabric, and outed himself as trouble.

'The band's management had always been very wary of me, right from the beginning,' he says. 'It was obvious they'd seen me as some sort of tough nut to crack. When carrots were dangled, and false promises made – which is how these things function – they could see I wasn't believing any of it. I was seeing, with my own sort of professional view, the way things worked.'

Such cynicism didn't play well; it rarely does in this milieu. After Robbie Williams was identified as a problem in Take That, the five-piece became four. But Cattermole doesn't want to complain unreservedly. He says there were as many good times as there were bad. If what he remembers today is mostly (but not exclusively) the bad, that's just how the brain works.

'We were filming the TV show for sixteen hours a day, day after day. It got draining because filming is exhausting, way more so than people who don't do it realise. The amount of energy it takes! You end up sleeping [for] hours afterwards because you've given so much to the process. Don't get me wrong,' he adds, 'I loved my days when we were filming the show, but the bits that didn't make me feel so good were things like being a long way from home, and being in a situation with other people that, hey, we may have had some laughs together and done some cool things, but they were not really people you would choose to be away with *all the time*. Again, don't get me wrong, I really, *really* liked everyone in the band, each in their own way, for different reasons, and hanging out with them in the end became the real fun part . . .' He trails off here, then veers onto a different tangent. 'But I'm going to be honest with you. I didn't have to flex too much to do the kind of work that was required of us, I suppose because of all the [theatrical] training I'd done, so it was an absolute cakewalk. I didn't have to concentrate, I wasn't even in the zone [for much of the time], because it was just too easy.'

In the studio, he became increasingly underused. He could sing, he had a voice; why not utilise it more? 'Surely I'd get to sing at some point, but then the songs they did eventually give me, and I've got to be careful here . . .' What he says next is that, essentially, he was offered album tracks, fillers, not intended hit singles. 'People think I didn't like the band, but that's all wrong. I actually think it was really great, and I'm really proud of it . . . but it's not something I wish to explore again.'

Cattermole quit in 2002, desperate for change. He went back to his nu metal group, now called Skua, and hoped that people would have short memories, that any fans he might have generated before S Club 7 came along would prove forgiving and welcome him back.

'I was a bit naïve there, I suppose. I wasn't aware of how ardent fans could be. We like to think that people can see us the same way we see ourselves, and because I've always believed in being an all-round performer, something that's very close to my heart, I didn't think it would bother people when I tried something new.

I mean, it's never bothered me when other artists switch from genre to genre, or from films to TV to plays, or whatever – and I actually do think we are living in a more accepting world now. But back then, it was hard.'

Skua secured neither a live following nor a record deal. Very suddenly, Cattermole was no longer earning a living. He'd killed the golden goose, newly fearful he'd made a terrible mistake. But then: no, he decided. *No.*

He was eyeing Robbie Williams: how had he done it all so *right*? The first thing Williams had released as a solo artist was a version of George Michael's 'Freedom!', largely because the song encapsulated everything he wanted to say to his fanbase, his critics and doubters. Cattermole appreciated the intent, but felt annoyed that Williams had got there first. 'All I could think was, well, I can't do that song myself, now.'

There was no offer of a solo deal, perhaps because there is little that falls more quickly from the collective memory than a former pop act. Even those that do go on to extend their careers do so through struggle. Cattermole struggled.

'I'm not a religious person, but having faith – in yourself, and in others – is kind of a very, very, very important thing. You know that kind of classic voyage people go on before they go to university – go to India to discover yourself? Well, I had that very moment of self-discovery myself, except I forgot to go to India. I should have, and I totally see why the Beatles went there. You've got to go somewhere to spiritually get yourself in the right place – for happiness, clarity and awareness, that kind of holistic approach that sometimes needs to be taken [with regard to] the situation you're in. Everything is so finely balanced, isn't it? It's like holding a feather very gently.'

Paul Cattermole never did travel to Rishikesh, but he did try meditation. Whether he had therapy is something he doesn't fully reveal. But he did find enlightenment of a kind.

He says: 'I think it comes from when you do actually hit rock bottom, when there is no further to fall. It's a tough place to be in. Drinking hasn't really been a big thing for me, but there has definitely been a problem with . . . with other things.'

He talks about a darkness, specifically inside him but also inside us all. 'We are all beings of light and shadow at the same time; we have a shadow self to our lighter being. I hadn't discovered the shadow side, I didn't even realise it was there, but it was something I was constantly running from, my entire life. I put it like this once, in a session. I said, "I've been running through the forest my entire life. I've been running from the beast, and every time I stopped to look back, it got closer."'

One day, he stopped running to discover that the beast was himself. We cannot run from ourselves. 'I had to stop and comfort the beast, and take it into my arms, and appreciate that we are all yin and yang.'

The session to which he refers wasn't therapy as such, but rather, 'a kind of spiritual healing thing'. He didn't get very far with the process, 'but I could probably do with a bit more, because there must be a way out of the kind of hell I found myself in. If I'd had my dream job, how come I wasn't living my dreams? How come I wasn't literally living the dream? How did that not happen? Management had kept telling me that this was the greatest stepping stone for me going forward, that they were going to look after me, they were going to do this, they were going to do that, blah blah blah. But, you know, even at the time I knew it was never going to happen, I knew they were false promises. And in a way I was glad, glad to be proved right.'

And in a way, he wasn't.

But he did his best, his damnedest. He played occasional DJ gigs, billed as 'Paul Cattermole from S Club 7'. He sang on television adverts, for children's colouring pens, a high street bank, Guinness. In 2008, he and his former S Club 7 cohorts Bradley

McIntosh and Tina Barrett formed S Club 3, a slimmed-down version, because the four remaining band members were unavailable or uninterested, conceivably both. Cattermole had been keen because certain managers over the years would tell him about the importance of 'legacy, legacy, legacy'. The venues this time around were smaller, with minimal riders, the smell of beer rising off damp carpets. Their first show was at somewhere called the Tokyo Club, not the one in Roppongi but rather Morley Street, Bradford, where in 2009 a young woman on a night out visited the women's toilets, passed out and didn't wake up again until 6.30 a.m. The staff had long since gone home. She had to call firefighters to set her free. 'I'm angry that Tokyo's didn't check the toilets properly,' she later said.

Cattermole: 'I did the shows for the cash, and it's not something I'd really write home about now.'

They only ever played intermittently, as and when it suited. Occasionally, other former S Club 7 members joined, then left, and during one lacklustre tour Cattermole injured his back, forcing an abrupt retirement from live performance. He was in a lot of pain, on medication, and found solace in comfort food. He piled on weight, and his self-image duly suffered. He feared that if he were ever to find himself on the paparazzi's radar again, it would be for the wrong reasons. He went back to touting himself for advertising work, but grew increasingly dispirited. If, as he would tell the panel on *Loose Women* in 2018, he'd happily deliver pizzas in order to make his rent, then that was easier said than done. The reality of being recognised while bringing a stuffed-crust twelve-inch to a house full of young people who might just remember him is not easily borne; likewise the desperate hope he might at least get a good tip out of it.

Being declared bankrupt proved a watershed moment. His mother had already tried to help by selling his silver, gold and platinum discs, but his own attempt to quietly sell his Brit Award on eBay failed. The whisper became a scream, and the scream a perceived cry for help. Perhaps, subconsciously, it was? News headlines followed, for there is always much mileage in the once mighty when they fall.

His tax bill at the time was somewhere in the region of £36,000, this at a time when he was earning just £15,000 a year. After legal fees, he owed closer to £92,000. He'd thought that if he could sell his Brit Award for as much as £30,000 – when you are desperate, dreaming is all you have left – that would at least help in the short term.

It didn't sell.

Cattermole either didn't pursue more reality TV stints after his dating experiences, or else wasn't asked to. He is trying to write his own music again, which he does with a certain obsessiveness. 'Oh, I can spend hours writing a song, hours fiddling with the kick drum sound. I heard that Mark Ronson does that too, so thank God I'm not the only one . . . You get this momentum, you don't know where it comes from, and suddenly it's two, three, four o'clock in the morning.'

Inevitable talk of further S Club 7 reunions unsettles him, and makes him nervous. While he doesn't want to look back, he also does, because it will be fun, nice to see his old mates, and could be lucrative, too. Each has gone off to lead their own lives, some are closer than others, and it's difficult to get seven people to agree on anything, much less at the same time.

'I want them to be happy, and I want them to do things that make them happy. Of course, I'd consider it an honour if I could sing a song or two with the rest of the band at some point, if they would like to do it.' His face brightens. 'I actually have a couple of songs I've been working on that I think could have potential for them; I think they're quite good, and one is particularly good. So I'd be interested [in a reunion], but I'd have to knock the gigs on the head – my back injury has given me an excuse for getting fat, I suppose – but a TV show, a Christmas special? I could do that.'

Meanwhile, he waits. In pop music, he says, all acts will, at some point, plateau. 'You will be tested on that plateau. The question is: do you have the temerity to bust through it?'

FIVE

INFAMY, INFAMY, THEY'VE ALL GOT IT IN FOR ME

11

Almost nothing in pop music is scandalous, not really. It's just music. It doesn't bring down governments, doesn't start wars, doesn't contribute to global warming – at least, not directly. It can certainly play on the sensitive disposition of individuals from time to time, and occasionally prompt a hand to clutch at the chest as if to catch a heart threatening to break free, but the heart is never going to actually leave its moorings. We like to exaggerate its effect, to afford it scandal and shock and awe, because it heightens our experience of it. And while it's true to say that Frankie Goes to Hollywood's 'Relax' benefitted from being seen as a piece of wanton perversion that would condemn us all to Hell, all it actually did was what pop music has always been *entirely* capable of doing: it titillated.

Pop music has always titillated. It first did so publicly back in 1956 when Elvis Presley sang 'Hound Dog' on American television. He didn't just sing it, he *performed* it, and the sheer physicality of his hips, the manner in which that obscenely mobile waistline seemed to ping off either side of the TV frame as if by static shock, was jaw-dropping, hypnotic and, for its time, giddily scandalous. Music had never been this sexualised previously. But all it really was was a man – albeit an unusually beautiful man, with more sex appeal than Bill Haley – dancing to his song while maintaining steady eye contact with the prime-time audience at home.

His appearance on *The Milton Berle Show* was immediately dubbed one of the most controversial in television history, which – as TV audiences across America scrambled to articulate just *how* shocked they were by talking about it endlessly, by writing about it in syndicated op-ed columns, and by wishing videotapes or YouTube had been around so they could watch it again – sent the twenty-one-year-old pop idol into the stratosphere.

Scandal was clearly a commodity, then, and thus was swiftly woven into pop's DNA as a key currency. If you want to get ahead quickly, shock. In the 1960s, Mick Jagger managed to scandalise by wearing blouses and getting arrested for marijuana possession. A decade later, punk remained very much a niche concern until 1 December 1976, when the Sex Pistols appeared on the Thames Television's teatime news programme, *Today*. The interview, a five-minute segment, quickly descended into what the newspapers the following day felt moved to suggest was an example of punk's 'filth and fury'. The host Bill Grundy was a man of a certain age who'd seen everything in life except that which he hadn't. And what he hadn't seen yet, ushered in, invariably, by the new genera-tion, he wasn't interested in. His view towards youth's latest trend was consequently best described as 'dim'.

A segment on punk was a sound editorial idea for a television show that liked to take the nation's pulse with open-mindedness, but to ask Grundy to interview the Sex Pistols was not, in retro-spect, the wisest decision. As the band and several of their friends, among them a young Siouxsie Sioux, faced the presenter with a collective expression they might have adopted for a school head-master, the conversation failed to find common ground. Affronted by their ineloquence, Grundy simply baited them, prompting the Pistols' guitarist Steve Jones to call Grundy first a 'dirty sod' and 'dirty old man', then a 'dirty bastard', then a 'dirty fucker' and, climactically, 'a fucking rotter', all on live TV. The nation, busy eating dinner on its lap and balancing a Tizer on the edge of the sofa, had seen nothing like it. And so, just like that, punk was anointed the most scandalous thing since scandal was invented. Bill Grundy lost his job, and a blueprint of sorts was firmly established: shock and awe was the way to go.

But this only really works if the public are naïve and compliant. By the mid-eighties, it was still comparatively easy – we were a sensitive nation; we weren't French, for heaven's sake – but, gradually, shock and awe became exponentially harder to achieve. We'd developed, at last, a collective thick skin. Those who continued to attempt to inflame morals through a particularly propulsive kind of pop music largely failed. We were too wise, too knowing. We'd already been burned, we'd seen it all before.

Still, some gave it a go all the same.

By 1986, pop stars might just have been running out of new ideas. This was bad news for those who had been trying to claw their way towards success for several years, who'd been bit-part players in successive scenes and were, by this point, simply exhausted, addled, and running on empty.

Operating on the almost-logic that people have short memories, and that if it had worked once, then why not again, one act decided to resurrect the punk ethos for two basic reasons: 1) in pursuit of reliable controversy; and 2) because they didn't know what else to do. But where there'd always been something winningly authentic about the Sex Pistols, at least in their initial intent, the band that called themselves Sigue Sigue Sputnik were the kind of punks one only found on postcards sold in London's Carnaby Street, or perhaps Madame Tussauds: peroxide mohicans, middle fingers extended, and safety pins where no safety pins should go.

The idea was that Sigue Sigue Sputnik would reinvent it all, and in doing so shock-and-awe their way into international consciousness, redefining eighties music with a thrilling soundtrack of supercharged steroid cartoon pop-punk, and that the world would stop, look and listen.

Or, at least, it would if Tony James had anything to do with it.

Miraculously, he'd succeed.

By 1986, at the age of thirty-three, Tony James was already old – certainly far too old to be sporting hair that looked like a flamingo's rear end. But he was playing a role here. The dark master of Sigue Sigue Sputnik, he'd convinced himself that his band really was the future, if only because, in the past, he'd tried so hard to make them so. The idea, he says now, was to look 'like the house band on the planet Venus'. In actuality, they more resembled a family box of Quality Street chocolates spilled on a pavement in the rain. Nevertheless, they would somehow go on to terrify and titillate – a vague 1986 version of scandal that 'we' wholeheartedly bought into.

'Basically, I set out to create my own rock 'n' roll fantasy movie, and it was very much like creating a film script. I could see it visually, musically, the way it looked. I'd learned from Malcolm McLaren' – an old friend of his – 'and so I thought I knew how you did it. It was going to be the group of my dreams, and my premise was this: what if I walked into a club in fifty years' time, and Elvis was playing with a band? What would they look like?'

He decided they'd look, and sound, like a combination of rockabilly, electronic, T-Rex, a bit of rock 'n' roll, and some dub. He wanted two drummers because his favourite group of the 1960s, the Pink Fairies, had had two drummers. 'I wanted a fertile soup into which I would pour these people [his fellow band members] and hope to grow it,' he says, gleefully mixing metaphors, 'to fruition.'

He looked to enrol those who hadn't been in a band before, who couldn't play musical instruments, but who looked the part: cheekbones, pout, and a little 'v' between the eyebrows whenever they frowned, as James would diligently teach them to do. The frowning was key. They'd wear clothes that would make punk look straight, and everything else about them would be so compelling that no one would be able to drag their eyeballs off them. A *spectacle*.

'I felt I could get away with anything,' James says. 'I just had an ideas overload, and there was no one about to rein me in. I was completely out of control.'

Instead of being ridiculed by everyone that came into contact with them (though this would happen in time, be patient), the reaction from record companies was one of almost delirious excitement. They believed the hype. For James, this had all been a long time coming. A decade previously, he'd been in Generation X with Billy Idol, and had been frustrated, and perhaps a little envious, when his frontman went off to become a rock star while he languished on the sidelines. But now his own day had come: Sigue Sigue Sputnik signed to EMI for a £1 million advance, then the biggest in history.

The buzz that accompanied their first single, 'Love Missile F1-11', was crucial if the label were to recoup their outlay. For the band to become famous, it had to court infamy, lashings of the stuff, and so, amid often purely nonsensical reports – many of them spread by the band and their team – of obscenity at live gigs and plots to assassinate Margaret Thatcher, the media duly played along, pretending to be horrified, which sold papers, which ramped up the band's notoriety, which got the single – not really punk at all, but rather a sort of epileptic sci-fi strut – heavy rotation.

The result: a Top 3 hit, and an avalanche of media interest. This came more from the tabloids than the music press, whose writers operated largely on a default setting of cynicism. But in the red tops, where scandal was valued above all else, they were liquid mercury. Meanwhile, they were unleashed on daytime TV in the crude hope of snagging their own Bill Grundy moment.

Instead, they had to settle for the warm jumpers of breakfast TV, where they were confronted with questions about make-up.

'We were on the front covers of fixty-six magazines across Europe in the first month of the group breaking through with that single, and we were hurtling towards number one in territories all over the world,' James says. 'It was intoxicating.'

Meanwhile, he concentrated on their grandest statement yet, which masqueraded as their debut album. His benchmark for this was *Led Zeppelin II*; he aimed to make a record, he says, 'that had eight "Whole Lotta Love"s on it.' In other words, eight songs, but all on the same theme. Here, however, James hit a problem. 'It's actually incredibly difficult to write eight songs that all sound the same.'

Difficult, perhaps, but not quite impossible. The band's debut, *Flaunt It*, did indeed feature eight songs, and all eight songs were clearly born of an incestuous relationship, each with the same foghorn tendencies, the same sonic relentlessness and, ultimately, the same empty palate. It was exhausting, which was perhaps the point. Its all-but-inevitable critical mauling upon release didn't stall the band's progress immediately, but rather elevated James, by now a self-identifying Svengali figure, onto even more mainstream talk shows, his band a genuine curio. Appearing on *Wogan* at a point when Terry Wogan's three-times-weekly BBC1 talk show was watched by millions, he was introduced as a manager in the same mould as Elvis's handler Colonel Tom Parker and his own hero, Malcolm McLaren.

'And I'm thinking: *Me?* Do they really mean *me*?' Suddenly, he was outside himself looking in, newly fearful that he couldn't quite live up to the ruse he'd concocted. 'I had no idea how to manage people! I had absolutely zero empathy – my wife always said I was semi-autistic – and I was hopeless at dealing with people in a group.'

And yet here he was, the master at his own ceremony, who now needed to step up, and *into*, his role. 'I just saw us as a great idea, in principle. But then it all got carried away, and it became crazy.'

For their next move, they did an unconscionable thing for the house band on Venus: they made a second album with the pop production-line producers of the day, Stock Aitken Waterman, the resulting artefact proving as bad in reality as it had been questionable in principle. They never got to make a third.

And then came *consequences*.

The first album had featured a lot of samples. Outside the world of hip-hop in the mid-eighties, few acts used samples, and there was little concept of first securing clearance for them. If, say, a snippet of a film sounded good on a song, it would be used. 'It just never occurred to anyone to check whether we were actually *allowed* to use it.' One snatch of dialogue they used came from the Stanley Kubrick film, *A Clockwork Orange*. The likelihood of Kubrick ever hearing it was slim. But life throws improbable curveballs. One day, the director was walking down his local high street when he heard the song coming from a shop, and heard, too, a couple of seconds of his film. Like Queen Victoria, he wasn't amused. He contacted his lawyers.

'And then all of a sudden, I was called into a meeting with business affairs people at EMI, who asked me whether we'd had clearance for the sample, and I was like: "Clearance? What's *clearance*?" Everybody'd just been so tied up in the tsunami of success, we never questioned *anything*.'

They now owed Stanley Kubrick money. Soon, it would seem as if they owed *everybody* money. On one American tour, they managed to spend $30,000 in a single weekend for their roadies – a crew of tall women with long fingernails – who'd presumed that the limousine service that had been hired for them could take them everywhere, day and night. Elsewhere, they were £350,000 in debt to their record label. Just a few months before, James had felt like a world-straddling rock star, on a par with his former bandmate Billy Idol. For a brief moment, he'd convinced himself that Sigue Sigue Sputnik were the biggest group on the planet.

But only for a brief moment.

At thirty-five years old, still full of Svengali-like, madcap ideas, but no longer the attractive proposition he once was, Tony James mulled over his dilemma: 'Do I crawl away and die now, or do I do something else?'

He chose the latter option. The band ended, and very quickly he joined the sinister goth act Sisters of Mercy, whose vampiric frontman Andrew Eldritch lived in a Transylvanian castle and bred bats*. James had originally wanted Eldritch as the vocalist for Sigue Sigue Sputnik, but some singers will play second fiddle to no one. They'd remained friends, though, and now James found himself second fiddle in Eldritch's band. The new Sisters of Mercy album was to be recorded in Denmark, far from the paparazzi's patch, which appealed to James. Also, the wage was decent. They'd record music by day, and play Scrabble at night, the abrupt lack of drama entirely welcome. The session was supposed to last six weeks, but Eldritch was a perfectionist: it dragged on for a full year. Afterwards, James was invited on the tour, and this excited him. He had ideas for it, but his ideas were neither sought in the first place, nor listened to now. James bit his tongue, quite possibly until it bled. When press came to interview the band, they interviewed its singer, not the guitarist with the colourful past. 'I was just one of the foot soldiers now.'

He returned to London, bought himself a central London mews house at a time when central London mews houses were

---

* Not factually true.

just about affordable to heavily-in-debt guitarists-for-hire, and explored his options. He tried to start other bands. He was offered a job in a record company – where Svengali types are worth their weight in gold – but he shuddered at the thought of crossing the great divide and working for The Man. Instead, he and another old friend, Mick Jones, formerly of the Clash and latterly Big Audio Dynamite, formed a band together in which they would play an equal role. They called themselves Carbon Silicon and hit upon the then-bewildering idea of releasing music for free – several years before online streaming services did likewise.

'As ever, I was ahead of my time.'

Carbon Silicon continued for ten years, releasing various singles and EPs. James considered it an entirely creative endeavour, and found it fulfilling, except when it came to touring. 'When you've been in big groups that played stadiums, it's really shit to go back and play a pub in Newcastle, and to have to get changed in the corridor or in the back of a transit van.'

When, more recently, he, Billy Idol, and Paul Cook and Steve Jones from the Sex Pistols, formed a punk supergroup, Generation Sex, billing themselves as *The World's Biggest Punk Act*, they got the rock-star treatment again, and James was happy: access to a private jet; the entire floor of a hotel in Los Angeles. This was but fleeting, of course, so he was mindful to enjoy every second of it.

Tony James found he still wanted more of everything: he wanted fame and infamy, he wanted to be the grandest perpetrator of scandal, and he wanted his music to be eternal. He could – and perhaps should, were he following the script – have been a casualty, but he never was. While there is certainly a part of him that remains ultimately unfulfilled, he exudes, as he approaches seventy, the satisfied calm that only comes from those who have lived out their dreams. He sports no flamingo bouffant these days, but rather some fetchingly grey tumbling curly locks that complement a trimmed goatee, and looks more advertising executive than former rock star. He's been married to his wife, Penelope, for thirty years, and has a grown-up stepson. And he is very comfortably well-off, living off the money from his extensive back catalogue. Generation X's most famous song in particular, 1980's 'Dancing With Myself', has proved itself one of *those* songs that gets endlessly rediscovered by successive generations, and is routinely used in adverts and films. They recently licensed it to a film for $1 million, and at one point in early 2020 it was being used across the world to help sell underwear, alcohol and cars simultaneously. He still has the mews house in London, and has paired it with a big house in the country.

'I never got fucked up by drugs, never did *any* hard drugs actually, and too many people in this game do,' is his explanation for why he looks, and sounds, as content as he does. For this, he credits his wife, who 'has kept me on the straight and narrow, and had a great, calming influence in my life.'

He accepts his limitations these days, too, and no longer wants to subvert much of anything. 'I know that people don't particularly want to hear new music from someone who is sixty-seven years old. Leonard Cohen might have managed to still appeal at that age, but most of us don't. And so the thing for the rest of us is: what do we do now? Me, I just want to be happy and content. I know I'm in my endgame now, but I've actually had a ridiculously successful career; I have financial security, and my back catalogue helps keep us in the mind's eye.'

He does like to remind himself of his achievements, but then who wouldn't? Sigue Sigue Sputnik were widely ridiculed at the time, and possibly misunderstood. In the years since, James has met all sorts of stars who have complimented him on his work, and the influence his outlook had on theirs, including Bobby Gillespie of Primal Scream, Jamie Hewlett of Gorillaz, Marilyn Manson and Bono, and each have told him that his band's swagger – and sheer bloody-minded intent – led the way. Others followed.

If lasting, meaningful success, in a medium that likes to devour its most boisterous characters then quickly dispose of them, is the respect of your peers, then Tony James, bowed but not forgotten, has at least that. The mohican served him well, after all.

12

'That was a quick learning curve, and it didn't work out well'

If the 1980s was, at least in part, the decade when style reigned over content, and subtlety only worked if someone funnelled it through a loudspeaker, then Transvision Vamp was that theory made flesh. Fronted by Wendy James (no relation to Sigue Sigue Sputnik's Tony James, unless she secretly is but isn't telling), they were a deliberately trashy pop act that spoke in slogans, and whose singer fulfilled the strictly stereotypical fifteen-year-old boy's fever dreams. Few people wore stretchy pink dresses that clung, often for dear life, with more flamboyant elan than James, and few managed to court the British tabloids with more carefree insouciance.

She was a Norwegian-born, west London-raised twenty-two-year-old who was never going to pass her time on the planet with decorum. In an era before social media, James inflamed the passions of, for a brief while, *everybody*, supporters and detractors alike, who had no real platform to alert the world to just how she'd affected them, but who tried nonetheless. She got *a lot* of letters, not all of them complimentary. If that stereotypical fifteen-year-old was unambiguously happy that James had hammered herself into global consciousness in much the same way Madonna had five years previously, there were many others who professed to hate her for her craven ways, her hyperbolic comments, her indefatigable strength and tunnel-visioned ambition. When she made it onto the cover of London's listings magazine *Time Out* at one point in the late 1980s, it was because she had topped their

Hated 100 poll, while in the *NME* she topped their 'gender traitor' list in a grimly tokenistic Women in Rock feature.

But this was all gravy to her, and in reply she would point you to her band's 1989 hit single, 'Baby I Don't Care'.

Despite her Nordic nation of birth, and her London coming-of-age, there was something very French, and very 1963, about her, like a cinema siren who'd just upset Jean-Paul Belmondo and given Roman Polanski the slip. At the age of twenty, two years before she found success with her first band, she was telling anyone who'd listen that nothing less than world domination would satisfy her. As a pop star, she expected to win a Grammy, and as an actress, an Oscar. She'd been just ten years old when Debbie Harry first burst onto the scene, but Wendy James was clearly taking note.

'I was a wild child back then,' she says. 'And as a young girl, I definitely, obviously, had the inclination towards music and performing. But rock 'n' roll didn't manifest itself as my comfort zone, or my vehicle, until I was about sixteen. Prior to that, I was playing in school orchestras, and singing in choirs. I just wanted to be on stage. But then the Sex Pistols came onto my radar, and Blondie, and I became a music fan, and then a lightbulb went on in my head, and I just thought: *This is how I'm going to get on stage. This!*'

Transvision Vamp were three male musicians in leather jackets bought second-hand along the Portobello Road, and the titular vamp up front. They signed a deal in 1986, and when their debut single, 'Revolution Baby', reached just number seventy-seven in the charts a year later, the future Grammy- and Oscar-winner hid her frustration well. Another single followed, 'Tell That Girl to Shut Up', a cover version, but *very* Wendy James all the same. This also failed to scrape the Top 40, but it was at least moving in the right direction: up. It was with their third attempt, 'I Want Your Love', sung in a manner that all too easily managed to reduce its target audience into gibbering wrecks and slavish devotees, that came good, and overnight the band was an international concern.

James was happy, yes. But surprised? No.

'It felt like the most natural thing in the world. We had a quicker rise than most bands, because most bands have to do several tours of dives before anything happens. But we signed our contract, made an album, put out a couple of singles, and by the time we'd finished our very first UK tour, were number five in the charts. That doesn't make you a millionaire – there's a way to go before that happens – so it's a gradual thing. But considering I started at sixteen with my best friends, there was never any doubt in my mind that it wouldn't happen at some point. And as much as Nick [Christian Slayer, lead guitarist and main songwriter] wrote most of our hits, I think a large part of the chemistry was coupled, obviously, with my character, and my talents – but also my drive.

'Everybody I know that made it,' she continues, 'had that drive: Chris Frantz from Talking Heads, Mick Jones from the Clash. They were all ambitious and competitive; they all wanted to win.'

Over the course of the next three years, they released three albums. *Pop Art* and *Velveteen* followed a strict formula of cranking guitars and lipstick kisses in slavish pursuit of giving the people what they wanted. Transvision Vamp were huge across Europe, Australia and in America, where James, so much more famous than either her band or her music, was idolised and objectified, and never taken as seriously as she felt she deserved.

But then came the third album, *Little Magnets Versus the Bubble of Babble*, in which James got to write her own songs for the first time. This was a different fish entirely, more reflective, less of the lip curl. The record company didn't like it – to the extent that they refused to release it, at least within the UK, a slight from which the band didn't recover.

'The whole band was frazzled by then anyway. We'd worked non-stop, much as you do in a pop band on a major label when they want to get as much out of you as possible. I would say, with a little bit of hindsight, that I'm glad we split up when we did,' she says, 'but then, in a parallel universe, had there been a manager who'd had enough wisdom to say to the whole band, but to myself and Nick especially: "You're absolutely burned out, take a year off, and don't even fucking think about music during that time, and then we'll see where your heads are at and if you want to make another album . . ." But no one ever said that to us. And so, unbelievably, the only way Nick and I had [to deal with it all] was to split up. I remember we were midway through an American tour, exhausted, and we just said: "Okay, let's end this when we get to San Diego." And we did. I was twenty-three.'

She hadn't won a Grammy, nor an Oscar, and so the posters of Wendy James that had been Blu-Tacked on bedroom walls across the world came unstuck and began, as old posters have a habit of doing, to wilt.

Over the years, James has been lost, a hermit, a Whatever Happened To . . .? She watched from the sidelines as one of her former band members, bassist Dave Parsons, went on to become a proper rock star in the British grunge band Bush. Her own reputation endures – she remains one of the more memorable stars of the 1980s – and so, while she is gone from the mainstream but not entirely forgotten, she gives a convincing impression today of living entirely unaffected by general consensus. In 2020, she released an album that ran to twenty tracks that she wrote, recorded and presided over with a rabid attention to detail, and the results gave her a huge sense of accomplishment. What more could she possibly need?

'The whole press angle never did mean anything to me,' she says. 'My life wasn't interfered with by journalists saying things about me back then, never, and it still isn't now. I had a boyfriend back then [the Clash's Mick Jones], and he told me, why would I give a shit if some journalist was bitching about me in a really sexist way? And I didn't. I literally didn't give a shit. I know how good I was, so you were absolutely free not to like it, and think that I might be a bit of a dick . . . but like I said, I had my friends, I knew that I was loved and respected by the people I also loved and respected, and so the whole maelstrom, whatever was going on about me in those days, I just didn't care. Still don't.'

And so when the woven rug of fame was whisked out from beneath her like a magic trick, ta-da, all she experienced was relief, a sense of, she says, 'thank fuck for that'. She could have taken the break she needed, but instead signed a solo deal, which she found herself embracing, even though the record company insisted she was still in need of some male guidance, a master and commander type to back up her X-factor appeal with well-honed songs. They presented her, not quite on a platter but almost, to Elvis Costello, who wrote and produced what would become her debut solo album, *Now Ain't the Time for Your Tears*, released in 1993. If her audience didn't like it, then neither did James herself.

'That was a quick learning curve, and it didn't work out well.' But in another way, it did. 'It was after that that I really stepped into my own shoes, and took control of my own career. I called time on that record after the first single came out because of my doubts, and that's when I also called time on my public life – in order, literally, to just sit at home and read books, watch movies, listen to music and refill the creative juices – just really to get in touch with myself.' She laughs. 'I hate that expression but, look, obviously there's a lot of change from the ages of sixteen to twenty-five, and that's when I started to fully embrace my musical powers myself and decide that, for me, from now on, I was going to write my own songs, for better or worse. *It's all going to be from me, that's what I'm going to do.* And I did.'

In her west London flat, she read her books, watched her films, separated from Mick Jones, and haunted the streets around

Portobello Road like the ghost of Christmas past. But she was happy; she'd made enough money and had earned her time to wallow and to percolate. There is an almost twenty-year gap between her first solo album and her second, 2010's *I Came Here to Blow Minds*, which, by its title alone, suggested an artist who was never going to be easily bowed.

One might wonder, and not unreasonably, what happens to all that soaring ambition and solid-gold self-belief after thirty years, especially when so much of it went ultimately unrealised – when no one did open an envelope on a shining stage to read her name out loud to an avalanche of applause, and when her band didn't reform to enthral and appal the world a second time, and when her fitful solo career has not yet taken off in a way she might have desired.

But self-belief at this level is a fascinating and enviable thing to behold. It sustains, irrespective of earthly forces, and in doing so allows the individual to keep going with much the same conviction. Wendy James never did ascend into Debbie Harry or Madonna status, but she is still here, still eminently true to her art, and even now, in her mid-fifties, remains as committed and focused as she ever was.

She says she's spent a lot of her time focusing on self-improvement. 'I'd never really written songs before, so there were a lot of failures, and things took a long time to get right. But I went at my own pace; I was in no rush.'

As is entirely typical for the artistic mind, she developed certain obsessive tendencies: the songs she wrote took her years, and the endless fine-tuning of them took more. She left London and moved to New York, and later to Paris, perhaps because, if nothing else, such locations played nicely into the narrative of glamorous pop stars, and 'London', 'Paris' and 'New York' look fetching in print. James was always good on the details. She hired musicians, studio engineers and producers, put each through their paces until, the way she tells it, their hair turned grey or fell out altogether. 'If you're not familiar with the way I work, you'd wonder what the fuck I did for such a long time, but, hey, it takes a long time to write an album.'

Her 2020 album, *Queen High Straight*, which was witty and droll and endlessly and almost parodically arch – like Lily Allen's mother, with a fag on the go and a grudge to nurture – took her three and a half years to complete. 'Everything had to be *just right*.'

At the time of writing, Wendy James has just over 1,000 monthly listeners on streaming services, which means an awful lot of work, at not inconsiderable expense, for precious little recompense or public recognition. So why bother?

Perched on her sofa in her smart Parisienne apartment, she looks and sounds unambiguously content. The impish sparkle in her eye that was present when talking about her early days of worldwide fame is still there; it's still *her*.

'Oh, the drive for me now is the pure fucking bliss of music, just music. I'm so happy right now, really I am. I may not be very wealthy any more, but apart from that, I've got everything I want. Also,' she adds, 'I'm still thin! While people [as they age] generally tend to get fatter and balder, I still look pretty good.'

She is also happy in her private life, in love, she says, 'with an artist, a really nice man', and after years filled with a sense of drama she mostly stage-managed herself, she feels at peace. In an ideal world, she'd like to be playing Madison Square Garden. But in its real counterpart, her corner of Paris will do.

'Most bands peak early,' she says, and believes that this is because, for most people, 'life tends to flatten you out after a while – you know, the regular travails of life. And then people have families, and that immobilises you to some extent. Having children does age you, and after that – well . . .'

Wendy James has never had children.

'No, I haven't. And that's why I'm still childlike, I think.'

13

'We made mistakes'

Infrequently, the infamy is actually warranted, especially when it spills over into real life, has precious little to do with any actual music, and threatens to ruin everything for its perpetrators.

It became increasingly easy to overlook the musical achievements made by So Solid Crew, the first UK garage act to enjoy mainstream success, because what happened with them *off-stage* became far more compelling. If violence was hinted at during the early part of their career – one lyric ran 'take you to the morgue', and was taken literally by some rather than metaphorically, which is curious when you consider that pop music lyrics tend to be *full* of metaphor – then by the time they were established, it was an intrinsic part of their story. So Solid Crew were trouble.

There was a core membership of nine – Megaman, Skat D, MC Romeo, G-Man, Oxide, Neutrino, MC Harvey, Asher D and Lisa Maffia – but there were floating members, too, and at any one time a live performance could feature as few as twenty, as many as thirty-two. They'd grown up in the housing estates of south London neighbourhoods Peckham, Brixton and Battersea, and in August 2001 they knocked Atomic Kitten off the top of the charts with their single '21 Seconds', a song that sounded threatening in a way punk could only dream of.

Such was the climate of multicultural Great Britain at the time that their appearance on *Top of the Pops* was readily viewed as an event that really did invoke scandal: angry young men who by some accounts led life irresponsibly, being made to look glamorous and aspirational; proof that crime pays. If critics needed evidence to back up what was then a fairly baseless suggestion of the ruinous influence this example of entrepreneurial urban youth conveyed, they found it. As So Solid Crew's success ballooned – their debut album, *They Don't Know*, sold 100,000 copies in its first week alone – so did the attendant controversy.

At one of their shows in Luton, a young fan was beaten to death. A year later, during a party they attended in Birmingham in 2003, two teenagers were shot dead, caught in the crossfire between rival gangs. Crew member G-Man was charged and jailed for possession of a handgun, while Skat D broke the jaw of a fifteen-year-old who had reportedly rebuffed his sexual advances. Asher D, who would go on to become the TV actor Ashley Walters, was imprisoned for possession of a firearm.

As Megaman would later say: 'We came from struggle.' Lisa Maffia would add: 'We were still living in the same grimy estates, seeing the same people – some of [whom] were awful.'

The trouble that followed them was blamed on the band themselves. If you glorify gun culture and violence in your songs, suggested then-Labour culture minister Kim Howells, what else can you expect? Howells called them 'idiots'. The Home Secretary David Blunkett, speaking about their lyrical content, deemed them 'appalling'.

Pretty soon, venues stopped booking them, fearful of further violent incidents. They were dropped from festival billings, just in case. Acts that had come up in the band's wake, walking through doors that they'd opened, did not want to share the stage with them. In 2013, they were reportedly removed from the Lovebox Festival at another artist's request. On Twitter, MC Harvey wasn't happy: 'We give artists careers, and they still treat us like cunts.' But perhaps these other acts were simply nervous, and didn't want the aggro? Because where others postured, So Solid Crew actually followed through – the real deal.

This is not, of course, the best way to forge a lasting career. So Solid Crew existed in a perpetual state of chaos. This might have been the point, initially – chaos has a certain cachet – but it also has an inbuilt detonator. Sooner or later, it will blow.

In this case, sooner.

Lisa Maffia, who was just eighteen at the time the group began, was the sole female member. She'd known various members at various times, and had dated G-Man. Half-Italian and half-Jamaican, she'd grown up in Brixton with her mother and younger sister, and had 'turned bad', she suggests, by the time she started her mid-teens. 'Got into *a lot* of trouble.' Falling in with that mainstay of every secondary school on the planet, the 'wrong crowd', she left at fifteen, and only sat her GCSEs later – when the wrong crowd had finally loosened its grip – at college. Here, she was to study art and photography, but couldn't afford the necessary equipment, and so ultimately left and got a job instead, working in Iceland (the frozen food shop, not the country – and on the tills, mostly). She wanted to enrol at a singing school, and because she couldn't afford the £145-per-term fee, managed to talk herself into getting the first ten lessons free, and was subsequently funded by the Prince's Trust. No one gets anywhere without a little grit. She spent two years at college, during which time she rekindled her relationship with the boys from So Solid. Aware that they needed a focal point, something to offset all the testosterone, they asked her to join.

Already locally famous, they now began to pick up gigs across Europe, and one summer were booked for an appearance at Ayia Napa in Cyprus. After their performance, a record company executive approached, wanting to sign them. The concept was foreign to So Solid Crew.

'We were like: "Sign us? What does that even mean? Sign us what?"'

In the meantime, she sang backing vocals for Oxide & Neutrino, two part-time members of the Crew, while working in an off-licence in Loughborough Junction, near Brixton, for cash in hand. She was nineteen. 'People would come in, buy a drink, recognise me and ask why I was there. I'd tell them: "I'm doing my job." I just didn't get the transition, didn't get that you had to leave your day job to become – well, to become famous, a pop star.'

By the time they signed, Maffia had it explained to her that her contribution was essential. 'My voice,' she says, 'made it all feel a little bit smoother.'

Megaman soon asserted himself as band leader and made, Maffia says, 'sometimes selfish, sometimes silly decisions that were detrimental to our careers. He had our careers, and our lives, in his hands. He obviously had his own vision, his own way of doing it, and things did get a little bit messy, yeah, because there was a lot of pressure put [on] him to make those decisions. We can't blame him, but,' she adds, 'there were some [choices] that I wouldn't have agreed to alone.'

The controversy became a problem, but, she says, 'fortunately for me, I was the only girl, so at the time of all that negative press, I fronted it with a sort of angelic, sort of soft approach, where I was apologetic, I admitted to our wrongs, and I also protested that we were young and misled in a lot of ways, being led by a lot of adults that didn't always have our best interests at heart. Or else they could've guided us a lot better.

'But then,' she reconsiders, 'maybe it was difficult for them too, because there were a lot of strong personalities within the band, and we were suddenly very rich and very famous by twenty. Imagine running around with over £1 million in the bank when you've come from a background of having absolutely nothing. None of us were born with a silver spoon, so when the money came, we enjoyed ourselves.

'We also made mistakes.'

They may have been collectively rich, but £1 million doesn't stretch very far when divided, albeit unequally, between twenty people, or thirty-two of them, or whichever number in between. Such were their touring expenses that it soon became obvious the band would never really profit from live shows. Maffia only started making her own money when the band was over and she signed her solo deal in 2003.

'I went and saw £350,000 in my bank account, and I didn't even know what that number was!' She did like the look of it, though, and the credit card was nice, too, the beep of acceptance that happened every time she swiped it through readers at plush department stores. So many beeps.

'Oh, I made some terrible decisions! Three cars in my drive at one point, and so much jewellery, clothes in abundance, holidays all the time, out with the girls every week – limousines! I was really rock 'n' roll with it, but then, you know, I was also very conscious of my future, so I got a mortgage, too. I wasn't like the boys. The boys just literally, you know, *lived*. I was smart, I suppose because I had to be: I had a child by that stage.'

By 2003, with their fame on the wane as the scene they'd helped create threw up multiple new and incoming stars, each member of the Crew drifted off, some with more purpose than others, to do their own things. Maffia's solo career would prove complicated: she wasn't an adept musician, nor yet a fully fledged songwriter. 'And I wasn't the perfect businesswoman, either.' Assailed nonetheless by offers, she said yes to almost everything that came her way: photo shoots with Duran Duran for some or other nebulous event; fashion shows across Europe. There was an album, *First Lady*, which produced a number-two hit single, but her third single reached number seventy-seven, and so that was the end of that. Later, she launched her own short-lived record label, and an equally short-lived clothing line. In 2007, she stopped everything when her mother got cancer, and took time out to look after her.

When Maffia returned to work a couple of years later, her renewed determination was ably matched by some newly entrepreneurial, almost Del Boy-like smarts. In the years immediately following the dissolution of So Solid, Maffia had realised that there was still good money to be made by doing nightclub appearances, ten-minute *hello-smile-wave-and-goodbye* jobs that would net her £4,000–£5,000 each, arguably the best-paid soulless work to be found anywhere in music. But the shelf life of such demand is as short as, well, a shelf, and the bookings soon evaporated. She was still a single parent, and still needed to work. To resuscitate interest in her brand, such as it was, she started up her own booking agency, herself the sole employee, and would call clubs across the country masquerading as the Personal Assistant to the one and only Lisa Maffia, formerly of So Solid Crew, now an international solo star and occasional fashion designer. Her PA's name was Celine.

Almost immediately, the bookings came in, and though she was offered far less money – now closer to £700 per appearance – it was a living. 'Celine' was so good at her job that she was soon booking similar gigs for sundry other So Solid alumni.

Later, dropping 'Celine', and retiring, at least temporarily, from music, she would open her own hairdresser's in Margate, deciding hair maintenance was a safer bet than the fickle world of showbiz. Running her own business would keep her busy, and she likes to be busy. 'I hustle,' she says. 'Never been afraid to hustle.'

14

'I'm a Gemini. Geminis are naturally quite fiery'

By 2006, pop infamy was back in its tired old comfort zone, in which the chief perpetrators smoked cigarettes and drank from cans of strong lager, wore skinny jeans and devoutly believed that their spirit of impish malarkey somehow constituted rebellion in all its incandescent forms. Musical theorists might claim that this happens sporadically and intermittently in different eras because the art form has grown moribund and arthritic, lacking in impetus and direction, and needs a kick up the arse. But it's just as often by chance. Sigue Sigue Sputnik's Tony James had, after all, spent the entire punk era *trying* to be punk (and briefly succeeding, with Generation X) before being given his chance to shine at a moment when British music was already in perfectly rude health, and really didn't need his continued involvement.

In 2006, however, music was, both intellectually speaking and in terms of how much it stimulated, decidedly *meh*. A band called the Kooks were enjoying a moment of something, likewise the reality TV singer Shayne Ward, while the Senegalese-American rapper Akon was riding high with a track called 'Smack That', which was about showing a young lady his Lamborghini on the tacit understanding that he could take her back to his place afterwards and 'possibly bend [her] over'.

There was no single unifying force in music, no grunge or Brit-pop, no hair metal or pop explosion. Just the year before, Mariah Carey had spent fourteen weeks at number one in America with 'We Belong Together', a suggestive R&B ballad of glissando vocal overtures that was nice, but not *that* nice.

Presumably, then – but by no means scientifically – out of such lifelessness do musical revolutions grow. While the world awaited this particular revolution to announce itself in jet streams, along came Towers of London, an 'it-says-here' punk act in skinny white jeans, with backcombed hair blow-dried and aerosoled, a lip curl modelled on Johnny Rotten's (but which looked closer in spirit to Shakin' Stevens'), and a bunch of songs designed to go off like a hand grenade. Proof? A single called 'Fuck It Up', and another, 'Beaujolais', in which lead singer Donny Tourette (not his real name) sang the line 'I am a man with mystery'.

On both record and in person they appeared in a perpetually sour mood: mistrustful, drunk, ready to ruck. If they hated 'us', they seemed to hate one another, too. There was much intra-band conflict, which centred mostly around Donny and his rhythm guitar-playing brother Dirk (not his real name either), who were forever screaming into one another's faces, or else throwing badly aimed punches.

If all this seemed curiously unconvincing, disingenuous even, it was perhaps in part because they were consistently being trailed by a TV documentary crew that filmed everything they did. And so there was a certain amount of acting going on here, or at least acting *up*. This was their USP: in an era of reality TV, where everybody who ever did anything did so while being filmed, they were doing likewise while in the business of being, purportedly, an Actual Band. Documentaries need spice, so Towers of London added spice. The more they tore it up on-screen, ran the logic, the more we might want to hear their music.

The band had landed their record deal in 2005, and a year on were having minor hits: 'On A Noose' reached number thirty-two, 'Fuck It Up' number forty-six. Their highest chart placing, number thirty, was with 'How Rude She Was'. Their first album, *Blood, Sweat and Towers*, was terribly earnest in its volume and intent, and was frequently silly and often helplessly entertaining.

Arriving at a time of musical blandness, the music press and tabloids alike descended upon them hungrily, not to hail them but to lampoon – to have fun riling them, goading them and generally throwing them to the sharks, the kind of unedifying spectacle that, regrettably, the music industry has always fostered and baldly encouraged.

Donny Tourette was twenty-five years old. Back then, he liked to suggest that he didn't care whether he lived to see twenty-six. 'I'm a Gemini,' he says now, fifteen years later, still very much alive. 'Geminis are naturally quite fiery.'

Towers of London did not go on to become a latter-day Sex Pistols, and nor did their impact prompt a new-century surge in the revival of anarchy. They'd been hoping, and planning, for millions of sales, but had to content themselves with closer to 40,000. Nevertheless, Donny Tourette *did* become a star in an emphatically modern sense: over-hyped, over-documented, unceremoniously dumped, and then left to pick up the pieces by himself. If Musical Youth were a cautionary tale for the 1980s, Towers of London were their equivalent in the 2000s.

'I spent most of my time ducking interviews,' Tourette says. 'I remember feeling so disappointed whenever I got asked to do yet another one, thinking, well, why don't you just go and interview the bassist, or the drummer? But they never wanted to do that.'

Tourette did make for an unusually compelling frontman: unfiltered, quick to react. The more you looked at him, the more you could sense fear in his eyes, and with it the suggestion that an all-too-human heart was beating in there somewhere, and that its frenzied pace was indicative of fight-or-flight. Even in his alter ego, his pantomime baddie, there was a sensitive soul lurking. And he was terrified.

He mitigated such failings – celebrities must be made of stern stuff – by drinking as much as he possibly could, at all hours. His record company essentially banned him from nights in, got him invited to red carpet events, onto high-profile support slots, and dubious events at miserable club nights. Everywhere he went, the paparazzi followed, because once drunk, he was easy to provoke. He felt like Princess Diana, hounded and harried. Was this really, he'd wonder more than once, what being a rock star was about?

Patrick Brannan had never really wanted to be in a band. He was happy being a fan. He and his older brother had been Beatles obsessives while growing up, then later transferred that obsession to Oasis. Watching the latter being interviewed on TV, his brother took note. *This* was what it took to be in a band, and to get noticed: write a bunch of good, if derivative, songs, then get your brother to sing them while intermittently punching him. Patrick, not yet Donny Tourette, resisted.

'Until one day, he beat me up – he was bigger than me – and so I gave in and agreed.'

This slightly reductive potted history might be missing some key facts, but no matter. It's the way he tells it; you get the gist. Patrick Brannan was now Donny Tourette, his brother Francis, Dirk. This was the late nineties. They'd been directly exposed to Britpop, but also maintained a lingering love for Guns N' Roses. A combination of the two, they thought, might just work. Due largely to the convenience of geography, they began to hang around Noel Gallagher's London house rather than Axl Rose's in Los Angeles. This was where many Oasis fans tended to congregate, in pursuit of osmosis, good vibes, shared bottles of gin and autographs. They were there one evening when Gallagher came home. Patrick, brazen in his confidence even then, told him that he and his brother were in a band, too. They sang him an original song, a cappella. Gallagher smiled, mumbled some encouragement, and fled inside.

Sometimes, even the merest encouragement is enough. Towers of London wrote song after song now, fuelled by their fleeting contact with greatness, but failed time and again to gain much interest. They wanted to write big, buoyant stadium anthems, but it wasn't happening. A change of direction, then: they became more inspired now by the Clash, the Ramones and the Sex Pistols, acts on a mission. They grew their hair, and blow-dried it mercilessly, somehow convincing themselves that this comprised a 'look'. (And it was, indeed, a look – albeit one from 1986.) They began wearing tighter and tighter denim, cutting off circulation and sperm production in the name of art.

'Noel Fielding, Russell Brand,' he says. 'They weren't rocking that look yet, and believe it or not, we'd never heard of Mötley Crüe.'

Pioneers, then.

Their deal, when it finally came, was with an independent label based in New York. The idea of committing their every act to film came shortly after, and soon this particular cat was chasing its own tail. Tourette was a man increasingly horrified by his adopted caricature, but unable to do anything about it. He was linked to women, some of whom he had relationships with, among them Bob Geldof's daughter Peaches, and several others the newspapers referred to as 'mystery blondes'. One of the less mysterious examples was Courtney Love, who was, claimed one tabloid piece, 'romantically pursuing the British rock star'. Another claimed that Tourette was partying with Love 'to make him look uber-cool'. Love herself was, by all accounts, furious at Tourette's ongoing efforts to get famous by his association with her, insisting that they had never even met. The truth was nowhere.

'They printed so many lies,' he says. 'My mum would see this stuff, and I just had to keep explaining to her that it wasn't real.' He pauses. 'It was almost never real.'

Their music by now had been swiftly discounted as a joke, a parody and, somewhat less controversially, as not particularly good, the amassed column inches repeatedly failing to translate into actual sales. The record company, fearing they'd never see profit from their initial outlay, moved into a code red situation. If they didn't now milk Tourette's infamy for all its remaining worth, there'd be tears before bedtime.

In 2007, Tourette entered the *Celebrity Big Brother* house. As far as good ideas go, this wasn't one. Towers of London may not have had much in the way of credibility, but *Celebrity Big Brother* would surely kill any they did have dead. To many, it confirmed only one thing: the sheer brazen desperation of Donny Tourette, so obsessed with even the most frivolous kind of fame that he'd prostitute himself shamelessly.

The truth, as ever, proved a little more complicated.

'Everybody thinks I just jumped at the chance [of appearing on the show], but I didn't. I turned it down many times. But they insisted.'

'They' were his record company, and this was their last-gasp attempt. Tourette could smell the desperation, and he wanted nothing to do with it. 'Nobody knows the real story about that, but I was literally blackmailed into it by the label.' They'd already withdrawn all their support and were threatening to strangle the band in perpetuity by not allowing them to release another record. In short: career suicide. 'So,' Tourette says, 'I did it.'

He entered the house alongside someone from Steps, Michael Jackson's older brother, a Page 3 model, and seventies easy-listening favourite Leo Sayer. Tourette quickly fortified himself with alcohol, immersed himself in the outdoor hot tub while fully clothed, and smoked cigarettes in a manner people only really do on soap operas. Leo Sayer commented that he looked like a 'harmless Johnny Lydon'. The more he strutted around the house as that first evening unfolded, the more he resembled a fatally wounded swan describing ever decreasing circles until collapsing into a heap. This was fun to watch, in only the most sadistic way.

On day two, by now comprehensively out of his gourd, his resolve broke. He bolted over the wall, refusing to return. The record company was apoplectic (he'd proved, if nothing else, a ratings winner), 'but by that stage I wasn't talking to them', and so he didn't care.

You might think that, by now, Donny Tourette had learned his lesson, if only because Patrick Brannan was surely still somewhere cowering inside of him. But no. There was more to come: the final and emphatic descent of the guillotine onto his brass neck.

Less than a month later, he accepted an invitation from the BBC music panel show, *Never Mind the Buzzcocks*, in which much of the comedy potential was sourced from roasting those celebrities foolish enough to appear. How best to succinctly sum up Tourette's faring? Like a shrimp thrown not onto a barbecue but into the open maws of hell itself. Rarely has a public figure squirmed more, seemed more out of place, or seemed more in need of his mother.

The band's record label did not recoup their losses. They went bankrupt shortly after.

Reliving all this now, he says, is hard.

'I couldn't really talk about this to anybody for years. Couldn't have a conversation about it at all. Even five years ago, it was still painful. But more recently, I've . . . Well, I mean, I guess time's a healer, right? But I've also got into things like spirituality and mindfulness, different ways of dealing with what happened to me back then, and things like acceptance, and no longer stressing over those things you can't change, but learn[ing] to embrace them instead, feel gratitude for them, even. Because, you know, I'm grateful for everything we had, but there are things I've implemented into my life now that help me deal with my past a bit more.'

His initial reaction to the fallout was severe. 'I was suicidal, you know. I was close to jumping off a fucking bridge.'

Now in his early forties, Donny Tourette has, like Emu after Rod Hull removed his hand, withdrawn from public life. He is Patrick Brannan again, no longer a freewheeling drunk but rather an entirely sober, friendly and keenly conversational person. He practices reiki and is convinced that the universe has a plan for him. He lives in Hoxton, east London.

After his dalliance with suicidal ideation, his sister came to his assistance, and locked him in her house to decompress. 'Everybody thinks you're bulletproof, but you're not. I'll tell you what the root of it was, and it's probably important, this. I was nervous all the time. I was terrified. In order to get up on stage, I had to drink; to do an interview, I drank; a photo shoot, drink. I was pretty much wasted constantly in order to have the confidence to do all the things I needed to do to be in a band. That's why I always seemed to have that layer of something else, that *fuck you*-ness. I was pretty much strung out for five years. Nobody who met me [during that time] would've known the real me. There was an insecurity to me, a lack of confidence.'

With hindsight, with age, he regrets plenty: the big hair, the careless interviews, the attitude. In mitigation, he suggests Towers of London were cursed. When they tried to break America after conspicuously failing to break the UK, they took their film crew with them, but then the credit crunch bit and the banks ran out of money, leaving their documentary doomed. 'But then everything we touched was doomed.'

Now not merely in debt but penniless, Tourette needed to work. He ended up on a building site. 'It all happened so quick, so quick. We'd been on the main stage at Reading and Leeds, all over the papers and TV, touring the world . . . and within two years of all that I was on a building site in a high-vis jacket, holding a sledgehammer, and just thinking to myself: *Oh my God, I've fucked it, I've really fucked this one, and there's no coming back from it.*'

The building site stint lasted three months. He knew that

whatever he did next, it had to be creative. 'I've always been an ideas guy.' He came up with a quiz show format that he sold to Sky, which went to pilot but wasn't picked up. He had more ideas, and his job now is to develop programme concepts for television – documentaries, game shows, music shows. His work as a reiki therapist is a side hustle, but one he loves. Processing his past, meanwhile, is an ongoing project. A few years ago, he took part in an ayahuasca ceremony, the South American practice of ingesting a psychoactive brew in pursuit of emotional and spiritual cleansing, 'because I wanted it to help me with the trauma I've gone through in my life, past and present, the band as well, and to be able to let go of it.' The ayahuasca made him vomit, as these ceremonies tend to do, the vomit both a figurative and literal purging. 'It just felt so good.'

He emerged with a clear vision, and he felt redeemed, reborn. He's urging his fellow former band members to undergo a similar purging now, convinced that, if they do so, then perhaps there *is* a future for Towers of London after all. There are already discussions for a film about their early days. If nothing else, you have to admire his optimism.

Life is a journey, he says. To help map it, he has attended spiritualist churches, consulted with mediums, and cried his eyes out at the revelations they prompted within him, which have enabled him to see, feel, and better process everything that comes his way. He looks back at his first stint in music, and shudders.

'I love my life now. Course, there's elements I still carry around that I don't like, and I'm working on that, and I don't want to sound like a cliché, but I'm always growing, and I'm at complete peace and bliss. There's still a lot of things wrong with me, things I'm trying to sort out, work out, but I appreciate what I have. I do a job that I like, I still hang out with the boys from the band, and I've landed myself in a good spot.

'It's just taken me a while to get there.'

SIX

THE PYRAMID STAGE

15

'Artists,' Alex Kapranos, singer with Franz Ferdinand, says, 'no matter what field they're working in, whether a visual artist, writer, a classical musician – it's a lifelong pursuit, right? But I'd say there's a slightly different perception in the field of the music I work in, an emphasis in the lead-up, in the beginning stages of public awareness [for pop stars]. But the way people perceive the life of an author, I think, is different. There, it's the _entire_ life which is the concern, and with someone like, say, Charles Bukowski, people were interested in what he was writing right up until the moment he died. It's considered to be a slow evolution, both as a personality and an artist, their body of work being a complete thing.

'But in music, in pop music, the emphasis is mostly on the beginning of a career.'

This astute observation would explain why, back in 2004, there was such a clamour of interest in, and excitement about, Franz Ferdinand, a Scottish band who took art rock and remade it in their own image more effectively than anyone had since, perhaps, Talking Heads – and why there is much less interest in them now. The clamour reached its climax around the release of the band's self-titled debut album. There was no such frenzy afforded fifteen years later for their fifth, which had the optimistic and almost self-help-like title of _Always Ascending_, because, as Kapranos explains, as a pop outfit they were considered, if not quite _old_ news by then, then certainly established enough for the fever to have passed. That debut album sold 300,000 copies in the first two months of its release in the UK, and over 1.1 million in America, and Kapranos was established – or perhaps more accurately had established himself – very much in the David Bowie mould: erudite, enigmatic, all cheekbones and elegance, someone who looked good in a suit, and who'd been born to be the receptacle of excessive stimuli.

Kapranos was nevertheless unusual for a thrusting young pop star back in 2004 for the simple reason that he wasn't particularly young. He was thirty-two. His band was unusual, too, because they sounded already entirely complete, the finished article. Where *could* they possibly go after the flamboyant strut of early singles like 'Take Me Out' and 'Do You Want To?' Their sound owed as much to alt rock as it did to Nile Rogers and disco; what was so particularly thrilling about 'Take Me Out' was how it changed musical direction halfway through to such dramatic effect you had to go back to listen to it again just to make sure your brain hadn't imagined it.

This was no overnight success, but rather the result of much private and secretive planning. Kapranos suggests that 'pop star' was his calling all along. 'I was twenty-seven, twenty-eight, when I realised, *Shit, this is what I do!* Okay, to call it a calling sounds a bit religious, but I knew that songwriting was what I did, and who I was. Trouble was, I'd missed the accepted timeframe, and so when I was younger, I was still just doing it for fun. By the time the band got together, the whole expectation of fame was kind of removed from the situation.'

They pursued music simply because they felt compelled to, because it gave them great joy, and because they knew they were good at it. So when fame did find them, and promptly elevated them to vertiginously lofty heights, Kapranos considered these developments entirely fitting, their fate fulfilled.

'Most artists aren't particularly candid about this, but I think most are massively ego-driven, no matter what their field. I have a theory that artists end up as artists because there's some kind of deep flaw within their psyche that they're trying to atone for, or trying to work out. The drive for recognition is part of the balance they're seeking. Usually, when you read biographies of musicians, that seems apparent – to me, at least. I know it's a sweeping generalisation,' he says, adding that people who pursue other professions can be just as conflicted, 'but those paths seem less driven by those big ruptures in the personality than in artists.'

In dealing with his own internal schisms, Kapranos was always lusting after that missing part of the jigsaw that would make him whole, and would make him make sense: fame.

'It's the lack of fame later on,' he says. 'That's the difficult part.'

If Franz Ferdinand *had* disappeared from public view after their 2004 debut, like some ill-fated actor who'd inadvertently overdosed shortly after making the perfect film, they'd have left a beautiful corpse, and would have slipped subsequently into endless mythologising. Their extended silence would, over time, have been strafed by intriguing wild rumour: they were secretly working with Kraftwerk, perhaps, or with Frank Zappa's hologram; or, no, they were shacked up together in a Californian commune, but no longer on speaking terms. Or maybe guitarist Nick McCarthy had been seen playing golf with Harper Lee, and at a screening of *Batman Returns* with Gore Vidal. Or Kapranos himself, alone in a tower and tortured like Orson Welles, was now living on an extreme macrobiotic diet that allowed him to maintain a twenty-eight-inch waist deep into middle-age, an achievement he'd flaunt in a rare Instagram post that was almost certainly *not* a fake account.

Nothing ladens gossip on the grapevine quite like a mysterious absence. The music they *had* made together, meanwhile, those eleven perfect songs on that perfectly swaggering debut album, would have remained pristine, eternal, a legendary benchmark, a time capsule, and myth's own soundtrack.

But, no, Franz Ferdinand chose not to disappear. Instead, they simply went about the business, as successful bands are wont to do, of making more music and then more music still, the errant fools.

A second album emerged, which did well to repeat its predecessor's effervescent spark, and allowed Kapranos to ascend into the role of a dapper man about town, doing fashion spreads in glossy magazines and even landing his own food column in the *Guardian*. But the glue that had bound the band together began to unstick. There was a four-year silence; at some point, Nick McCarthy left. Kapranos began feeling his age.

'There's a celebration of youth in music, and in sport, isn't there?' he says. 'Your physical capacity will wane over the years, so for a sportsman or woman, you might not be able to run the length of a football field at the age of thirty-seven the way you had at nineteen. Similarly, in the world of music, whether we like it or not, the perception of what we hear is based upon how musicians look, *physically* – something that's, of course, played up by marketing, whether a poster in the back of *Smash Hits* magazine years ago, or a music video watched today on YouTube. People want a pleasing image to look at while listening to music: a nice set of cheekbones, a winning smile.'

Kapranos would give this much thought over the years, as interest in the band waned, his food column was cancelled, and glossy magazines dressed up other young-buck singers instead. He came to the conclusion that there is little within the pop field as distasteful as a middle-aged pop star who manages to denigrate their back catalogue, or at the very least dull its edges, simply by continuing. Almost no one is exempt from this fate, he says. It happened to Johnny Cash, to Leonard Cohen, Neil Young – even David Bowie, who struggled to remain relevant in the 1990s. A seventeen-year-old pop fan does not want to look towards someone in their forties to help articulate life for them. But there are other problems, too. When that seventeen-year-old pop fan reaches their forties, they perhaps no longer need to have their feelings articulated by *any* musician; they've learned to do that for themselves. They might have become jaded, or at least not quite as susceptible, or impressionable, or as prone to look up to singers any more. They've grown up. Instead, when they continue to listen to music, as they surely do, they crave the music of their youth to remind them of more innocent times. They want David Bowie at twenty-five, not David Bowie at fifty-five. Correspondingly, an Alex Kapranos in his mid-forties can get left on the shelf.

'And that's a shame, really, because I personally have always loved those artists that can, and do, articulate those emotions as we go through life: that passion and love, and all manner of other trials, but from an adult perspective rather than a teenage bubblegum one. ABBA was very good at doing that, though I never felt they got the full credit.

'I have the same emotions about writing songs today as I had when I was fifteen, but in many ways the process is more far-reaching now. I have more experience, I can communicate better, I'm a better musician, and I know what I'm doing.' But he's a realist, too. 'I know that nothing can quite match that first buzz of realising that this is something you can actually do, and that's why, I think, fame is quite anxiety-inducing. It makes you question the process of what you do, and that gets harder the longer you do it.'

Over the years, he has experienced several episodes of crippling self-doubt. He counterbalances this by maintaining his ego, which, he insists, 'is totally out of control, gargantuan, massive – just like every other musician who ever graced the stage.' He laughs. 'You need the arrogance and the swagger to get out on a stage in the first place, you need to have ideas above your station, the ability to think on a grand canvas. You need to be prepared to alienate your friends and family in order to follow your dream, even when that dream gets in the way of ordinary life.

'Fame,' he says, 'is like a wave. You go up, and you go down. But what's its destination? I'm hoping that the end of my career is my grave, that I can remain an artist until the day I drop, either on stage, or in the studio. It's an appealing idea.'

Franz Ferdinand have been far quieter of late, their music the recipient of less rapture, individual solo projects muted and ruminative and under the radar. Kapranos has accepted this, but music for him still completely defines his identity and sense of self. 'I never wanted anything to come in and take any sort of role in my life that would ever edge out making music, and so I don't let it.' Before being in a band, he did all sorts of work: he was a van driver, a welder, a pretty decent chef. 'But none of those jobs ever felt like a career. *This* – music – this is what I do, come what may.'

After McCarthy left the band, he didn't for a second think of ending it. Franz Ferdinand is bigger than the sum of its parts.

'Say the rest of the band were killed in a private jet as it flew down to Glasgow in poor visibility,' he says, 'or the helicopter they were on ran out of petrol. Then, yes, I would probably stop the band, but even then I wouldn't stop being an artist. I could never stop writing, or playing, music. There are times I can write five songs in three days, and other times I won't write anything in six months. Sometimes, I can become bored, too, so a lot of this is about pushing us into new perspectives, and new techniques.'

This is why, in 2014, the band got together with another legendary art rock group, but one with far more years than them, Sparks, to work on the FFS project. Sparks, made up of brothers Ron and Russell Mael, who were almost twice Kapranos' age, brought something new, something fresh, and made him look at music as if it had just been created that day. There was something revitalising in this. 'It's like doing a puzzle. Nobody wants to do the same puzzle time and again, so you need a new one, right?'

Alex Kapranos is a man with obsessive tendencies. Most of them are fleeting – learning the craft of making fine cider, for example, 'the best in the world', and then losing all interest with that and getting into baking bread instead. Or woodwork, or . . . *something*. His brain has to be engaged, and that engagement must encourage him to lose all sense of time and space around him. This probably makes him murder to live with, but such is the way of obsessives.

'I need the satisfaction that comes from doing something new, and then, when I reach a level of satisfaction, I move on to do something else.' Most frequently in life, that has been music. 'I never want to adopt that glazed expression,' he says. 'I never want to be the singer in a heritage band, dragging my artistic corpse behind me. It's important to maintain a sense of reckless-ness, and if you don't mind fucking things up every now and then, the recklessness can be exciting.'

16

At more or less the same time that Alex Kapranos was between musical projects, learning how best to cultivate apples in the pursuit of premium cider, Snow Patrol's Gary Lightbody was experiencing something else entirely, something all mega-successful artists must fear at some point in their lives: writer's block.

This all happened when he was still comparatively new to Los Angeles, the Northern Irishman having invested the multiple zeros of his newly handsome bank account into Californian property. He now counted plastic surgeons among his neighbours, and stood in line on daily coffee runs next to A-list actresses in Lycra running gear. One of the more intriguing factors of most if not quite *all* rock stars is their conviction that they never truly fit in to normal society. Instead, they embrace their outlier status in the expectation that success makes them at least appear superficially cool and worth knowing, whatever their peccadilloes. Lightbody, a sensitive man riven with insecurity, had always struggled with cool, and so LA was always going to be problematic for him, a city built on an edifice of perceived perfection, and which hid its myriad dysfunctions well. He tried hard to blend in and felt it keenly when he failed. He failed more times than he succeeded.

In an upmarket clothes store in his new neighbourhood, he bought himself a leather jacket, the first he'd ever purchased. It was shiny, black and aromatic, fitted around the shoulders, tight across the torso, and bifurcated by a sparkling zip. It was the kind of chic manly outerwear that puts one in mind of low-slung motorbikes on open West Coast freeways. Obscenely expensive perhaps, but he'd bought it in the spirit of his new identity: rock star. May as well try to look the part. Thing is, a good part of Lightbody's charm was that he had never particularly resembled a rock star so much as a mature student who plays computer games all night long. His hair was forever an untameable mess, and his smile, whenever he offered one up, was sheepish, as if he was embarrassed about the way it shaped his lips. His general aura, and it was not an entirely unappealing one, was of crippling self-consciousness. Just before flying out to the States for Snow Patrol's first big US tour, he was interviewed for an American magazine in a canal-side café in London's Camden one cold winter's morning. The interview revealed him to be not the latest superstar-in-waiting, coupling the effortless charm of Chris Martin with the insouciant cool of a Libertine, but rather someone who'd just rolled out of bed with a headache, a hangover, and an inability to speak in full sentences. Star quality wasn't lacking so much as entirely absent.

But, hey, these days, needs must. Gary Lightbody was now a singer whose songs had sold millions worldwide, making him rich beyond his wildest dreams. Yes, his busy schedule was keeping him all too frequently single, and curiously unfulfilled, and increasingly fond of drink to the point where fondness looked more like reliance, but LA had always been a place of reinvention. Effort was required.

On the day of its purchase, he took his leather jacket from its hanger, he put it on, and he went out.

'I went to a bar,' he says, 'to meet some friends.'

He arrived, permissibly, a little late. They were already there, off to one side, standing in a wide circle, old friends and new, people he'd met through work, through touring, through mutual appreciation. He ordered a drink and compelled himself to relax. Gingerly making his approach, he saw that the crowd comprised someone he hadn't met before but whom he immediately recognised. It was Stephen Merchant, co-creator of *The Office* and someone who, at six foot seven, always towered over everybody else in his company.

Lightbody caught the eye of one or two friends, and said hello, but he'd not yet penetrated the circle, not yet alerted everyone to the fact of his presence. This wouldn't have happened to Bruce Springsteen, to Bono, or Lady Gaga, but never mind. He patiently waited for the present conversation to run its course, at which point he would say hello to all. A moment later, the tall man noticed him. He leaned back on his long legs, transferring his weight to the balls of his feet, and very deliberately took in the leather-clad Lightbody.

'*All right!*' Stephen Merchant said, in his familiar rolling Bristolian tones, 'Mad Max has arrived.'

Mass laughter, not a dry eye. Lightbody physically diminished, curling into himself until he was almost spherical. 'He just completely buried me in front of everybody. The one and only time I had any rock-star confidence about me was completely decimated in the space of a few words. My one dalliance with rock 'n' roll behaviour,' he says, shaking his head, 'never to be repeated.'

Gary Lightbody was born in Northern Ireland in 1976, and was making music by the age of eighteen, first in a band called Shrug, then Polarbear, and eventually Snow Patrol. If solo singers tend to work hard on fostering a sense of self-confidence because they need to, then it's easier in a band. In Snow Patrol, much like Peter Perrett in the Only Ones, Lightbody was one of several. The confidence was collective. The others bolstered him.

'When you start a band at the age of eighteen, you think you'll be famous by next Tuesday lunchtime.' But there were to be ten years of Tuesday lunchtimes before anything like that began to happen. Lightbody, refocusing his ambitions, decided that overnight success was a death-knell; stealth was better. The band played live as much as they could, sometimes to as few as thirty or forty people. If any 'fans' hung around afterwards, the band would ask whether they might be able to crash on someone's floor for the night; they couldn't afford a hotel. Whenever his parents worried whether he was making enough money to pay the rent, Lightbody was conscientious enough to reach for a white lie.

In the late nineties, they signed to an independent record label – taken seriously at last – but by 2001 were dropped. If he'd been looking for a sign to consolidate his talent, this was it: he surely had none. He took himself to the job centre, where he was assessed for his ability to operate within the workplace. After the day-long course, it was recommended he seek employment in a call centre. His parents approved: this would constitute real work.

He lasted two days. 'That's how useful I am to society when you take the guitar away from me,' he says.

The band got back together.

'One last try,' he told himself.

Snow Patrol returned to the songs they'd been working on that had got them dropped from their contract, in the dogged belief there might be something worth salvaging. Besides, they'd not written anything new. These songs would go on to form the back-bone of their breakthrough album, *Final Straw*, and the singles that would be released from it, among them 'Chocolate', 'Wow' and a shimmering ballad called 'Run', each of which would go on to be sung by millions in stadiums around the world.

By this stage, Snow Patrol were ten years old. How many bands last that long before breaking through? Lightbody couldn't think of many, though those he did come up with – Pulp, the Flaming Lips, Mercury Rev – gave him hope. The band still had a manager who believed in them, and the manager introduced them to a producer who went by the name of Jacknife Lee. Lee saw the promise in these songs, stripped back the annoying indie sensibilities, and embraced the melodies contained within.

'He told us,' Lightbody says, 'that choruses were nothing to be afraid of.'

All of a sudden, there was definable promise, and *Final Straw* hung heavy with an emotion that felt both true and earned. They were picked up by a major label, Polydor, and the album came out in 2002, the same year Coldplay put out *A Rush of Blood to the Head*. Timing, in music, is often everything, and the world seemed to fall in sync in its desire to listen to songs that dealt in heartbreaking resonance, and whose rousing choruses allowed a mass singalong.

Final Straw was a hit, first in the UK, then right across the world. On the precipice of thirty, Gary Lightbody now had a successful 'job'. His parents were relieved, while he himself experienced a dizzying vertigo. They were now playing arenas, 'and we had no idea how to play to that kind of crowd.' A year later, they supported U2 in even bigger venues. Lightbody would spend every night on the side of the stage, watching how Bono worked the audience. He took notes. Bono, he saw, wore leather jackets.

But the comfort zone he'd now found himself in did not seem to have much solace in it. 'We were just very aware that this could be taken away from us at any time, and that in fact it – the success – might be a mistake. I was waiting for someone to tap me on the shoulder and say: "Actually, sorry, it's not supposed to be you guys, so if you could just move out of the way, that'd be great."'

Humility is a good characteristic in anyone, but too much of it leads to an inferiority complex. 'You're never fully cocksure, or confident,' he says. 'So you'll find no footage of me entering a room like, say, [the UFC fighter] Conor McGregor. I love someone's ability to do that, and I revere it, but it's so far from what goes on in my own head.'

He did find an outlet for his angst, though, and poured it into the band's next album, 2005's *Eyes Open*, sufficiently self-aware to know that his increasing frailty could be used to his band's advantage. It sold eight million copies, with its lead single 'Chasing Cars' going on to become the most-played song on British radio of the twenty-first century. This was superstar status. Superstar status tends largely to anoint only the truly remarkable – the Beatles, the Rolling Stones, U2, Beyoncé, Adele – acts that, with perhaps the exception of the tangibly relatable Adele, seem not so much human as super-human. But Lightbody never felt that. They'd been on the road almost constantly for eighteen months by this point and had become, he says, 'insane, each of us collectively in the middle of a series of nervous breakdowns at any given moment. It was fun to be in such a big band, and we laughed like idiots for most of every day, but there was also so much tension, so much.'

The record company, thrilled to have stumbled upon such an unlikely cash cow, wanted more, and as soon as possible, but Lightbody was spent. Surprisingly, he was bored, too. Their next album, *A Hundred Million Suns*, did not have another 'Run' or 'Chasing Cars' on it, but was rather more meditative, deliberately less rousing, less stadium-friendly. One track, 'The Lightning Strike', ran to sixteen minutes.

'At its best,' he says, 'a song is a pure expression of whatever is in your mind or your heart at the time. You can't do it again, and if you try, if you set yourself down that particular path, then you're no longer making music that's entirely true to yourself, and you end up trying to make music for someone else. I never wanted that.'

Another long tour followed, then another album, this one representing a 'change of direction', something no record company wants to hear, in any circumstances, not now, not ever. Fans were encouraged to be open-minded about a record inspired by dance music, that even had certain goth overtones to it. The hardcore could see what they were trying to do, and secretly wished they weren't hankering after what everybody else was: more of the same.

Gary Lightbody needed to get his head altogether. He moved to Los Angeles, in part because that's what people in his position do, in part to revive him in new ways. Perhaps writing songs would be easier from there?

Seven years of silence followed.

In 2013, the American singer and writer Henry Rollins officially quit music. Rollins had been in the West Coast hardcore punk band Black Flag from 1981, before fronting his own act and then going solo. Though his tattoos and machismo brought to mind levels of testosterone comparable to a Navy SEAL – his neck was the circumference of a great oak – he was sensitive, and gentle, and didn't mind showing it. He wrote poetry, and by the 1990s was more famous for his spoken-word performances than his musical ones. He was the author of a number of critically revered books inspired by a difficult upbringing, and through which he learned to channel his anger into something more positive and redemptive. To many, he was an icon. But by 2013, he'd had enough. '[Music] used to compel me,' he said, concluding, 'I've moved on.'

Gary Lightbody had been a fan of Henry Rollins. When he heard that the singer had retired, that Rollins had 'had his songs' and that there were no more, this resonated with him. Then it panicked him. 'I kept thinking, *'Fuck, fuck! Is that what's happening to me? I haven't got any songs left? I'm fishing in a dry well . . .?'*

Rollins was fifty-two, Lightbody not yet forty. This was too soon, surely?

His initial plan, such as it was, was that living in Los Angeles – alone, perennially single, probably nursing the memories of his most recent broken heart – would encourage the next album to come quickly; not one the record company would necessarily crave, perhaps, but one he felt he needed to make. 'An exploration of our roots,' he says. 'I got heavily into early Irish history, and wanted to delve deep into our past. I thought that was really interesting, not to make a traditional Irish music album so much, but an album with at least an echo of the past. So that's what I set my mind to.'

Had he confessed this to his label at the time, he'd have heard the retreating echo of a thousand horses' hooves, as the division responsible for maintaining their profile in a way commensurate to, say, Coldplay – who were not busy making an album that explored *their* ancient Home Counties roots – galloped over hills and into the distance. Best, then, he never let on, but rather continue to explore his impetus in private. However, it's not easy making traditional music of any nationality without it sounding like the worst of parodies, and, anyway, the songs were not coming easily to him. During the increasingly tortured process, he came to realise that what he was actually trying to do here was find his *own* roots, his *own* identity, not simply to make an album of pop songs. 'I'd literally been running away from myself for years, so I had to try to find some semblance of who I was.'

This process took him close to three years, during which time his drinking became a cause for concern. 'It was a mess.'

Lightbody believes he was probably already on the road to alcoholism, that it might always have ended up a factor in his life, but sensing that the band had peaked, that they may never headline festivals again, undoubtedly weighed heavily on him. Drink, however temporarily, eased the burden and pushed it into the margins. His fellow band members were settling down, occupying themselves more easily; one of them, guitarist Johnny McDaid, now also living in Los Angeles, was in a relationship with the actress Courteney Cox and had become very close with Ed Sheeran, the two of them writing songs together and keen to continue the partnership.

Lightbody had not found lasting love himself – or rather he *had* found it, but kept losing it. Though never truly alone – he had many friends in LA – he felt adrift in a manner that gave him a freedom he'd much rather have traded in for something else. Late nights became later nights, and when he rose the morning after, it was already afternoon, the Californian sun taunting him with its cloying radiance, holiday weather but no one to enjoy it with. He'd reach for his laptop, cringe at the empty document's flashing cursor, then start drinking again.

He says: 'It made me feel impotent.'

Mulling over Henry Rollins' decisive action, Lightbody one day wrote a song, in the fog of hangover, called 'Don't Give In', which sounded precisely like what it was: a plea to self. It worked. This was the first battle won in his ongoing personal war of attrition, and ended his songwriting drought. More songs came after that, and then an album, *Wildness*, in 2018, which remains his favourite Snow Patrol album, and which sold steadily but not stratospherically. 'But we're still able to play the same tours, we still get into the charts, and so that's okay, I'm fine with it.'

Like Alex Kapranos, he remains invested in his craft, but no longer wants to do it to schedule, or to order. No more lighters-aloft ballads. He doesn't want to repeat himself, is happy to leave the past behind, and feels only fitfully saddened by its passing. He's made his money, and no one can take his back catalogue away from him. The pressures he once felt, many of which he'd piled on himself and which, much like his leather jacket, really didn't do him very many favours, have finally receded.

He may at one point have watched U2 from the side of the stage every night in order to pick up tips, pointers and inspiration, but he didn't go on to become Bono. But that's okay.

Most people don't.

17

**'I love the upheaval; I love emotional disasters; I love
mismanaging every relationship I've ever had'**

Despite those few exceptions that prove the rule, there cannot be
too many long-term prospects for the kind of rock star who finds
their niche wearing the sort of spandex most people would flinch
from on the grounds of taste, decency and functional eyesight.
And so, if there ever was a genre for which the advice 'enjoy it
while it lasts' was designed, it's hair metal. Hair metal has a long,
complicated, and often hilarious, past, and was mostly left dead
and buried by two things, both of which occurred within the
space of a week in late September 1991: the implosion of Guns N'
Roses into the world's most bloatedly humourless rock band with
the release of *Use Your Illusion I*; and the main stage arrival of
Nirvana with their second album, *Nevermind*. The latter's pared-
down economy was so throat-grippingly effective it compelled all
remaining hair metal outfits to please make their way to the door
marked EXIT in a disorderly fashion.

It seemed that the genre was never going to attempt a return
until, somehow, in the early 2000s, it did. Its resurrection came
from an unlikely location: Lowestoft, an English coastal town
110 miles from London. The band were called the Darkness, and
were proponents of the genre with the kind of tongue-in-cheek
cheek that many would suggest could only ever have been the
product of sardonic Brits. It's entirely possible that a band never
took itself *less* seriously than the Darkness, but as is always the way
with comedy, the band's collective efforts to raise a smile, and to

entertain, served to mask just how adept they were at what they did – skilled, even.

Regardless, they'd have been wise to enjoy it while it lasted, too.

The Darkness converged at the purely imaginary point at which Queen's Freddie Mercury careened into Aerosmith's Steven Tyler and Spinal Tap's David St Hubbins outside the portaloos at a Monsters of Rock festival, each looking the other up and down and wondering who was taking the piss more. In the video for their 2003 signature tune 'I Believe in a Thing Called Love', they knowingly plundered every caricature of every bad hair metal and rock act there'd ever been: Lycra jumpsuits opened to the navel, long hair, tattoos and handlebar moustaches. But where so much of this sort of thing invariably involved more style than content, 'I Believe in a Thing Called Love' was determinedly joyful, the most fun pop song in an age.

'That takes a certain amount of charisma, you know,' says singer Justin Hawkins on playing the role of a frontman who stands on stage with legs akimbo and one arm held high, convinced he's in full command of his audience. Fortunately for him, Hawkins was possessed with that charisma. He'd grown up wanting to be Freddie Mercury all along, and as an avid teenage gig-goer would note with interest just how few frontmen could manage what Queen's singer so effortlessly could. Instead he'd see terror in their eyes, the cowed stares of those who could sing, perhaps, but not engage with a crowd. Hawkins thought that if he was ever going to rise into such a position himself – and it was by no means clear he would – he'd ensure that his concerts would be collective experiences, everybody whipped into a frenzy through the sheer force of his personality.

Hawkins did grow up to be a singer in a band, and he was true to his word. He knew his task would be difficult – fan worship is earned, not a given – but then he always had a backup plan in the early days.

'If there was an awkward silence – which is excruciating for the singer – I decided I would take my clothes off, or else I'd cry. I always had that up my sleeve.' He never did find an occasion to cry, or strip naked. 'The catsuits I was wearing were so skin-tight that the audience could probably see my knob through them anyway. So it would have been a – well, a small reveal, if you will. But I actually always looked forward to things going wrong, I suppose because I wanted to feel that visceral fear' – in the knowledge, he adds – 'that I'd be able to slay that genuinely horrible moment.'

If his band managed to avoid such discomfort, it was because they'd struck a rich vein. The Darkness proved themselves very popular, almost overnight. Their debut album, *Permission to Land*, which comfortably sounded like nothing else around it at the time, was an instant hit, 1.3 million copies sold in the UK alone, their *School of Rock* posturing reminding everyone that, when done well enough, and with sufficient knowing, heavy metal could have widespread appeal.

A dream start, then, but Hawkins had another ace up his sleeve. Slavishly following the rock 'n' roll script, he knew that there needed to be drama, too. And so if the Darkness were going great guns, he'd have to stage a gunpowder plot.

'If I have ever experienced contentment in life, of any sort, then I have to sabotage it,' he says, not so much with pride – although there is a little of that, too – as simple, incontrovertible fact. 'Why? I suppose I love the upheaval; I love emotional disasters; I love mismanaging every relationship that I've ever had, including the good ones, the ones I had with the people in my band – one of whom was my brother, Dan.'

For the past seven years, Justin Hawkins has lived in Switzerland, not as a tax exile but as a former husband to a Swiss woman with whom he has a daughter whose life he wants to be a part of. The marriage didn't last, at least in part because of his predilection for those emotional disasters.

'I've given up trying to modify my behaviour with other people, or to make it somehow less of a rollercoaster. I embrace the chaos now, but,' he says, 'I know that I upset a lot of people along the way.'

There is a certain reductive upholding of rock-star cliché here, that people who make music for a living are somehow configured differently, do not cleave to domesticity like the rest of us, and so can fall back on this natural inclination of theirs, something programmed into their DNA, as an excuse, a cheap get-out clause. It isn't particularly imaginative, it's a cop-out, and you do want to say: grow up. But Hawkins insists that he cannot help sabotaging things, can't resist striving to ruin the good in order to make it bad. 'I suppose because I won't find the important things in my life as rewarding otherwise. I've got a lot of really unhealthy traits.'

Occasionally, he'd ruminate on these traits. Why were they there? Why all the sabotage? Had he not had them, perhaps he'd never have become a rock star in the first place. Perhaps his band might never have found success. He knew enough to accept that the person he was made him the person he became, but over twenty years after his band's breakthrough, he's now counting the cost of such extended erratic behaviour. It wasn't until 2019, while chatting to another singer from another band while both were on tour in Australia, that there came a chink of light. The other singer told him: 'Listen, mate, I think you might have ADHD.'

'He recognised some of the "qualities" in me as the same as his, that I had something that should be treated. But the way I'd always treated it was to just enjoy it, really.'

With consequences, though. Two years after their breakthrough, one of the band's founding members, guitarist Frankie Poullain, left. He was swiftly replaced, and the band released another album, but then Hawkins himself felt it necessary to leave after a stint in rehab for cocaine and alcohol abuse. After he came out, he elected not to re-join the Darkness but to focus on his own project, Hot Leg, whose immediately faltering progress made the band's eventual reunion, in 2011, all but inevitable. Very few bands ever fully recover from a mid-career hiccup, and so it was to prove for the Darkness. Something about their collective impetus had changed; no longer did they have infinite patience for one another. They merely tolerated each other now. Meanwhile, that initial burst of novelty they'd all enjoyed in the early days had passed into something more drudge-like, more everyday. There were scars and a lingering discontent.

Hawkins had always been the impetuous kind, and so in the midst of his band's slow – if inevitable – descent, the singer fell in love and got married. It would have been wise not to bring his rock-star mentality into this private union, but since when had he shown wisdom?

'When I was happily married,' he says, 'I didn't write a single thing worth listening to. It's a truism, really, but you don't notice it at the time. When you're in a relationship like that, you want to impress the person you're with. So you modify your tastes, your outlook, you try to impress them – and absolutely nothing good comes from it, ever. I firmly believe that the best way to write stuff,' – *good* stuff, he means – 'is to have stuff inside you that is fucking you up.'

That hoary cliché again. The Greek philosopher Aristotle, years ago now, wondered: 'Why is it that all men who are outstanding in philosophy, poetry or the arts are melancholic?' A couple of thousand years later, James Kaufman, an American psychologist who studies creativity, coined the term 'the Sylvia Plath Effect' to echo Aristotle's conviction that there is a high prevalence of mental illness among artists. Kaufman thought this particularly affected poets, but there is much anecdotal evidence across all mediums: writers can also tend towards the quietly ruminative and depressive, while musicians suffer similarly, but not always so quietly.

Despite the Freddie Mercury obsession, Justin Hawkins never wanted to be a singer. His earliest ambition was to be a guitar player, and he approached music as a technical exercise, a problem to solve. 'That was always my speciality, really: finding a musical problem, and then finding my way around it. It's using music as a sort of excavation or tool, I suppose. I loved learning the language of it, and always felt I could spend my whole life exploring it.'

He never had that indie earnestness that afflicted so many of his peers, and so, while they may have been gigging in formative bands on the pub circuit in pursuit of both experience and credibility, Hawkins was plying his trade making symphonic arrangements for TV shows and adverts, writing music to accompany campaigns by IKEA, the Church of England and *Britain's Got Talent*, or to promote things like chocolate bars and whiskey. When the Darkness formed, he simply channelled his energies into a more performative outlet, recalled his childhood love of Freddie Mercury, and gave it his all, not in the figurative sense but rather the literal: he gave it his *all*, no matter the cost.

'This is, in many ways, a ludicrous existence, and I know I annoyed a lot of people because my histrionics were seeping into everything I was doing – I lost a lot of friends – but it's a journey I had to take. Normal life is not an option for me, it's not what I want, not even something I think I'm capable of. I'm a rogue person,' he says, 'and I'm a musician first. Everything else comes second.'

In 2014, he went back to rehab. He didn't go through the recovery process in the traditional way, didn't bother with meetings, has never done the twelve steps, but he did at least take to heart some of the accompanying advice. He realised he'd done lasting damage to many of the relationships in his life, particularly the one with his brother, 'and so I did what I was supposed to do. I realised that behaving the way I was behaving, and doing those things to my body, was not an option any more, so I stopped.'

Sobriety left him guilt-ridden, which was compounded by a late-arriving identity crisis. He was, by now, belatedly convinced that the way he was living – which was the way he was *supposed* to live, given his profession – was killing him. Can you be sober, and sensible, and still a rock god? Was that even permissible? (Aerosmith's Steven Tyler has been sober since 2010, so the answer is: yes.) 'No two ways about it,' Hawkins says. 'I'm lucky to be alive. Trouble is, I don't feel lucky.'

He reached, then, for civilian solidity, and focused on being a father, determined to make something good out of something – a marriage – that he'd managed to sour. The next part of the script he was following, unwittingly or otherwise, was to remain clean. (Steven Tyler spent thirty years trying to stay clean.) Hawkins being in Switzerland helped. Conversely, his geographical distance enabled the band to get back together, too, in its original line-up, each member aware of, and reconciled to, their reduced status, but grateful all the same. Hawkins says he would rather be performing at festivals in the middle of the afternoon, in a tent, to a devoted set of fans, than on the main stage trying to keep hold of passing trade. He doesn't have the luxury of choice, of course, but it serves his continued sobriety well that he takes satisfaction from now being a mid-table concern.

Otherwise, however, he remains as dogmatic as ever, someone who gets cranky, and out of sorts, if music is not the thing he does to fill his days. His home studio, which offers views of the pine forests Switzerland likes to boast of in postcards, is filled with guitars, keyboards, amps and microphone stands. He gives the impression of being radiantly happy, of someone doing precisely what they are supposed to be doing with their life. When he says he no longer cares about the high-stakes game that is perpetual radio-friendly popularity, he sounds entirely convincing.

'Oh, we could've followed up that first album with exactly the same, or something similar but more polished, but then, you know how *polished* goes, right? It just gets gradually more and more so, until all you have is *polished*. Case in point,' he says. 'Coldplay. Another case in point: Maroon 5. Both started out as rock bands, but not any more. They stayed on top by being radio-friendly. There's no way a rock band would ever *want* to be on the radio; that's not something you should be aspiring to. And if you have to get the synthesisers out,' in order to stay on the radio, as both bands cited have, 'then count me out.'

Problematic as his personality has proved over the years, it's also proved his fortune, and Justin Hawkins, while not someone you might readily wish to marry or try to remain best friends with, has retained plenty of that initial charisma. Sometimes, what makes you such a complicated human being is also what makes you so compelling an artist. He suggests that he is embracing the 'chaos of single life', which is presumably just how he likes it. But towards his fellow band members, each of whom now live a short flight away, he works hard to stay reverential. The façade may have cracked, but he doesn't want it to shatter. He routinely offers them songs for consideration, and they then decide collectively which ones are good enough for the Darkness. Those that aren't, he squirrels away for later use. The manner in which they communicate is cordial, well-intentioned, mostly tantrum-free – *careful*. Now into his mid-forties, Hawkins has happened upon the art of diplomacy. *Better late than never* is one way of looking at it. It's helped him rekindle his relationship with his brother, and this pleases him.

'It's very difficult to come between me and my brother at the moment, and I feel sorry for the other guys in the band because me and Dan are very much in sync. That's actually partly why I enjoy my job so much now: I don't feel conflicted any more. I just want us to make great uplifting music, together.'

And to do so still on festival stages, in a lurid catsuit more see-through than it strictly needs to be, with his legs apart and arms aloft, delivering cock rock for the masses as if nothing else matters in the world to him but this, only this.

Perhaps nothing else does.

18

**'There was clearly psychological damage,
and I just couldn't do it any more'**

Approximately twenty-six miles outside of Los Angeles is Topanga Canyon, a laid-back neighbourhood that's like 'an ageing hippie [that] refuses to wash off its natural character', according to the *LA Times*. This is where Tim Booth resides, works, and breathes evenly from his diaphragm each morning, offering up as he does so a wholly convincing impression of living the good life. He has been here on the West Coast of America for fifteen years, and radiates health and positivity in the way that natives to California do. At sixty-one years old, he remains not just fit but almost tauntingly so: he will occasionally post naked-from-the-torso-up photographs of himself on Twitter, and while you may want to laugh, to poke fun even, the emotion you mostly feel is envy. He makes bald look good, and goatees look not entirely silly.

Booth is the singer from James, long Manchester's most idiosyncratic act, and among its most lastingly successful. While many of his era have either disappeared completely, overdosed fatally or else grown into grumpy old men whose social media feeds are full of conspiracy theories, Booth has very deliberately wended his own way, and has thus fashioned for himself a robust afterlife. He's still a singer in a band that won't go away, yes, but he has done other things, too: he's a trained dialogue therapist, and a dance instructor who leads people into epiphanic trance states that leave them with a palpable glow.

He'd be handy to have around during a power cut.

•

By 2002, twenty years into their career, James began to implode, finding themselves in the midst of irreconcilable differences. It happens, but few had anticipated it of them, because if bands tend to follow a formula, James followed their own. They were a profoundly musical bunch of Manc misfits fronted by a Yorkshire-man who'd originally harboured thespian intent and, together, they seemed less pills and thrill-seekers than a quasi-religious cult whose music was anthemic but meaningful, packed with message and roughage, and who by the 1990s were perfectly capable of filling stadiums.

Booth was a compelling focal point, and resembled a messi-anic cult leader whose vibrating interpretive dance moves hinted at ecstatic possession. Famously, around the time of their break-through hit single 'Sit Down' in 1991, he could command a hall of 5,000 to do just that during the song – sit down – as if awaiting his benediction, or at the very least some communion wafers and wine.

He'd been born a sickly child, with a liver disease that went undiagnosed until he was twenty-one, a factor that transformed his adolescence into a long period of suffering. At thirteen, he turned bright yellow – jaundice – and spent the next several years in and out of hospital. 'I just thought I was this person who got sick,' he says.

As with many who struggle with long-term health condi-tions, the more doctors failed to diagnose the problem, the more deeply he went in pursuit of his own cure. He immersed himself in alternative medicine – which, in the early eighties, was a Wild West frontier: extreme, eccentric, not covered by BUPA – and he also dabbled in religion and spirituality. He was devoutly sober, a vegan. He joined James initially as the tambourine player, and was later promoted to singer.

'We were totally idiosyncratic, weird, awkward, and fame-avoiding for much of the time, almost making sure we didn't get success,' he recalls. They spent the eighties a well-kept secret. They were the Smiths' favourite band, and developed a reputation as a must-see live act. When Madchester happened, they could no longer keep hidden. They toured with the Happy Mondays; Shaun Ryder's crew, aware of Booth's abstinence, regularly tried to spike his tea with acid. James started having hits – 'Come Home', 'Sit Down' – all their idiosyncrasies falling fluidly into place.

Their inspiration had come from an unlikely quarter: Bruce Springsteen and the E Street Band. 'My heart had always been with the punks and the nihilists, and the self-destruction of living in such a bitter, fucked-up world – in my head, at least – but then someone dragged me to see Springsteen, very much against my will. I didn't like his music that much, but I just thought it was incredible, all of it, this incredible band where every one of those members could have been famous in their own right but were together making uplifting music that just made you feel so much . . . *joy*.

'All that went against a lot of my . . . You know, I'd thought that music was about expressing your darkness, that real art was *all about* darkness, and yet here was somebody, Springsteen, who didn't look like he was a tortured artist at all. Of course, as we later learned from his memoir [*Born to Run*, published in 2016], he did actually suffer from depression, but back then he was making just the most uplifting music. And that was revelatory for us, so we essentially formed our own E Street Band, an English, *indie* E Street Band, with a brilliant trumpeter, a brilliant violinist, an amazing keyboard player, and that gave us all these incredible orchestral possibilities that could take us in any direction we chose.'

For many years after, James did just that. They played halls, then arenas, then stadiums. They survived Madchester, had hits in America, coasted far above Britpop, and were still firing into the

2000s, not so much challenged by their longevity as perpetually renewed by it. Their songs were distinctive, in thrall to no one but themselves, and *very* James, this curiously enduring act, which just kept going.

Throughout all this, Tim Booth was perhaps the only rock star who could justifiably have been sponsored by Whole Foods. On only one occasion did he dare risk a beer before a gig. He didn't like it. And only once did he snort a line of coke. He didn't like that, either, preferring instead to attain his own natural high through the medium of dance. He remained mostly celibate, too, and would only very rarely agree to sex, with a willing participant, on the mutual understanding 'that it had to be a meaningful human relationship.'

He didn't speak for the rest of the band. The more pious he was, the more leathered his bandmates got. He couldn't really blame them: touring the world can get rather boring, and ascetic purity isn't for everyone.

But soon it began to show. Their live shows became stilted, the band incapable of veering off the set list – something they'd previously prided themselves on – simply because they were too wasted to do anything but go through the motions. There is no more unedifying a sight for the only sober one at a party than a room full of coked-up drunks. Booth became increasingly impatient, then angry, then disillusioned, then heartbroken, this special thing they'd built organically, from the ground up, now in pieces around him. He had to act.

'There was clearly psychological damage, and I just couldn't do it any more.'

So he quit and, for emphasis, left the UK, too, heading for Los Angeles and other distractions: a collaboration with the film composer Angelo Badalamenti, and, later, a tentative pairing with another rock outlier, Suede's guitarist Bernard Butler. He resurrected his love of acting, and landed a small part in the Christopher Nolan film *Batman Begins*. He settled in Topanga Canyon, focused on his family, his trance dancing and his meditative states, and felt at peace with himself and the wider world around him.

He remained settled and content until 2005, when he did a rather foolish thing: he went to see Bruce Springsteen and the E Street Band in concert. During the show, Booth felt the physical rush of nostalgia, an onslaught of old memories, and the taunting realisation that seems to affect so many musicians at certain points: that as good as their current life now was (in fact, it was better in many respects), it was still lacking that singular, individual thing that had once turned everything so gloriously technicolour – in Booth's case, James.

Various members had reached out to him over the years, enquiring with feigned disinterest whether he might ever fancy giving it another go, but he'd always resisted, no matter how covertly tempting. But this time he didn't.

This time, he got on a plane, and went back to Manchester. He went back home.

The break, it transpired, had done them all good, each having the necessary time to mull over what James had become, their part in its downfall, and how they might yet make it good again. Individually, they'd made amends, fixed personal crises, and weaned themselves from addiction, only to find an emptiness awaiting them – a hole that needed filling.

The initial reunion was awkward in a way that will be immediately familiar to anyone who has ever arranged to meet up with old friends after a significant period: at once fond but self-conscious. But bands have a trick to fall back on that those in normal life don't: the music. Here, initial conversations didn't have to run dry and into uncomfortable territory, the scabs of old wounds too quickly picked, because they had their instruments to hide behind. They could communicate in song. Booth, keenly sensitive to this, had arranged to meet them at a rehearsal space in Manchester; in other words, at work. They got the manly hugs and cursory pats on backs out of the way quick, along with the comments about how tanned Booth was looking, all that Los Angeles sunshine, etc., and then they took their places, plugged in, and began to play.

The magic was still there, and this was all the bond they needed.

'But I had one overriding rule,' Booth says. 'That we had to write new songs, good songs, and those good songs had to be as good as the old ones. I couldn't just get back together for the sake of it. There was more to this than nostalgia, than just becoming a heritage band, which, for me, is the kiss of death. It means you've got nothing else to offer, and I always believed we did.'

A pinned tweet on Booth's Twitter account reads: 'Most bands do a theatre set of the same songs each night in the same order. James change it up each night from an arsenal of 100 songs. That's how we generate our passion. If you come see us live – try to let go of hearing your particular favourite or disappointment will follow.'

In the years since they reformed, they've released six albums that very assiduously haven't traded on their back catalogue but rather each time attempted something new. They remain a big festival draw, and so while in one sense nothing has changed, everything has, too. *Booth* has changed. He's no longer sickly and callow, but in rude, robust health. He looks like Sir Ben Kingsley doing something vigorous by Shakespeare. During his hiatus from the band, he studied a practice known as voice dialogue therapy, the premise of which suggests that we are not one person but rather an entire orchestra of sub-personalities forever fighting for control. During voice dialogue therapy, you talk to each sub-personality to learn how they are squabbling amongst one another, which of them is driving the car, which locked away in the trunk. This helped him, he suggests, not only to understand himself, but his *selves*. Elsewhere, he trained to become an acting teacher, with an approach based on the Meisner technique (named after the American theatre practitioner) that aims to help students 'get out of their heads' in pursuit of behaving more instinctively in their environment.

His shaman dance tutorials, meanwhile, continue, and he sits in on his wife's sessions – she's also a shaman – most Saturdays, when she leads up to 200 people in something called consciousness expansion.

'I'm interested in those therapies that straddle the boundary between creativity, therapy and, for want of a better word, the metaphysical interest that changes people's lives, and the crossroads between the three,' is how he puts it.

Tim Booth's grandfather was a World War One hero. He won the George Cross, and went on to live a settled and seemingly peaceful life until he reached his seventies, when, out of the blue, he suffered a breakdown. His grandson believes that this occurred because he'd tried to suppress the trauma of war for so long. Eventually, the body buckled. Trauma is locked into our bodies. At some point, it has to come out.

Booth ultimately believes that each of us is here to deal with our trauma, and to process it. 'We're very good at self-deception bullshit, and we all have our blind spots, but the trick is not to walk away *from*, but rather to walk *towards* our weaknesses. And the trick is to keep walking into them, because often there's amazing riches there.'

A nod, a smile, and something beatific happens to his face, a light lit from within. Both eyes blaze; the grin makes dimples. Whatever mysterious code is required to lead a life of peace and love and serenity and fulfilment, the singer from James appears to have cracked it.

SEVEN

THE TROUBADOURS

19

**'I think I'd thought that just being *me* was enough.
Perhaps it wasn't, not any more'**

On June 15, 1995, on an overcast day in London, a barge was pulled slowly down the River Thames towards a nice photo opportunity at Tower Bridge. On top of the barge stood a statue of the pop star Michael Jackson, constructed out of steel and fibreglass, and standing at thirty-two feet tall. He was in a warrior-like pose, and cast in military dress, bandolier criss-crossing his chest, fists clenched at his hips, while he gazed blindly off into the middle distance, where there was a Tesco Metro, a petrol station and some rather nice converted warehouse apartments.

This slow and showy voyage was arranged to publicly announce that Jackson had a new album out, *HIStory: Past, Present and Future, Book I*. The exorbitantly expensive marketing campaign (costing $30 million) was undertaken by his record company Sony after Jackson reportedly told them to 'build a statue of me'. There were nine such statues built, and they sailed through Paris and Berlin and Milan and Los Angeles, because a new Michael Jackson album – and Jackson was the self-styled King of Pop, remember – required the world's attention. The statue, which was of course entirely preposterous and singularly failed to re-endear him to those who simply took it as confirmation that his marbles were continuing to scatter far and wide, nevertheless achieved its aim: the world sat up and watched.

When the Barbadian singer Rihanna was gearing up to release her album *Unapologetic* in 2012, back when she was eyeing

Beyoncé's crown with the conviction that she'd swipe it soon enough, she, like Jackson, decided she wasn't simply going to allow it to quietly enter the market without accompanying fanfare. An idea was hatched by her marketing department, some blue-sky thinking that would later be reconsidered a wheeze and then, ultimately, a farce and farrago, but which at first was embraced with nothing less than rabid enthusiasm: she would charter a Boeing 777, and invite 150 members of the world's press to join her on a seven-day tour, visiting seven countries to play a show in each. During each connecting flight, and depending on her mood, the assembled journalists would be lucky enough to have her 'play' stewardess, serving drinks and snacks, and exchanging banter, thus affording them a very up-close-and-personal audience with an international superstar.

It was billed a 'unique, glamorous experience', presumably by someone who'd never spent an extended amount of time in a metal tube sitting in a cramped seat with minimal legroom while breathing recycled air and trying not to get caught smoking in the WC. Rihanna never did interact with the media as fulsomely as intended, either in the air or on the ground. During most flights, she refused to come out of First Class, and the longer she hid, thereby denying the press their promised stories, the more alcohol the journalists consumed in mitigation; one hack was later judged to have had an 'episode' when he stripped and streaked through the plane, perhaps upon the realisation that there could be nothing *less* glamorous than awaiting the appearance of a diva at 37,000 feet when all that diva really wanted to do was parachute out of there.

Nevertheless, *Unapologetic* – which by now seemed aptly titled – was an event that did not go unnoticed when it came out.

And when the seventeen-year-old Billie Eilish released her debut album in 2019, there was a collective global anticipation so frenzied that fans counted down the minutes until it was uploaded onto streaming sites at the stroke of midnight, before immedi-ately listening to it with a feverish intensity until all lyrics were committed to memory, and eternal reverence pledged. The young singer was duly corrupted forever as a result – convinced, as she now must have been, that this was simply what happens when you release an album: the world goes a little bit mad, and feels forever altered afterwards as a result. What you make makes shockwaves, and you get to watch it ripple.

That's how it works, right?

Actually, no. That's not how it works most of the time, nor for most acts. Yes, the fanbase gets a little excited and people make a note in diary planners; radio playlists may accommodate accordingly, and there might just be an appearance on *The One Show* confirmed, but, generally speaking, the world fails to fall into rhapsodic sync, or grind to a standstill, or require a jetliner to spread the word.

The pop landscape, illustrious as it is, is mostly made up not of those totemic heroes who get to create earthquakes but more by those able foot soldiers, the eternal support acts, the admirable grafters who've remained true to their craft even when everyone – but, crucially, not *quite* everyone – has deserted them. Like those Japanese soldiers who continued to defend their patch of land long after World War Two had ended, they plough on as if still under order, doing what they always did, because it's what their training taught them: in this case, releasing a series of albums that document life as it is lived in real time – youth into midlife, married life into neuroses, crises into old-age renaissance. There will always be an audience somewhere, and often a grateful one.

Certain singers appeal to us because they are *one* of us, even when they very clearly aren't. Take Bruce Springsteen. For all that he's an uncommonly gifted chronicler of the blue-collar experience, the ultimate rock 'n' roll everyman, he's also nothing of the sort. He admitted recently that all he's ever been is an actor who *plays* the part in song. When was the last time he actually worked on a highway, or toiled on construction? Conversely, it's the foot soldiers – the support acts, the also-rans – that have remained far closer to their source material; they really are one of us. They continue on in the face of adversity, a reduction in circumstances, and an increasingly necessary reliance upon their mercifully loyal fans – and they do so, as we have seen elsewhere, because that is what they're here to do. They're the troubadours: more paragraphs than chapters, but no less noteworthy for that.

It may not always be pretty down here, but it's admirable work, and in their endless artistic excavations, they frequently summon up pearls that remind us of nothing less than what it is to be alive.

Lloyd Cole, still in possession of a fringe he needs to regularly flick away from his eyeline, recalls walking around central London one day in the mid-nineties in his fine suit and expensive leather shoes, something that, as a member of one of the area's private clubs, he did a lot of back then. He was a handsome man, Lloyd Cole, if your idea of handsome was foppish, with cheekbones to ski off, and a mouth always pursing towards its next cigarette. He favoured the kind of suit jackets a geography teacher might sport, but which, worn by Cole, looked raffish and bestowed on him an intellectual appeal. You'd take one look at him and fancy he could recite anything by Baudelaire, in the original French.

On the streets of Soho he was used to causing a commotion – a cheap pun here, perhaps, but apt in the circumstances nonetheless. Heads would turn whenever he was out in public, fingers would point, and Cole would work hard to stifle the smile of satisfaction he felt: that he was known, admired, even worshipped a little.

But that had stopped happening now. Now, he could walk through these overfamiliar streets unnoticed and untroubled, as unremarkable as everyone else. The shock of this dropped barbells into his stomach. 'Thing is,' he says, 'I was still selling quite a lot of records, and doing okay, and things were fine, they were. But there I was anyway, somewhere near the Astoria, and thinking to myself: *Oh. Oh! Before, I was a magnet, every head turning my way. And now – now, it's stopped.*'

He made it to his private members' bar, ordered a stiff drink and contemplated existential concerns for the rest of the afternoon. He was thirty years old. He'd not that long ago left his first band, Lloyd Cole and the Commotions, after which he'd moved to New York, made solo records, and had felt revived. But now this.

'I realised I was rudderless, without new ideas. I think I'd thought that just being *me* was enough. Perhaps it wasn't, not any more.'

The very worst thing about this hypothesis? That perhaps he was right. The scenery changes, and you get left behind.

There is footage online, dating from March 1990, of a certain Wayne Hussey, singer with the Mission, the furrow-browed goth band from Leeds whose lugubrious music sounded like an articulated lorry moving slowly through heavy traffic. In the clip, he is behaving the way rock stars have traditionally been expected to behave across all public forums: like an entitled arsehole. He's appearing on a late-night TV talk show, and, in his defence, is being ambiguously goaded into such a state by the host. While it's tempting to lay exclusive blame at the TV presenter's door – this particular presenter has form – it's nevertheless factually true to point out that Hussey had arrived on the show drunk. He is slurring, and clutching a wine bottle from which he is encouraged to take more glugs, as viewers watch what it's like when, for certain pop stars, the good times pass and oblivion beckons.

This was two long years after the Mission's high-water mark, which they reached with their hit single 'Tower of Strength', lyrically a rather tender love song, but which behaved as all great goth songs did, like a satanic hymn of foreboding doom.

Hussey had served a long apprenticeship before things coalesced nicely for him, but by the new decade, the Mission, and the genre from which they'd sprung, was over, and Hussey was in debt and on the dole. 'That particular journey,' he says, 'had come to an end.'

He could have dug in his heels, refused to budge, and stewed, but rock stars are often given the chance to escape and, like bank robbers, they often do. In time, Hussey moved to California, watched his marriage crumble, and then seized upon the offer of a tour of South America, as sometimes it's worth escaping twice. In Brazil, things came good: he met the woman who would become his second wife, and realised that there was an existence for him here, far from home, where he wouldn't necessarily be able to reinvent himself, but at least would not be judged exclusively on past glories. Goths aren't supposed to favour the sun, but Wayne Hussey always did like a good pair of sunglasses.

'I live near the sound of church bells now,' Hussey says. And although his livelihood has been undeniably reduced, he has managed to stay true to himself. The majority of us will not get to live out our wildest dreams; if we're lucky, though, we'll achieve a version thereof. 'All I ever wanted was to be a musician, and I did it. I'm still doing it. Nobody has taken that away from me.'

As he talks, the church outside his window announces the top of the hour.

'The bells,' he says.

Lloyd Cole would never run quite so far, but perhaps he didn't need to. He'd been a very distinctive proposition in the eighties, Derbyshire's – specifically, Buxton's – answer to Manchester's

Morrissey. Both were seen as antidotes – necessary ones – to pop's kitsch sparkle and plastic sheen; they were poets in the land of limericks.

'When we started out in 1983, 1984,' Cole says of his band, 'I had, in equal measure, massive naïveté and massive self-confidence. I thought I could do what I wanted to do, but in reality I didn't know how to do anything at all. I just happened to be lucky enough to hook up with four people who were very good musicians.'

He was a lyricist you wanted to read as much as a singer you craved to hear. 'She says a girl needs guns these days / On account of all the rattlesnakes,' he sang in 'Rattlesnakes', a track that would go on, in its chorus, to reference Eva Marie Saint and Simone de Beauvoir. 'She's got cheekbones like geometry and eyes like sin / And she's sexually enlightened by *Cosmopolitan*,' went 'Perfect Skin'.

Fame came quickly. 'Oh, but I complained a lot of the time, and I suppose I was quite the snotty arsehole. You want to be a pop star, but then you complain when people follow you around in the streets. But *of course* that's going to happen, and you want it to, but you still complain, and then you notice it when it goes away, and then you panic.'

He'd always striven for a certain level of control, not just over his band but his career. If anyone was going to structure it, it would be him, not outside forces. There was an album, then a second, then, perhaps too quickly, a third, and they were great, and big hits, but Cole grew bored, and yawningly disillusioned, and rashly decided to quit the band and head out on his own. Precocious talent had taken him this far, and he felt confident it would now take him further still.

A comparatively wealthy young man – pop pays well when you feed it sufficiently – he moved to New York, bought himself an apartment, and turned the kitchen into a home studio. He sourced new musicians, those who might give his imminent solo work a more louche, loose sound, more rock and less pop. His debut album, self-titled but commonly referred to as X due to the sleeve art, was the work of someone no longer prepared to resemble everybody's favourite geography teacher. A line from the album track 'Undressed': 'You look so good when you're depressed / Better even in your current state of undress'. Another: 'You were sitting there smoking my cigarettes / You were naked on the bare stone floor.'

The cover featured a black-and-white image of the artist in a morning-after-the-night-before pose, the suggestion here of whiskey and Marlboro cigarettes, of someone unafraid of the prospect of minor sexually transmitted diseases.

All of this, he suggests, was deliberate. 'I wanted to make a rock record, not the poppy stuff any more. I was twenty-seven years old, living in New York, getting over the depression of the band splitting up, my splitting up with my girlfriend, and I was intent on meeting new people.'

The reinvention suited him at first. But then that mid-afternoon stroll through the streets of Soho, on a visit back to London, confirmed his creeping fears: that his popularity was now a fraction of what it once was, and that, worse, he no longer rated himself. 'Creative integrity is difficult to maintain.' Perhaps, he thought, people had had enough of him because he'd written everything he'd needed to say?

'There are a lot of musicians about whom you might think, I've got enough music by that guy now. But if you look at Dylan, Prince, Bowie – in their prime, every album was different, every album still pushing boundaries. Of course, not everyone can be as amazing as a Bowie, or a Prince, and I don't delude myself in that department, but you do have to hold artists like that up as examples for yourself. And if you fail,' he adds, 'then at least you fail with good intentions.'

One might be able to suggest, with all good intentions, that Robert Howard has been failing in this manner for many years now. Once, he was Dr Robert of the Blow Monkeys, a gilded eighties pop act with political affiliations all too easily overlooked due to the simple fact of his physical beauty, and whose biggest hit singles, 'Digging Your Scene' and 'It Doesn't Have to Be This Way', were the sound of pure sunshine. The more Howard pushed to be taken seriously – the band's third album, *She Was Only a Grocer's Daughter*, was a reference to the Prime Minister Margaret Thatcher, and not intended as a compliment – the more his record company pushed him front and centre as someone for girls to scream over.

'They touched up photos of me, changed the colour of my eyes so that I'd look more like the geezer out of A-ha [Morten Harket],' Howard says. 'And so there were more and more teenyboppers turning up at our gigs. But they were short-changed, because we weren't like that at all; we weren't what they were expecting. We were coming from a different place entirely.'

His band joined the Red Wedge movement alongside Billy Bragg and Paul Weller, reimagined their sound and style, but soon watched their appeal reach its sell-by date, sending the singer down a familiar path: unemployment, drink, bankruptcy, misery. 'We're all tortured, man,' he shrugs. 'Everybody wants to be immortal – they think they can find a foreverness in music – but it doesn't matter. The number your song got to in the charts? Doesn't matter. Whether you'll be remembered? None of it matters, it's all rubbish.'

For a time, he played bass guitar for Paul Weller, appearing on Weller's *Wild Wood* and *Stanley Road* albums, and then, at the age of thirty-nine, by now married with two children, he decamped to southern Spain with his family, in need, he says, 'of an adventure, something to start me back into life a bit.'

In Spain, he lived simply, not quite off the land but miles from Waitrose, and filled his time by maintaining a furious work rate. Though few people paid him any mind – or, for that matter, *paid* him – he has gone on to self-release ten solo albums. The Blow Monkeys did eventually get back together, once all their children had come of age, and occasionally they play the nostalgia circuit, but the old days are not something that motivate him as much as the present does. His wife tells him to keep at it. 'Even if no one's listening, she tells me, *do it*. And so I do, because she's right: every new song I write is a signpost, and it gives you focus. That's why I do it. I don't need the appreciation of strangers any more.'

20

'The worst-case scenario is becoming famous for something you're not proud of, or desire to outgrow'

Robert Howard faced the musician's familiar dilemma: remain within the box into which you were first placed decades previously, or else go your own way, and to hell with the consequences. This does tend to suggest that early success is a straitjacket, that the winning formula you happened upon at that point in your career is the same formula that must continue to define you forever, irrespective of how you may feel about it now. It doesn't allow for change, for evolving, and, as such, it constricts. There isn't very much that's creative about that. When Del Amitri, a Scottish act whose initial breakthrough was predicated on a deliberately commercial understanding of radio-friendly, middle-of-the-road rock, decided two decades later to step out of their comfort zone and make an experimental electronic album, they were greeted with the sort of consternation that turns hair grey. How dare they hack off the hand that feeds? Not everybody gets to be Radiohead, after all.

When the band presented their new venture to their people – management, label, assorted trusted friends – many thought it must be an elaborate joke, the punchline of which wasn't immediately clear. Band members who grew whiskers and willingly wore cowboy boots didn't make this kind of music, did they?

Did they?

'We played it to some people,' says the band's singer Justin Currie, 'and it didn't go down well; it didn't go down well at all.

So we lost all our courage, I suppose.' The initial aim was to 'deconstruct this whole pop-rock thing. We were bored of it. But other people suggested otherwise. I guess we didn't fancy career suicide.'

Del Amitri, who have gone through several incarnations since forming in 1980 – a jangly pop outfit until they became increasingly switched on to American acts like Bob Seger and the Eagles – found success in 1989 with their album *Waking Hours*, which merged keening melodies with lovely, literate lyrics. But it was their 1995 single 'Roll to Me', a deliberately more simplistic proposition, that, in some sense, sealed their eternal fate. Based upon a rather cutesy harmony, and littered with words that didn't so much tell a story as simply sound pleasant when strung together – 'And look into your heart, pretty baby / Is it aching with some nameless need? / Is there something wrong and you can't put your finger on it? / Right then, roll to me' – it ran to just two minutes and twelve seconds. Though it only reached number twenty-two in the UK charts, it eventually climbed into the American Top 10 and became something of a staple on US radio – largely, Currie believes, because of its brevity. Whenever there were just a couple of minutes before the news at the top of the hour, and DJs wanted to fill it with something brief and uptempo, 'Roll to Me' fitted the bill. It's been a staple on US radio for three decades now.

'That song has allowed us to pay our wages for over twenty-five years, and allowed us to stave off day jobs. It just keeps getting played, and so we keep earning off it – not a lot, but enough.'

Like, in truth, the vast majority of bands, Del Amitri weren't interesting enough to be fawned over by the music press, which reacted to their absence of controversy or incident by ignoring them. 'Purveyors of nice music' rarely make for strong headlines. Currie initially bristled at this, but later learned to be relieved by it. 'It was weird being in that liminal place, out of obscurity at last and somewhere in the mainstream, but still outside the glass bubble of the big-time proper.'

The success they did secure was enough to keep them coming back for more, and Currie kept reminding himself that this constituted good fortune, a happy situation. But he was already beginning to feel hemmed in.

'Some really successful artists can be liberated by enormous success, and can escape the audience's expectations and go on to make genuinely great work,' he says. 'Or they can be imprisoned by it. The worst-case scenario is becoming famous for something you're not proud of, or desire to outgrow. Forging a creative career is for the very brave, and we never had that . . . and so the oddest thing is to find yourself facing an audience, most of whom do not share your musical tastes. You start to wonder: *Are we the thing that we wanted to be, or the thing that the market made us?* That's not a very pleasant question to consider, when you started out as punk, and are inspired by much more left-field music than the majority of your audience would either contemplate or tolerate.'

Lacking the bravery, he suggests, of Bob Dylan or Thom Yorke, he ended up committing his band to being 'honest plodders, giving the audience what they want. There's no reason to go all Heston Blumenthal on their arses, is there?'

There is, of course, another option: retreat. Go into hiding, or go your own way; refuse to play the game any longer. The Irish singer-songwriter Damien Rice has done that repeatedly in a very sporadic career, releasing just three albums between 2000 and 2020, ignoring demands and pleas for more, and instead disappearing off the music map as successfully as J. D. Salinger did the writers'. There is a story, possibly apocryphal but quite possibly not, that Rice was so appalled when the *X Factor* band Little Mix scored a massive number-one hit with their version of his single 'Cannonball', selling over 200,000 copies in a single week, that he donated the profits to charity, not wanting to be sullied in any way by something that Simon Cowell had had a hand in, and that people might immortalise through karaoke.

Rice's precursor in many ways was Liam Ó Maonlaí, singer in Ireland's Hothouse Flowers who, back in the late 1980s, went from promising street musicians on the rain-slicked streets of Dublin to being anointed the 'hottest new band in the world' by *Rolling Stone* magazine. Hothouse Flowers were a whirling dervish of bluesy folk with stadium pretensions and a fetching singer who looked like he'd been dreamed up by Kerouac or Ginsberg, and who likely didn't always wear shoes.

'I got a sense of what it was like to be able to silence a room very early on in my life,' Ó Maonlaí says, 'to take people on a journey, because that's what traditional music does: you and everybody else in the room go on a journey with it for a few minutes. And so when we became famous all over the world, we didn't have to question our confidence in what we did. We knew how to hit the very centre of every room we played; we knew how to open that vein. You can't really verbalise what it is – that energy to *hit* – but that's exactly what we were doing.'

One of their earliest TV performances was on, of all things, the *Eurovision Song Contest*, offering up what might have been some melodic relief in the interval between competing representatives. From there came *Rolling Stone* magazine's lofty pronouncement, a global record contract, and an international hit single in 1988 with 'Don't Go', which was folk music for people who didn't like folk music. But the speed at which all this happened was too fast, for the singer at least, and he came quickly to the conclusion that it had got out of hand, and that *all this* was not what he had signed up for.

'You can smell a song that's written to make money,' he says, 'just as you can hear a song that was written because it had to be written. But the best songs are those that force their way out of a group of people who just happened to have met. *That's* the feeling I always liked, like you were on the edge all the time, on the very elements of, of – *creation*. It's mind blowing when things like that happen, and you owe it to yourself, to the work, to stay on that edge.'

Pushed far from the edge and into something that resembled a comfort zone – they were famous and had money and tour itineraries that stretched the world and went on for years – Ó Maonlaí lost sight of himself. After the release of their third album, *Songs from the Rain*, he says, 'my disenchantment with the ruthlessness of the business had come to a head.'

He needed to walk away, but never had the opportunity to do so. When his father died, he found his chance.

'I realised that I'd actually earned the right to say to the guys in the band: "Look, we've given them [the record company] seven years. I don't know my ass from my elbow, I haven't seen four seasons at home in that whole time, we've been worked like rats . . ." I was loving it all, sure, but it was relentless, too. If I hadn't stopped, if it had gone on indefinitely . . . I don't know what person I'd have become.'

He put the band on hiatus, went home, and 'looked inward'. His first realisation was that the music business wasn't designed by musicians. 'You don't need to break the law to rip off a band. Oh no, you can stay *well within* the law, but then that's because it was designed by people who want to make the most out of somebody as quickly and effectively as possible.'

Relieved to be free of it all, he took a year off, and the year became two. He grew a beard, returned to nature, and felt the grass under his shoeless feet. He resumed playing in a traditional sense, for himself, with friends, ad hoc performances in local bars, and falling back in love with music in the process. At some point, perhaps inevitably, the band did get back together again, but now no longer under the aegis of paymasters.

A decade ago, he found himself in debt, and owing at least six months in rent, a mortgage being something he'd never quite achieved or been particularly interested in pursuing. He didn't want his young family to be rendered homeless, and so he did that intriguing thing musicians of a certain level can do with enviable ease: he got rich quick, all over again.

Even acts that have fallen out of public consciousness and into hard times have a history they can readily trade upon. There will be those that never forget, who continue to carry a torch – and, crucially, will happily pay to be reminded of the good old days. 'I was never afraid of just being spat out,' Ó Maonlaí says, 'because musicians have been here throughout history. Even before we lived in stone houses, the musician was here. They played for the wealthy, and they played for the poor, without discrimination, a natural thing. As a musician,' he says, 'you are always the driver of your own destiny.'

So when his landlord explained just how much in back rent he owed, he simply called up his booking agent, arranged a couple of Hothouse Flowers gigs, and watched, less with relief than simple satisfaction, as both sold out. The bailiffs were never called.

This is how he continues to live his life today, following his muse, even if it does occasionally take him down cul-de-sacs, and doing what feels right in, he says, pointing to somewhere close to his gut, 'here'.

'We've been going for thirty-five years now as Hothouse Flowers. There could be another ten albums, or there could be none. It's fluid, uncertain, and I like that uncertainty, that sense of the unknown. To acknowledge the unknown, to look at it in the face – that's all I ever needed.'

It's an approach that has brought him something he insists money never could buy: peace.

'If somebody offered me €1 million to put a song I wrote on a petrol advert, or a sanitary towel, or whatever, I wouldn't do it.

I would not do it. The ultimate thing, for any musician, is to trust what you're doing. Trust has taken me this far and, seriously, I don't think I've ever been happier than I am right now. I may not be living in a part of Ireland where I'd most like to be – I'm not by the sea – and the place I'm renting could use a huge overhaul, but I've enough money to put food on the table, so what more do I need? What more does any musician need?

'Money?' he says witheringly. '*Money*, for what's most sacred to me? You can't put a price on that. So, no thanks, on your way, I'm fine as I am.'

When Lloyd Cole decided to leave New York – he was married by now and raising a growing family who needed space – he moved to Massachusetts. A change of locale, it seems, is important for the transitioning artist. Here, he felt certain earthly pressures lift, and the freedom to follow the creative impulse wherever it led. Occasionally, he delved into the avant-garde – a succession of electronic instrumental albums whose chief sound effects were blips and blops, like rain falling onto a bald head – and he did these not to satiate his audience but because *he* wanted to, and because he'd long realised that his audience was perfectly happy to dip in and out of his oeuvre every few years without committing to absolutely *everything* he did. When you've accepted the disappointment that you will never be Prince or David Bowie, it actually offers up a little freedom.

Cole is fine with this, he says. 'People just don't want middle-aged pop stars. We want novelty, or we want grandeur; we don't want the dull stuff in between. We find old people charming; they become venerable, iconic. But we tend not to find middle-aged people charming.'

Justin Currie holds similar beliefs. Artists, he says, 'tend to write their best songs between the age[s] of twenty-three and twenty-seven. Bob Dylan says that he could not write the songs he wrote back then today, because they would be different. I suppose it's a combination of youthful arrogance, of not knowing the rules at all, and so you just try everything. But as you go along, you learn the mechanics, you rehearse more, you entertain an audience, and it all becomes more of a conscious job. That's why most of us tend to peak in our mid-twenties, I think, and I think that [more artists] should own up to that, to the fact that the most interesting music we make is during that period.'

Which must cast heavy shadows over the rest of their creative lives?

'Well, in an ideal world, you make your pile early, and then fuck off,' he says.

That's the thing, though. Not everybody makes their pile in a timely fashion, and even those who do don't necessarily yearn for an early retirement of golf and trout-fishing.

Justin Currie is approaching sixty; Lloyd Cole is already there. This is a time traditionally – but not uniformly – of creaking bones and tired limbs, angiograms and increased propensity for diabetes, and so on, leading to eventual infirmity, and then – statistically speaking, at least – death at seventy-four, scattering widows in your wake.

But for musicians like these troubadours, this is also a boon time because it means, according to Lloyd Cole's reasoning, that they are at last approaching their second coming. This is the time they've been impatiently waiting for, when they will find themselves abruptly admired again: for their tenacity, their commitment, and for still toiling at their craft. If David Bowie was able to leave behind the embarrassment of Tin Machine in his fifties to ascend into near majesty in his sixties, where everything he did glittered like gold, likewise Leonard Cohen and Tom Jones

– and Bob Dylan, who at the age of seventy-eight scored his first number-one album in America – why not them, too?

Aim high, says Cole. Aim high, and if they fail, then they at least do so with good intentions.

There is much mileage in good intentions.

21

'It's a question of temperament'

When Tanya Donelly quit music, she became a doula, working with new mothers. When Natalie Merchant quit, she opted to teach underprivileged schoolchildren to express themselves through creativity, her conviction being that little in life feeds the soul quite like art. Both women exited the music world within a few years of one another. Neither was pushed: their respective scenes were slightly poorer for their withdrawal (though both quickly rallied), and each felt, to varying degrees, an ultimate compulsion to return at some point, but in very different ways and strictly on their own terms. Their days of being easily manipulated marketable entities were emphatically over.

Donelly had come to prominence during a period of rude health in America's early nineties indie scene, when her band Belly unexpectedly shucked off cult status for mainstream chart success. Hailing from New England, she had previously played in Throwing Muses with her step-sister Kristin Hersh, and then in the Breeders with former Pixies' bassist Kim Deal. In those bands, she'd very much been the left-of-centre guitarist who'd been good on backing vocals when she hadn't been able to exert sole control of the microphone herself. But Belly was hers alone, a sugar-spun alt-pop confection whose songs were twisted fairy tales studded with poisoned tips, the kind Tim Burton might have serenaded Helena Bonham Carter with in the early days of their courtship.

The band was supposed to remain in the margins, with the cool kids in the flannel shirts and graffitied Converse and the grow-your-own-weed supply, but then something happened. 'There were these little vortexes across the country back in the early nineties that, for one minute, hit each other, and lit each other up,' Donelly says. 'Chicago, Seattle, Boston. All of us were supporting the other, and everything we did supported everyone else. It was a good climate, but I really think that we blew the doors open by mistake, a fluke down mostly to good timing.'

The band's first album, *Star*, became a chart hit, and found itself Grammy-nominated. 'Which was weird, because *Star* was a weird-ass album. The way I write songs, my lyrics . . . I'm not a hit-maker, you know? So when it did become a hit, it felt far more to do with the era than with me.'

Whisked along for the ride, she was soon nurturing an eating disorder and drug problem. A year after their second album, *King*, she'd had enough and split the band up, craving the kind of ordinary existence her parents had led. 'My father was a plumber, my mother a secretary, so I was used to the concept of working your ass off your whole life.'

So she got a proper job. A doula is not a healthcare professional, but rather someone trained to support an individual through pregnancy, and what happens immediately thereafter. Having recently had children herself, Donnelly wanted, she says, 'to do something dramatically different, something focused on somebody else, not me. I guess I wanted to be of service.'

A couple of hundred miles south, Natalie Merchant was experiencing a similar compunction. Not so much tired of being a musician as of existing within the overly corporate world of music, she stopped singing in order to become a teacher of sorts, exploring music in its purest form with children who might otherwise never get exposure to the arts in such direct form.

'I love these kids so much,' Merchant says, 'and I want them to feel regal, and they do. They treat the costumes we make for them as if they were golden, and the shows we put on' – which are cross- and multi-cultural – 'bring a real sense of belonging and participation.'

If doulas don't get paid as much as rock stars, then you imagine peripatetic performing arts teachers, who visit predominantly rural schools in blue-collar towns where industry has long been outsourced and where unemployment is high, must get paid even less?

'Oh, I don't get paid,' Merchant says. 'It all comes out of my own pocket.'

Natalie Merchant's band, 10,000 Maniacs, came of age in the mid-eighties alongside R.E.M. and the Indigo Girls and, later, Suzanne Vega and Tracy Chapman, earnest and wholesome outfits all, Democrats surely, and deft at what they did. If 10,000 Maniacs brought folk rock to an emerging generation of liberal music fans largely uninterested in the otherwise excessive artifice of rock – the Greenpeace stall they took with them on tour always enjoyed heavy footfall – then it seemed fitting, almost appropriate, when Merchant's style was repeatedly likened to that of a librarian rather than, say, Stevie Nicks.

'I remember once, in the early days, going to a photo shoot for a popular culture magazine. They'd decided that because I was young, and had a decent figure, that I should model some of these new bathing suits that were made out of – chiffon, I think. This is what the stylist had decided for me. I looked at what was hanging on the rack for me to wear, and I just burst into tears. The stylist told me to just cooperate, and then tried to get me into the bathing suit . . .

'I made up a lie, and told her my aunt had just died. I left.'

Later, the record company, still adamant that she ditch the bookish schtick, suggested they rename the band Natalie Merchant and the 10,000 Maniacs, allowing her unambiguous centre-stage. The singer declined, and she grew used to declining much else she was either invited or urged to consider. She grew tired of the realities that clung to successful bands: a different city every day, a different hotel room every night. 'I discovered that I'm actually a really devoted, introverted house-person. I like going to the store, to the post office. I missed having the same person in the street greet me. I missed it increasingly.'

And so, in 1992, at the height of her band's success, she simply quit. This was ostensibly in order to pursue a quieter life. Not unlike Liam Ó Maonlaí, she closed the door, both literally and figuratively, and started to make music the way she wanted to. Unfortunately for her, however, her debut solo album, 1995's *Tigerlily*, sold five million copies, making her more successful than she'd ever been. 'And then came the treadmill again.' Having spent her twenties in a different city every day, a different hotel bed every night, she now spent her thirties doing likewise – until her mid-forties, when she stopped – this time, properly.

'I just thought: *I can't do this any more*. I had a daughter by now, and I just wanted to raise her. So I went home.'

Today, she spends at least half of every week volunteering in class-rooms for the Head Start programme, a US initiative that provides comprehensive early education for the children of low-income families, and the rest of her time stitching the costumes and enabling extra rehearsal times for the end-of-year performances each school puts on. All the funding for this comes from Merchant herself, and her lack of musical work means that she is currently living off her savings. 'But I live pretty humble, so that's okay.'

People remark frequently that they find it strange – admirable, too, certainly that, but strange nevertheless – that a former darling of the folk-rock scene would so willingly walk away from what wasn't merely a successful career but an enduring one. If per-formers are required to possess unusual levels of self-obsession – because how else would they be able to do what they do? – then what on earth had happened to hers? Her answer is that she didn't walk away, not fully: after *Tigerlily* came a further seven solo albums. But Natalie Merchant was always an activist at heart, and, for her, music was a way to speak publicly on the things she cared about most. As well as highlighting the work of Greenpeace, she's done benefit shows for Doctors Without Borders. Her school programme initiative, then, is merely an extension of this: communicating through music, albeit on a far smaller, and much quieter, scale.

She rarely gives interviews any more, has said pretty much all she needs to say on the subject of herself, and has happened upon something that takes up almost all of her time because it feels so worthwhile. She was raised Catholic. Vestiges of that education have remained.

'There will never be a lack of children who are not being served well enough,' she says, 'and in a lot of the rural communities around where I live, people are still very, very poor, and are just going to get poorer still.'

How then, she asks, can she *not* try to help, 'to do whatever I can?'

She still gets fan mail, sent electronically these days, and often she reads it. Avid followers want to know when she might return to the stage. Occasionally, Merchant considers the question herself. Her daughter has grown and is off at college. She has more time to herself. But can she be bothered with it all again? And does she have anything more to say?

Now in her late-fifties, Merchant is very much of the old school. She doesn't want to record an album in her spare room like everyone else does now; she wants to book out a studio, with a noted producer at the controls. But all this costs money, specifically *her* money, as Merchant has long preferred to fund her own records.

'But whatever I spend, I will need to earn back, and these days there is no assurance that I will, or any guarantee on how long it will take. So it kind of inhibits me from making the kind of albums I'd want to make. When I think of "Natalie Merchant Inc.", singing, songwriting, hiring bands, producing records and planning tours – well, it's a massive production. You know, I've had managers in the past twenty years who'd say to me: "Just go out and play your hits in the bigger venues." Because, of course, that way would mean regular money, and it would be safe, but I've always tended to prefer smaller venues, and I've always liked to pick my songs from throughout my entire catalogue. Also, I haven't had a drummer for fifteen years. I got tired of having to be louder than the drummer.'

She prefers these days a cellist, a string quartet, a gentler accompaniment.

'I was lucky enough to make lots of money back when I was selling lots of records. I know that there are plenty of artists who also made a lot of money but who still feel compelled to go out there and still do it, keep making albums and keep touring, and that's fine. It's just a question of temperament, I guess. But I do look at these people, people like Bob Dylan and Paul McCartney, and I think to myself: *If I were you, I'd just go home and enjoy my garden, and my grandchildren . . .* So yes, it's a question of temperament, and theirs, clearly, is different to mine.'

22

Death by reality television has become a popular, if fairly inexplicable, pursuit in the twenty-first century, indulged in by all manner of once vaguely famous faces desperate to lose the 'vague' in favour of becoming celebrated again. It doesn't always turn out that way, but then it's not really designed to. The individuals who say yes to the offer of a largish cheque tend not to consider the quid pro quo, the financial incentive contingent on throwing away whatever good reputation you'd managed to build up by exposing sides of your character you'd hitherto done well to conceal. That's why we're watching, after all: for the car crash. We're not watching to see sensitive souls playing at being sensitive souls, we're waiting – as they prowl the diary room, the jungle or, if it's Channel 5, a surprisingly spacious motorhome as it totters towards Prestatyn – for the incidents of crazy behaviour, the racist faux pas, the revelations of misogynistic leanings.

Often, we don't have to wait long.

Of course, most house- and jungle-mates did become wise to this eventually, undergoing strenuous media training beforehand in pursuit of brand protection, but it wasn't always like this. In the early days, those who became *contestants* used to be largely ignorant of the dangers contained within. They paid a hefty price.

In 2006, a white label twelve-inch took the club scene by storm. The song, called 'Thunder in My Heart', had a certain throwback disco appeal, while the vocal, which was strained and impassioned, more alto than bass, rang a familiar bell. It maintained a consistent Saturday night popularity, and soon found its way onto the radio as the work of a new artist by the name of DJ Meck. Meck, real name Craig Dimech, had wanted to launch his own dance label, and for this he required a profile-raising hit. So he reworked 'Thunder in My Heart', a mostly forgotten chestnut from 1977, and with it found swift success.

It was only after several plays on Radio 1 that the identity of its previously nameless singer was revealed: Leo Sayer, a friendly, easy-listening relic from a time before punk, whose credibility had always been conspicuous by its absence. Sayer, by 2006 living in Australia, had been approached by Dimech for permission, which he'd readily granted, happy to be remembered but with little idea that the song would catapult him back into the limelight. He was fifty-eight years old, and hadn't had a hit for decades. He still toured regularly, considered himself a 'big fish in a small pond' in his adopted Australia, and while he'd always hoped for a revival, this didn't necessarily make him a betting man.

The purported 'big reveal' of the song's vocalist did not hinder its appeal but rather emboldened it. When something is so unashamedly kitsch, it becomes post-modern. Sayer was flown over for a series of promotional duties he threw himself into with all the zeal of an artist half his age. He recalls finding himself on a Saturday morning kids' show lip-syncing the song, and enjoying the process enormously.

'There was another band in,' he says. 'It was a boy band, Blue, and there were all these girls screaming for them.' By the end of the show, he suggests, 'everyone was screaming for me!'

For some singers, being remixed and repackaged for the approval of a new generation would prove unconscionable. As the urbane singer-songwriter Joe Jackson – an artist who, in the late seventies and early eighties, was labelled a British Billy Joel due to the level of sophistication in his lushly crafted songs, and for the piano accompaniment, too – insists: 'I only ever want to act my age. Of course, if you want to be a star still, and be adored, it's a different story. But that was never something that appealed to me. This industry,' says Jackson, 'breeds neurosis, and I never did want to be neurotic.'

And so someone like Joe Jackson continues to go about his business quietly and untroubled, still writing and recording but hopeful that no one is about to remix him any time soon and make him have to go through all *that* again. But Leo Sayer? Sayer was thrilled. He'd stewed in the middle lane for too long. To feel young and thrusting again – to have a hit single again – was a lifeline, and a particularly sweet one at that: an old song of his spanning generations, confirmation of its classic status.

'Thunder in My Heart' went to number one: Sayer back on *Top of the Pops*, cocking a snook at anyone who'd ever dared write him off.

'It was amazing! It must be a bit like the way Bob Dylan felt [when Dylan's 2020 album, *Rough and Rowdy Ways*, was an American chart-topper]. To finally get a number-one record after all those years, eh? He must have been smiling, too.'

Success tends to breed more success, at least in the short-term. If Dylan declined to step onto this particular conveyor belt after his late chart resurrection, then Sayer was all over his. His record company needed little encouragement to release another greatest hits collection, the same line-up of already-familiar songs, but now with a brand-new remixed smash included. He felt inspired to tour, to write new music, to explore his expanding options.

One such option was television. He was invited to take part in *Celebrity Big Brother*, about which he suggests he knew very little. He was assured that it was popular, and would probably do wonders for his profile. The money was good, too.

He agreed, and shortly after entered a house full of people, purportedly famous ones, who were unknown to him, but who, to everyone else, were vaguely familiar: the former model, the former TV presenter, the former pundit – in other words, the usual suspects.

Over the next few days, he began to realise just what it was he'd signed up for: silly games designed to ridicule and demean, and mind games intended to prompt division. Sayer, a grown-up, an artist who'd recently had a big hit, felt sideswiped, bewildered and hoodwinked; no one had prepared him for this. Was *this* what constituted celebrity these days? It was all so *facile*. He refused to play along, to be so willingly manipulated.

This erstwhile family favourite, with his high voice, mop of curly hair, and a smile that could turn his cheeks into ripe apples, went scarlet with indignation on our TV screens, and his comfortable PG-rating quickly became an 18. He raved and ranted and sulked. He swore – *a lot.*

'I'm afraid I didn't handle myself very well,' he says now, in a quiet voice. 'I went a little to pieces.'

Much of what he claims about the show is thrillingly scandalous, and probably libellous, but he insists, as many have before and after him, that he was a victim of judicious editing and duplicitous scheming, and that all his best bits weren't shown, anyway. 'They painted the picture they wanted to paint.'

When he stormed off the show, the tabloids couldn't write their headlines fast enough. 'Everything slipped away from me in England after that,' he concedes.

Sayer flew the 10,573 miles back home to Sydney, where no one could hear him scream.

For someone who stood no taller than five foot three, Leo Sayer was once quite the pop colossus. *Melody Maker* had made him their face of 1974 for good reason. He sang charming, heavy-bellied ballads like 'When I Need You' and 'More Than I Can Say', while on 'You Make Me Feel Like Dancing' he employed a falsetto every bit as tight-trousered as the Bee Gees' own.

'But as time goes on, you fall out of favour – with the press, the critics,' he says. He knew to expect this, 'and of course it doesn't worry me any more, but at the time it was a concern. You realise that people are getting on with another kind of music, and that they don't really, sort of . . . well, you're not novel any longer, and artists do have to be novel, don't they? They have to be exciting, new, and very now.'

He moved to Australia, not just for the big fish/small pond situation, but because he liked the place and its sunshine. Though the rest of the music world had moved on without him, he never stopped grafting. He worked throughout the eighties and nineties, doing forty- to fifty-date tours, often two shows a night. He had survived 'crook' managers, recorded with Roger Daltrey, dined with Paul McCartney, and over time became a literal one-man band, learning how to produce himself, and how to play most of the instruments he needed to record albums. He recorded many.

There were always places he was popular. Vietnam, for example. He'd toured there back in the early nineties, replacing a scheduled Michael Jackson tour after Jackson pulled out last minute. 'I'm still as big as Jackson was, over there,' he says, a claim that might not be entirely true, but the point is this: he saw an opportunity, and made it work for him.

The minor 2006 renaissance did have positive long-term effects, and he remains a curiously evergreen proposition: his songs are streamed almost two million times a month, which is more than many younger, hipper acts.

'I'd like to be a bigger artist, sure,' he says, 'but I'm not going to sacrifice my private life in order to make it into the charts any more. I'm lucky. I'm still respected in the industry, I think, and by certain rock critics, and I still have my audience, and my peers respect me, too. And I haven't had to prostitute myself very much since that *Big Brother* thing, so I do like to think that I'm still here purely on merit.

'I'm just happy now making my own records, my own decisions, and being in control of my own life.' But he does continue to dream big. 'Oh, I'd *love* to have another number-one record before I'm eighty, in 2028. That's what drives me, and I'm always trying to prove myself. Hey, if Bob Dylan can do it, can turn back time at [almost] eighty, then, fuck, why not me?'

There may be any number of reasonable explanations as to why not, but Sayer's drive can hardly be faulted. He is old now, but he won't slow down.

'I've had many relationships in my life, but I've never had children. So my songs, they're like having children, which I send out into the world. It's a bit like David Hockney, the artist. He brings out paintings he painted way back in the sixties, and people go: "Wow! Look at that! That's brilliant, it's lovely!"

'Every now and then, I hear my songs on the radio, and it's a wonderful feeling. I give myself a little pat on the head and go: "Yeah, that's good, isn't it?"'

23

For some, the routine expression of one's art represents nothing less than a higher calling. Or at least they claim it does, with such brow-beating conviction that they come to believe it themselves, and then convince the rest of us, too: that music really is a vehicle capable of lifting the entire world up out of the humdrum and into something spectral.

For three decades now, CeeLo Green, Atlanta-born and raised by ordained ministers whose oratory skills were conspicuously passed down to their son, has been singing songs specifically designed to help lift the collective spirit.

'There is much, much suffering in the world,' Green says, describing a wide circle with his extended index finger, then pointing up to the clouds and perhaps even beyond, 'and so I have to do more to make people happy. If I'm truly going to be a shepherd for people, then I have to show them the dynamics inside themselves.'

To date, he has done this most comprehensively with 'Fuck You', a song about being spurned by a paramour who prefers men with more money. The song's hero, Green himself, is upset by this, and feels dejected and worthless until he decides, to adopt the popular American vernacular, to own his own shit and get truculent on her – well, on her ass. The repetitive expletive of its title was wrapped around an utterly joyful Motown harmony, thus elevating the track into an anthem of self-worth and self-empowerment for all who heard it and chose to make it their own.

It was a smash hit the world over, its ubiquity on the airwaves throughout 2010 made possible by the radio edit that replaced the profanity with the more palatable 'forget'.

'Fuck You' was not CeeLo Green's first experience of chart success. That had come four years previously, when he'd teamed up with hip US producer Danger Mouse for their collaborative project, Gnarls Barkley, whose signature tune, 'Crazy', a song that addressed the themes of mental health set to an irresistible groove, behaved much as 'Fuck You' would a few years on: huge success, everywhere. Around the same time, he had a hand in writing another monster, 'Don't Cha', for the Pussycat Dolls. For a time at least, everything Green graced went gold.

He didn't simply happen upon this breakthrough; he worked at it, toiling away since the early 1990s, initially as a member of the Atlanta-based hip-hop and funk act Goodie Mob, before going solo and trying to find his niche. Short and squat, as bald as a bowling ball, and with eyes that followed you around the room, he was not typical pop star material, but rather resembled a cartoon character come to vivid, pixelated life. His voice, though, had a commanding presence all its own. He often had to raise it to be heard, and his experiences in music were to strike a familiar note: frequently misunderstood, often overlooked, and routinely deemed not appealing enough, not hot enough, not good enough. But, clenched fist, he showed them.

'One of the secrets to my success has been to not take myself too seriously,' he says. 'So when something happens that can be considered a happy accident [like finally achieving the mainstream success he'd always considered his due], then that's something to be happy about. I never wanted things to be ordained or predestined; I never wanted to be in total control. Total control is sobering to the point of dissatisfaction, and I wanted to be intoxicated – with emotion, and the vitality of the opportunity, because each opportunity is alive, just like the hours in a day. That day is alive, the day itself: *alive!* It's alive with the particles in the air, with the day, the wind, the effects in the environment. It all plays its part, a living, breathing organism and ecosystem that you just have to breathe in, and adjust your eyes to.' He pauses for a moment. 'Am I making sense to you?'

The successes he did go on to enjoy often seemed happy accidents; they were not easily repeated. Gnarls Barkley went their separate ways, and 'Fuck You' did not pave the way for further hit singles. The Pussycat Dolls got other people to write their other songs.

'Making hit records, making it look *easy*: that is the actual talent to have. You know, everybody that aspires to be an artist is really only ever one song away [from finding that magical formula], but look at how many people never discover it, or never have that moment transpire in their lives. I was already a professional artist for ten years before I got to that point. It's a long trudge uphill, and a lot of people give up before then, right before their promise is [realised]. And why? Because we have to survive! We have to survive day to day! Domestically, we have children, we have mortgages, and so on and so forth, and a lot of people depend on their dreams to support them.'

In other words, it's difficult. 'It is! But fortunately I've had a support system, a large amount of people who were attempting, and aspiring towards, the same thing, that same collective goal.'

He compares his own achievements to climbing a mountain. When he got to the summit, he planted a flag. And, 'there's this inability to breathe. You have to get acclimated, and that can be very unnerving, and uncertain, and unfamiliar, and just completely foreign. You become fearful, not in a sense of you're scared to be where you are, but fearful in the sense of self-preservation. It's like, *Okay, what do I have to do to survive here, if I plan to stay?* So you meet and greet, you socialise with others who are just perhaps passing through, and others who have gotten comfortable there, and perhaps complacent. Because there's a thin line between being comfortable and being complacent.'

Though he insists he never got complacent himself, neither was he given much time to get too comfortable. 'Let's face it, I have walked back down to that valley, yes, but then that's because I've got family in the valley, so I've got to go home and see my family; I didn't want to be separate from the synergy, because that's the starting point for me right there. The synergy is, you know, you don't always have to be part of your environment, you can also [let it be] part of your imagination. But the environment itself,' he says, tapping the side of his head, 'that's the intellectual property.' He asks again: 'Am I making sense to you today?'

When he was sixteen years old, Green's mother, a firefighter, was paralysed in a car crash. Before she died, two years later, she endeavoured to pass on to her son all the wisdom she'd accrued in life. He has carried it with him ever since.

'I'm possessed with the intelligence of that individual, the articulation, the competence, the core fundamental values. Basically, what I'm saying is that she transitioned just in time for me to receive that inheritance, and for me to carry on my journey.

'My career,' he says, 'has been an expansion. I'm rooted in who I am, and so anything that I've done is testament to elasticity. I stretch.'

He's had to, because his journey, for all its imbued wisdom, has been, at times, a problematic one, which one could suggest that he was the progenitor of. CeeLo Green has a temper, and he doesn't suffer fools. He does not like to receive bad reviews, or rumours that dare question his sexuality. In 2012, he was accused of rape, and pleaded no contest in court to supplying ecstasy to a woman who had woken up in the singer's bed, with no memory of what had happened following their date in a restaurant the night before. Due to lack of evidence, the case was dropped.

Upon becoming rich, he became profligate. He invested in businesses, and lent his name to brands – like fizzy drinks and batteries – which made him richer still. 'Hey, it costs a lot of money to be CeeLo Green. It takes an operational budget. I need watches! Private jets! I need limos, I need mansions!'

This, it might be argued, is a particularly American reaction after having had success in one medium. You branch out, and, in doing so, extend your shelf life because you remain in the public eye. Advertising long-life batteries may not ensure that you manage to write yourself another hit single, but it does increase the chances of being asked to advertise something else in turn, which maintains fame's buoyancy, and opens you up to more opportunities still. For some, this is an appealing place to find yourself in – essentially, showbusiness.

In this respect, Green describes himself as a 'scholar' of the industry. It's not just about art and craft; it's about 'finding the right rhythm. I know the creators, the curators, the pacemakers. I'm dynamic in that way, and I know how to monetise that.'

But the more he became a brand, the more his art was diluted. Any sense of mystery and magic was gone; there were too many dollar signs. Wealth brought comfort, and he grew a little too focused on an opulent lifestyle when perhaps he should have been concentrating on the real reason he was here: music. But, hey.

'I'm kind of jolly, like a big Viking, and I live the life of excess,' he says. 'We should all have a season to indulge, shouldn't we? The trinkets, the spoils, and to have a little fun. Who wants to be a prude about that? Also, I share it' – the trinkets and the spoils, he means – 'with as many people as I can, because, you know, fame does fleet.'

It does. After one of his bursts of mainstream success came to a dwindling endpoint, he found himself dropped by his record label (he suggests they reached a mutual decision), but this didn't matter, because 'the roar of the crowd doesn't want to see you play it safe. They know I'm a daredevil for the sake of their enter-tainment, and they want to see me survive another stunt, or crash and burn.'

In a career spanning almost thirty years, he has released a dozen albums, had two defining hit singles, lost money, made it back again, stained his character, and somewhere along the way convinced himself that all of it constitutes a kind of higher pur-pose. By his reading, we'd all do well to listen – not just to him, no, but to singers everywhere, and not just for their benefit, but for ours, too. 'Music is life!' he insists, throwing exclamation marks into his speech as if anyone remained in any kind of doubt. You, at the back there: pay attention. Sit up straight.

'We don't have to deal with the redundancy of the day to day, of the rhythm of the road,' he insists. 'No! Let's make an adventure out of it! Let mortality be your motivation! I do all this for the fun and the fundamentals. And I *am* going to be happy, when all's said and done. How many people live in fear and stagnate until they die? I want to be fearless! I'm not concerned with the physical stuff [because] everything is perishable. I'm here for the spiritual. As long as there is suffering in the world, I want to try to do more to make people happy.

'I'm a daredevil,' he says again. 'And I have the audacity to keep trying.'

24

**'Some girl was crying because I was now apparently
doing *disco*'**

Meanwhile, elsewhere in music's broad and accepting church, someone else was attempting their own version of nurturing the muse.

It was 1990, and Suzanne Vega was in full stride. She'd been one of the more unlikely stars of the previous decade, a time largely dominated by glamour and a more-is-more ethic that made this somewhat school ma'am-ish artist appear tiptoeing and timid by comparison. Her glacially poised acoustic folk was a throwback to more analogue times, her wardrobe *Anne of Green Gables* prim, and her cut-glass New England vocal was the only possible sound that could have come from such pallid, pursed lips. While Madonna was singing about being touched for the very first time in a manner that distinctly suggested otherwise, Vega's was an altogether more subtle form of hypnotism, her lyrics – an example of which would cost a small fortune to reprint here – delicate and poetic.

Like trees towards the end of November, then, she was absent of adornment, exposed to the elements. It suited her. When she started having actual hit singles, it seemed unlikely but also entirely deserved, and 'Marlene on the Wall' and 'Tom's Diner' – the latter later remixed as a dance track, bringing her to a whole new audience and significantly horrifying the original diehards convinced she'd sold out – established her very much as part of the musical firmament. By 1987, Vega says, 'every door was open to me. Every gig I did sold out. I played [New York's] Carnegie Hall for two nights, Radio City for one night, all in the same year. Everything was great.'

By 1990, she was ready to take things to the next level. For her third album, *Days of Open Hand*, she began to develop a fuller sound, the concept of 'proper' studio production now appealing to her, a testament perhaps to her growing confidence and self-awareness, an eagerness to step into her rightful place and assert herself accordingly.

She announced her biggest tour to date.

'My manager had big plans for the tour: a very ambitious set designed by a set designer; we had trucks and buses, I had a crew, and a band; catering; a backup singer; a woman to do the clothing. All of this was, you know, huge for me. And the venues were going to be really big, too.'

Vega had spent her life preparing herself for this. Having grown up in Connecticut as the daughter of a minister and a schoolteacher, she'd chased a record deal for eleven years, never changing her style or approach – or her make-up – until she was eventually signed, her success proving that attention to detail could be every bit as resonant as flash and flesh. Suzanne Vega was famous for her songs, not her personality, and not her face. At the height of her chart success, she could – and did – stand outside record stores, in front of posters of herself, while her music was being played across the shopfloor, and nobody would take a second look. When she paid for her shopping with a credit card, store clerks would tell her that she shared her name with a singer, and almost never make the connection. 'And that was okay with me. That suited me fine.' But after 1990's big tour, all that would surely change.

On opening night, however, she saw that the venue was just a third full.

'And I thought: *Where's the rest of the audience? Maybe they're still out in the lobby . . .?* But, no, that was it, there was no more audience. And that's the way it went the whole tour.'

By this stage in the pop landscape, what had once been a sparsely populated field was now full to bursting, Vega's success having re-alerted the industry that there is little more powerful in music than the lone singer-songwriter with a guitar and access to their own vulnerability. In other words, she had competition.

'We had Sinead O'Connor, we had Tracy Chapman, Tanita Tikaram, Martika . . . A lot of women, basically – but especially Sinead O'Connor. It seemed like every city I went to, she was also there, playing the next bigger venue to mine. And so suddenly I realised, oh, okay, so that's how this is going to be from now on.'

The tour, which was supposed to last for two years, was cut short after just a few months. It made for a miserable time. 'One week I had to let the backup singer go, and then the girl who did costumes. And then we decided to stop travelling with the set, and so had to fire the crew that carried the set around. We just kept losing pieces of the production as it went on. But I was mostly aware that we were losing money, *my* money. And at the end of the year I had to work out something with my manager because we'd lost really quite a bit. It was,' she says, 'frustrating.'

Defeat not an option, she remained sanguine. Time to morph into a different kind of artist, perhaps. Quickly, she made another album, *99.9F°*, which sounded even more robust than its predecessor, and played with different styles, too. She hadn't really done that before. But then this was how you survive: by evolving.

'Oh, but some of my fans *hated 99.9F°*, they hated it, hated the sound of it. My brother was selling T-shirts on that tour, and telling me that one time in the lobby afterwards, some girl was crying because I was now apparently doing *disco*.' This brought her pause but, she says, 'I had to stick to my guns and do what felt right.'

She'd gone from selling three million copies of an album to one million which, back in the 1990s, was considered a failure. Immediately there were consequences. The record company, she says, 'would no longer send a car to pick me up from the airport, so that became something I just had to deal with myself.' She laughs. 'That's how annoyed they were with me.'

By 1997, now closing in on forty, there was another shift, a promotion that couldn't help but feel more like relegation. She was an *elder stateswoman* now. The figurative podium upon which she stood was gazed upon by yet more new competition, all of them younger: Alanis Morissette, Jewel, Fiona Apple.

That year saw the inaugural Lilith Fair, a travelling music festival founded by the Canadian singer-songwriter Sarah McLachlan, comprised exclusively of female solo artists and female-led bands. Vega, whose mainstream appeal had further receded, was invited to take part. She was married now, and had a young child, whom she took with her, erroneously presuming that other singers might do likewise. But no.

'I was pretty much the only one that came with my child, but then a lot of the girls hadn't had children yet – Sarah McLachlan and Paula Cole had children later – and so I was sort of an object of curiosity, all these women, the singers, saying: "Oh, what's it like to have a child?" I felt like I was, I guess . . . *respected?*'

She was aware of what her presence on the tour conveyed: a kind of hierarchy that spoke more of her previous achievements than her current prospects. 'I knew that I was selling a lot less albums than the other women, and it was made clear to me that the reason I was on the main stage at all was because of my stature, not because of my record sales. I was always the opening act, but I was still very proud to be there. Lilith Fair was playing to 20,000 people a night, way more than I had on that tour in 1990, so it was a little bittersweet.'

Almost twenty-five years later, Suzanne Vega has come to accept the natural way of things, as all career musicians do, her slow and possibly inexorable shift into something less sparkly but perhaps infinitely more interesting for her. She can still move around in public unnoticed and untroubled, still releases albums that are lauded, and continues to push her own boundaries, most recently a Broadway project inspired by the life of the 1950s American writer Carson McCullers.

'I still care about appealing to an audience, but only up to a point now, and beyond that, I don't care. That's just the way it is. Would I like another hit?' she wonders. 'I wouldn't say no, but I'm not going to chase it.'

This is the best answer, of course. The troubadour's spirit is to not chase anything. You simply go about your business and wait for the world to spin slowly on its axis until eventually it comes back around and finds you – still there, waiting patiently.

EIGHT

ONE-HIT WONDERS

25

'All of us are looking for validation'

Every act may crave a hit, but nobody wants to be a one-hit wonder. *Do* they? It offers only a particularly distinctive respect, almost quizzical, as if to say: *how did that happen?*, and as a mantle to be lumbered with, it does tend to stick, and not always in a good way.

This is perhaps because a disproportionate number of one-hit wonders are novelty songs – lions sleeping tonight, push pineapple shake the tree, save your love oh darling save your love, polka-dot bikinis, and all the da da da's and the blobby blobby blobbies – so the pearls amidst this swine (and there are many) are considered aberrations, flukes, and just get lumped in all the same.

When, for example, Cornershop had theirs in 1997 with Fatboy Slim's hyperactive remix of their song 'Brimful of Asha', it taunted them, thrusting a determinedly left-field cult act who'd otherwise been quietly fusing a DIY punk ethic to Indian rhythms into a spotlight so harsh it almost burned singer Tjinder Singh's mutton chops to a crisp. Succinctly, they were not *that* kind of band, as anyone who'd been a fan of their earlier work – including songs like 'Wog' and 'Kawasaki (More Heat Than Chapati)' – could attest. They didn't know quite what to do with a younger, poppier demographic of fans, knew it couldn't last and were really quite grateful when it didn't.

Similarly, big-hit-then-*nothing* status left early-eighties post-punk trailblazers Tenpole Tudor struggling amid drugs and intra-band acrimony as they failed to make good on their sole hit,

'Swords of a Thousand Men'. And the worldwide hit US soul duo Charles and Eddie scored in 1992 with 'Would I Lie to You?', a song spun entirely from silk, ultimately afforded them a cruel taste of something they'd forever after be denied: a career.

'That was hard,' Eddie Chacon says now. 'It was really hard.' Charles Pettigrew and Eddie Chacon had both spent upwards of a decade experimenting with formulas before concocting that particular potion, and then found they couldn't again. Pettigrew withdrew into silence; Chacon managed to land a gig writing songs for Danish artists. The pair would occasionally talk about a reunion, but after Pettigrew died of cancer in 2002, Chacon was bereft. 'One day, I just went into my home studio, turned everything off, and didn't go back for ten years,' he says. 'You make art for art's sake, it's true, but all of us are looking for validation, and so when that validation stopped coming, I had to face the very sad [realisation] that nobody was listening any longer.'

Life for him wasn't over, though, so he needed to reinvent. He became a photographer, initially of erotica – his wife was understanding, he says – before specialising in fashion. For the next ten years, he was happy, and busy, doing something else entirely.

But then: the itch. It came back. It always does. The older he got, the closer mortality loomed, the more he found he wanted to return to his first love. When a friend introduced him to a producer who'd worked with credible young artists like Frank Ocean and Solange, and who not only knew who Chacon was but was keen to work with him, Chacon decided it must be serendipity, kismet, distant planets realigning.

The result was a muted but, he insists, deeply satisfying comeback in 2020 with an album, *Pleasure, Joy and Happiness*, that was suffused with a melancholy Marvin Gaye might have admired, and his former cohort Charles Pettigrew would have been proud of. Its melancholy, Chacon stresses, was its selling point. 'It's something a fifty-seven-year-old would make, not a younger man, and I love that; I *embrace* that.'

One reason he returned to music was to lay to rest his demons, to suggest if only to himself that there was more to him than one song, one moment in time. Another was that his one-hit wonder had given him glory; he wanted more glory. 'It's like boxers,' he says. 'When you've been a champ, people call you champ for the rest of your life. So you want to get back into the ring. And when you've had a number-one record, friends still say to you: "Hey, what's up, pop star?" You miss that, and so you try to replicate it.'

Cornershop, whose members have probably never used a boxing metaphor in their lives, went the other way after their hit single, and fundamentally did *not* try to replicate its assumed glory.

They were already one of the UK's more intriguing acts by the time Fatboy Slim sunk his teeth into them. In 1997, they'd just released their third album, *When I Was Born for the 7th Time*, a major critical hit upon which 'Brimful of Asha' was a fetching love-struck homage to the Indian singer Asha Bhosle, its hazy guitar groove conjuring up an image of melting molasses. Too slow to be a single – it also lacked a bassline – they released it as such anyway, and shrugged amiably when it reached number sixty in the charts.

Norman Cook, who had been a member of eighties indie darlings the Housemartins before reinventing himself a decade on as a superstar DJ and highly imaginative producer, and, later, as Fatboy Slim, immediately liked the record, picking up instinctively on what it lacked. He wanted to remix it. 'We liked Norman Cook, liked his stuff, and while we weren't sure what he'd do with the track, we did want to hear it,' Singh says.

Cook's method was as inspired as it was basic; a lot of the best ideas are. He simply sped the song up, transforming Singh's voice from a lugubrious cod-country croon into a cartoon helium squeak, and added a bassline onto which he dropped acid. The result, Singh says, 'whacked you around the head all the way through; it was unrelenting – and a sure-fire hit.'

It topped the charts in several countries around the world, and if Cook was satisfied with a job well done, Cornershop were blindsided. Not all bands are made for, or suited to, being courted by radio stations and Saturday morning TV. They tried, but they stuttered, blushed easily, felt out of place, and wondered what it all meant. What were they supposed to feel now, and how was it supposed to transform them? Should they stop singing songs about Kawasakis and chapatis – and politics and racism – in favour of more palpably mainstream fare? One of their earlier tracks was a song entitled '6 a.m. Jullandar Shere', a psychedelic wig-out with Punjabi lyrics that stretched to seven wildly hypnotic minutes, which probably wouldn't have translated easily on *Live and Kicking*.

'I think we might have confused people by what we were presenting,' Singh says of subsequent live shows, where they suddenly found themselves playing to a very different crowd. 'Brimful of Asha' would go down well; the rest of their set, less so.

When it came to making new music, they elected to do so under the guise of a different band name, Clinton, thus allowing them an autonomy they felt Cornershop no longer had. They wouldn't start another Cornershop album for five years. Two decades on, and the vast majority of people who know them for their hit single know nothing else about them: they are reduced to a pub-quiz question for which the answer could just as easily be 'Crazy Frog' or 'Las Ketchup'. Tjinder Singh is entirely happy with this; it's allowed his band a career. Once, the very fact of that song's endless heavy rotation felt problematic to him, compromising him in ways he'd never envisaged a Punjabi punk act from

Leicester could be, but no longer, not now. Now, he says, 'I feel only gratitude towards it. When I hear it in supermarkets today, it's a nice treat, actually.'

By the time Peter Cunnah had his hit, he'd already been a jobbing indie guitar act for a number of years, and was briefly signed to U2's label Mother, a moment of bright light that quickly went dark. He only came to write his sole contribution to popular culture as a reaction to crying at his desk during a short-lived office job, which he feared had signalled the abrupt end of his career. A passing colleague suggested to him that things could only get better. She was right: they could.

In 1994, the Northern Irishman's band D:Ream were number one for four weeks with the determinedly optimistic 'Things Can Only Get Better'. It had been a minor hit the year before, but after Cunnah remixed it, inserting a pounding piano intro ('the full Elton John') and thus inadvertently inventing something briefly known as 'handbag house', it hit a rich vein. The success promptly broke the band: Cunnah was keen to embrace pop stardom and all its trappings, while his co-member Al McKenzie decreed it a sell-out, and walked. Cunnah followed the mainstream trajectory, supporting Take That on tour, thrilled at having written a song the whole world was singing. It was all he'd ever wanted.

But within two years, the hits had dried up, his management had locked horns with the record company, and Cunnah considered himself a casualty. 'What's that thing soldiers have?' he asks. 'PTSD. I had PTSD, so I just walked away from the business, I'd had enough.'

He had at least been sensible while it counted. The moment profits from the single had started to come in, he'd invested. He bought flats, then houses. 'I could afford to retire at thirty-six.' And for a while, he did.

Three years after the big hit, and a year after his retirement, 'Things Can Only Get Better' was granted a curious postscript when it was adopted by the Labour Party, then *New* Labour, after the party had convinced itself its election campaign required a catchy theme tune. The UK had had seventeen years of Conservative rule, and so things, they felt it pertinent to point out, could only get better. Labour's handlers knew that one way to motivate youthful voters – traditionally a demographic that didn't always exercise its right at the ballot box – was by affiliating itself to popular culture. By 1997, Britpop had been co-opted to represent a national mood of optimism, the suggestion being that, culturally, Britain was booming, so why not politically, too? If the then-Prime Minister John Major was seen as increasingly grey and ineffective, a relic from a Britain that still remembered ration books, then prospective new Prime Minister Tony Blair was young and thrusting and visionary. He used to play guitar; he quite liked Oasis and Blur.

Both the lyrical leanings and the joyful melody of 'Things Can Only Get Better', then, were in keeping with this prevailing, and infectious, mood. Cunnah was initially game. He gave his permission, and even appeared at several Labour Party events to perform the song live in front of an audience of politicos whose myriad abilities did not include a capacity for dance.

On 2 May 1997, Labour won the election by a landslide, and Peter Cunnah took full possession, though he didn't know it then, of a forever-poisoned chalice.

'I've a love–hate relationship with that song now,' he says. 'It's been my meal ticket, for sure, but, you know, Tony Blair is basically a walking war criminal. I've had people say that my work is tainted as a result, that I'm somehow complicit, which I find very, very hurtful.'

The song never fully leaves him, even though he often wishes it would. He moved back to Ireland recently, a sort of homecoming. People recognise him there all the time.

'I have a swear box for that song now,' he says. 'Every time somebody spots me in the street and says, "Pete, you know, things can only get better", it's another pound in the box. Within two weeks of moving back, I already had twenty euros.'

26

'We were never good at being told what to do'

Pursuing anything quite as crude as hit singles was never within Chumbawamba's purview. Music for them was a platform from which they could espouse their political views and highlight issues they considered worthy of public attention. In early April 1982, in a comparatively well-appointed squat in Leeds which had both running water and functioning electricity – because, says Allan 'Boff' Whalley, Chumbawamba's guitarist, 'we were never simply all about cider and Pernod, taking drugs and bare floorboards; we were anarchists, yes, but we were entirely self-sufficient, too' – the five members of the band were gathered around a television watching Margaret Thatcher announce that the country was at war with Argentina over the Falkland Islands. Incensed that the Prime Minister would use this far-off conflict for political gain when it might otherwise have been solved with diplomacy, they wrote songs as a means of protest, went on marches, and generally made their feelings known.

'We didn't want to be normal,' Whalley says of the band's intent. 'We were watching the news a lot, were not happy with what we were seeing, and wanted to sing about it, to demonstrate.' And so the group that had once been called Chimps Eat Bananas became increasingly politicised. Frequently, they'd meet Billy Bragg on picket lines.

Their music was perfectly suited to people who lived together in unrented accommodation and shared a communal toilet: a mixture of faithfully traditional folk, some highly strung melodies, and occasional shouting. Though they were together-enough to sign to a label (the independent One Little Indian), they routinely distributed singles for free, or else wanted their seven-inches to come with books attached and filled with photographs, a prohibitively expensive idea that their record company's marketing department didn't always look favourably upon.

'This kept happening a lot,' Whalley says. 'Creativity versus commerce.' Their arrangement nevertheless carried on happily for a decade. The band had its audience, while the rest of the world had no idea they existed; both factions perfectly content. But then the label ran out of money, and so the album the band had recently completed, their eighth, entitled *Tubthumper*, found itself homeless. Any notion that this was a record that would actually salvage the label was never entertained, for the simple reason that improbability rarely is; its bosses, having heard the demos, including the almost-title track 'Tubthumping', weren't overly impressed.

This might have surprised Chumbawamba somewhat, as they thought they were doing something different. 'We were trying to write songs now about everyday things rather than merely political statements,' Whalley says. 'We were writing about the resilience of everyday people who, you know, fall over, get drunk, but get back up again. That was the idea behind "Tubthumping". But it certainly wasn't about us trying to write a hit, or anything.'

For a while, they considered self-releasing. What's more anarchic for a band that existed within the record industry than to operate entirely on their own principles, long before the internet developed to the point where that was a viable alternative for all? But a tape of the album somehow found its way to EMI in Germany, who liked what they heard and offered to sign them – for £100,000. To suggest this was a surprise development for people still used to queueing for the loo in the morning in a shared space would be an understatement.

The collective called a meeting: what to do? EMI represented The Man, as corporate as corporate gets, and as such was to be feared, mistrusted and loathed. However, they couldn't help but wonder: *Yes, but what if . . .?* What if they were able to infiltrate the industry from the inside, remaining true to their roots, and causing trouble?

They knew that their operational manner would come to discombobulate their new label bosses soon enough, that a meeting of minds was never going to occur, and that the union would inevitably fail, but in the meantime: what fun they could have.

But then something unexpected happened. 'Tubthumping' was released as a single, and its nagging refrain of 'I get knocked down / But I get up again', proved to have universal appeal, and so in 1997, the fifteenth year of the collective's determinedly erratic career, they had themselves a monster. It would go on to sell over three million copies.

'We weren't expecting that,' Whalley deadpans.

This was the point at which fame should have corrupted the band just as surely as it corrupts almost everybody else, dazzling them with its glare, and belatedly revealing to them just how thankless a task anarchy really was when compared with the glorious superficiality of the pop star's life: of red carpets, the best hotels, and first-class travel.

But here's the strangest thing: Chumbawamba remained true to themselves.

And anarchic fun was most certainly had.

Though they may not have realised they'd written such an obvious hit, 'Tubthumping' was clearly the kind of song radio was invented for: maddeningly repetitive, helplessly addictive, and with lyrics that celebrated the fortitude of the human spirit. Its sole subversive streak was fundamentally juvenile: the choral refrain was often misheard as 'kissing the night away', when actually the word used a 'p' instead of a 'k'. This meant that every time daytime radio played it, the word 'pissing' was heard over and over again. Subversion with a very small 's' indeed.

Chumbawamba was an act that could, and frequently did, swell to eighteen members. Because all profits were split equally, no individual would ever get rich, no matter how many singles they sold. But then money had never been their overriding concern, and so the sudden financial windfall, which could easily have corrupted them – it has others – changed nothing. What did change was their reach, their capacity to influence. They had a platform now, and intended to use it.

'We were never good at being told what to do, or just say[ing] yes to everything,' says Whalley. 'And we said no a lot.'

The song was recognised by the Brit Awards, nominated for Single of the Year. This wasn't of particular concern to the band: they'd spent the previous few months involved with striking Liverpool dockworkers, performing benefit gigs and standing alongside them on picket lines. They invited a couple of them to the Brits, thinking that, if they won, the dockers could go up in their place and air their issues.

Chumbawamba didn't win; All Saints did, for their single 'Never Ever'. The next best thing, they quickly decided, was to enjoy all the free champagne. Why not? At some unfocused point of the night, their table became aware of the presence in the room of the MP for Lancashire North, John Prescott. There was no particular forethought for what happened next, simply drunken impetuosity, something to convey their opinion of a politician they didn't admire with unambiguity: they emptied a bucket of water over his head. 'It really wasn't premeditated,' Whalley confirms, 'and there are no photographs of the incident itself, just in the moments afterwards.' The pictures, which made the front pages of the papers the following day, showed Prescott soaked and furious.

EMI was not happy. They advised a personal note of apology to the public servant. This was refused. 'That's what we'd been aiming for all along, anyway: to get up people's noses.'

A few months later, they released a new single that highlighted another hitherto unanticipated change of direction: a freestyle doo-wop about the then-Prime Minister, Tony Blair. The band had recorded it without their label's knowledge, their intention being to release it for free, making it ineligible for the charts. Once they'd done this, they delivered 2,000 copies of the CD single to employees at EMI's headquarters in London, essentially to say: *Look, see what we've done now!*

It is entirely probable – indeed, how could it be anything else? – that at this point in their relationship, EMI must have rued its German counterparts' lack of foresight: Chumbawamba were not major record company material, but rather an uncomfortable thorn in their side, gate-crashers to a house party who were refusing to leave the kitchen.

The label boss retrieved each copy that had been distributed amongst his staff and sent them straight back to the band. Their reaction? 'We were filled with childish glee.'

They were dropped shortly after.

Things reverted pretty much back to type from there. Chumbawamba became again a micro-operation, existing on a budget, and making music – and statements, always statements – as and when they saw fit. They did not have another hit, were never again recognised by the Brit Awards. But 'Tubthumping' was not about to go away.

In the years since, there have been endless requests to license the song. Almost always, the band say no. On specific occasions, they do make exceptions. One year, the US car company Chrysler offered them £100,000 to use the track on a TV ad. The band knew there'd been a long-running dispute at Chrysler's Detroit plant, its workers striking for better wages, improved conditions. They agreed to license the song, then donated all the money – very publicly – to its striking workforce. 'Chrysler were infuriated,' Whalley notes.

TV talent shows like *The X Factor* and *Britain's Got Talent* have routinely requested use of the song over the years, for their contestants to sing. Saturday night television enjoys a singalong. They offer a lot of money and, when they are summarily turned down, more is offered, sometimes life-changing amounts. But the answer remains the same: no. 'I don't like Simon Cowell, I don't like what he stands for, and so the more money they offer,' Whalley says, 'the more fun it is to turn them down.'

They were once offered somewhere in the region of a million dollars for the song to be used in either the World Cup or the Olympics, Whalley can't remember which. But the band didn't like the working practices of either, and so never got to cash the cheque.

In 2012, they called it a day. They'd been together for thirty years; time to do something else. Singer Alice Nutter pursued a successful TV writing career; Whalley started running competitively and, like his former bandmate, enrolled on a screenwriting course.

'There's a point when music becomes, not undignified exactly, but just the *thing you do*,' he says. 'That's the point you have to dream up something else for yourself. You have to challenge yourself, constantly.'

He considers success a double-edged sword, something that fixes you in the moment, and that serves largely to hinder your future progress. 'Look at Andy Warhol, a genuinely experimental artist until he became successful, at which point he simply repeated the same trick time and again. A true artist wants to try different things.'

Whalley was fifty-one when he retired from the band. He liked that he had no idea what to do next, even if his young family might have craved more financial stability (unlikely, if they viewed life through the same lens as he). He wrote a couple of short plays, then started a community choir. He is currently writing a book. He still loves running competitively. What he misses of the old days is a sense of the collective spirit, 'the magic that happens when like-minded individuals get into a room and put their heads together.' But reforming the band, the de facto position of all musicians at some point, would, he suggests, be 'weird'. Chumbawamba is dead, resurrection a biblical fiction.

'The bands I loved, when they split up, I always thought it was a beautiful thing. And those bands that I loved who then got back together – well, it never felt right. I don't blame them for doing it, but it's just not for me. I want us to remain within the context of when we were important, when we were on to something. And that was then, years ago, not now. I've no interest in rehashing anything. Best to look forward,' he says.

27

'It's all about early dysfunction'

1981, London. A not-so-young twenty-six-year-old survivor – but not proponent – of punk was at last living out his dream as a gainfully employed pop star. A face seemingly full of cheekbones, and a chiselled jaw that sat squarely beneath a set of bug eyes, Ed Tudor-Pole was busy hollering out a song that might have invented karaoke, had karaoke not already been invented elsewhere by somebody else. 'Swords of a Thousand Men' was the kind of rallying cry designed to be yelled from the terraces by crowds who couldn't hold a note in a bucket.

People liked it. It went to number six in the UK charts. By all accounts, Ed Tudor-Pole was his real name, and – notionally, at least – he was as posh as the surname suggests and had spent years, *years*, trying to crack this particular nut.

'I'd watch *Top of the Pops* as a kid,' Tudor-Pole says, 'watch the bands, and think, I know why that's a hit. And then I'd think, I can do that, and I can do it better, too.'

Music, for him, was a means by which to escape his otherwise miserable existence. If anyone's asking, Tudor-Pole has a theory about why some people find themselves turning towards music in pursuit of self-expression: the more Dickensian your childhood, the more likely it is you will want to perform.

'You'll find that, almost certainly, a miserable childhood leads to a desire to go onstage. No question! It's all about early dysfunction, about those who feel they have little else to lose. The less you have to lose, the more reckless you become. And that kind of bold behaviour,' he suggests, 'tends to work rather well in the world of rock 'n' roll.'

Tudor-Pole's mother was haughty, cold and summarily cruel. 'She was nasty to me, nasty every day – not sexually or anything, but she never smiled, always was angry.' He learned to cower, to try to make himself invisible. 'But I was lucky: I could go and visit my dad and stepmother from time to time. It was cool there.'

The respite this offered was largely due to his father's television set: wood-lined, deep-backed, a bulging black-and-white screen. It was 1964, and little Edward was nine years old. He'd watch the music shows and feel a pleasurable fever whenever the Rolling Stones came on. At the appearance of Mick Jagger, he'd inch closer to the screen, and gaze in awe, and simply think to himself: *Yes*. There was something hyperbolic about the Stones, humanity in excelsis, and something about Jagger's lascivious manner seemed to suggest that life without consequence held a certain appeal.

A decade on, Tudor-Pole had grown into his name: whippet-thin, those big staring eyes, a particular set of the jaw. Having already convinced himself that all of life was a stage, he'd attended RADA, landed a bit part in the seminal punk film *The Great Rock 'n' Roll Swindle* in 1977, and was at one point mooted as a possible replacement for Johnny Rotten in the Sex Pistols, before ultimately forming his own band, Tenpole Tudor, convinced that infamy – of the long-lasting, even legendary kind – was his for the taking.

'You have to have aspirations, right? Not that I ever quite dared believe they'd come true, but having gone to drama school I didn't know what else to do. I wasn't very good at punk, really, but I did quickly become convinced I could write better songs than any of them did.'

He wrote 'Swords of a Thousand Men' on the tour bus in early 1980, in the cubicle-sized toilet, with the conviction that creation requires a certain privacy.

'It's a tight fit, the khazi,' he says, 'but when you're writing songs, you need to be alone: just you, and your guitar. And the coach was terribly crowded, everybody smoking, and so even though the toilet stank, I could pretend I was on my own in there.'

He began by picking out chords inspired by Norman Green-baum's 1969 hippie epic, 'Spirit in the Sky', and kept going. From nowhere, he then plucked out lyrics about the Grand Old Duke of York and his 10,000 men, liked where this was going, and watched, fascinated, as the song appeared to write itself. Playing it back afterwards, at home, both alone and in front of his band-mates and friends, he could feel it levitate before him. He'd *done* it: had wrenched himself out of familial misery and created his own narrative. This song, he knew, the result of his own ripe and burgeoning talent, would bring him all the love he'd been denied as a child. There was magic in that. This was omnipotence.

Now all he had to do was write another one.

It never happened, not in any tangible sense at least. Tudor-Pole blames nobody, but if he were to, if he *had* to, he'd blame the drummer. If there is a single member of any band that seems to come in for more opprobrium than any other, it's the drummer, the one who invariably causes the most upset or discord, and is either the first to leave or else the most easily replaced. Perhaps there's something in the individual's disposition, someone who spends their professional life hitting things with sticks, that renders them less capable of existing diplomatically within polite company?

'It's always very hard to keep a band together,' Tudor-Pole says. 'You just have to have one negative character in the band, and with me, it was the drummer. That was the bone of contention.'

This particular drummer never took the hint. He didn't quit. And so Tudor-Pole, in a fit of extravagance as typical to the aver-age singer as obstinance is to the drummer, split the band, and stalked off on his pipe-cleaner legs, convinced that he could start again elsewhere. He found, however, that he couldn't just create another act with his former's instinctual chemistry, and neither was he able to write a song that contained so much propulsive magic. Panicked, he fell back on acting – if life's a stage, Tudor-Pole knew all about curtain calls – and began auditioning. He hated the process, because most actors do: 'It's demeaning.' But he kept at it and, eventually, four years later, landed the small role of Ed the Ted in the 1986 film *Absolute Beginners*. Months later, he made it all the way to the final two hopefuls auditioning for the lead role of an independent feature funded by George Harrison called *Withnail and I*. Tudor-Pole thought the script terrific, and he felt a kinship with the character of Withnail he'd never managed to locate within Ed the Ted. This film, he thought, could launch him internationally. He'd never have to sing 'Swords of a Thousand Men' again.

'But Richard E. Grant got it. He got to play Withnail,' he says, adding, 'whereas I got to *live* Withnail.'

In other words, a trained actor – and, briefly, a pop star – reduced to the state of a bum, a could've been, a should've been, an almost-was. His professional existence has been peripatetic ever since: the odd thing here and there, the occasional TV job – in 1993, he was the host of the TV show, *The Crystal Maze* – and, along the way, many hopes raised, only to be cursorily dashed. In 2008, he appeared in a *Harry Potter* film but was later edited out; he enjoyed the briefest exposure in the second series of *Game of Thrones*, playing a 'ranting street preacher'. Also in 2008, in a film called *Faintheart*, he played what IMDb lists as 'Lollipop Man / Death Metal Singer'.

'By the end of the last century, most of the acting had gone down the drain,' he admits. 'And I hated acting anyway; they're all such cunts. It's such a frivolous profession.'

And no one gets out of it unscathed. To harden his disposition, he girded himself with drink, allowing days to merge into years unless they were all simply *very* long months; it was easy to grow confused. He was never really a bum, though, just serially disappointed, let down, professionally unfulfilled. But he did have relationships; he did have a son; he lived in an enviable London postcode, N19, where there were a lot of pubs whose regulars knew his name. Briefly, at some or other point, don't ask him for dates, he started another band, 'but I was on my uppers, the guitarist was a junkie, and the bass player never turned up.'

Musicians, who needs them? Not Ed Tudor-Pole, not any more. He took a solo gig – this was Sunderland, probably 1994 – and the show offered him a glimmer of hope, something to cling on to. Standing on that stage, the sole focus of attention for the couple of hundred people who'd been nice enough to turn up, gave him an adrenaline rush he'd first felt back in 1964 watching Mick Jagger on TV, and then again in 1981 when he'd appeared on *Top of the Pops* himself. The rush, a mixture of pheromones and testosterone and unfettered radiance, was a feeling he wanted to replicate. And, he now realised, he could. He simply had to *perform*, to play live again, not necessarily always in Sunderland, but as often as he could, and wherever would have him. Nostalgia could be monetised; he could trade upon the music fans' love of their musical youth. He could play the hit, and the almost-hits, to those that remembered him, and he could do so over and over again.

'And so that's what I did, every week, for the next fifteen years, somewhere in the UK, mainly up north, places like Scotland, sometimes Wales, literally every weekend. I played shows, and I played shows. They paid for my boy's school fees, they earned me a living, and I was having fun! It filled my time. For fifteen years, I did nothing but go to rehearsals every day. I practised my scales, I got nervous for the gigs, then I did the gigs, then I felt elated, and afterwards I felt knackered, then I got back to normal again, and then, fuck me, because guess what, the next day another gig was coming up . . .'

Who knows how many times he ran through 'Swords of a Thousand Men', but each time the crowd went wild, and they were kindly, too, to any newer composition he fancied airing. 'At these shows,' he says, 'and all those nostalgia festivals – because I did those too – music isn't really the main thing at all. I remember talking to some Yorkshire lass at a big punk do – and I still hate punk, or almost all of it – and I said to her: "Do you actually like all this stuff?" And she said: "No, it's mostly a horrible racket". But she just wanted to be there, in that time again, to wear those old clothes again, to see her old mates again, and to catch a few of her favourite bands from that time.'

If it provided a welcome diversion for her, then to Tudor-Pole it offered nothing less than salvation, an ability to eke out a living from the thing he loves best. If his fans refuse to forget his sole hit, then he shan't, either. Without it, he'd be propping up a bar somewhere.

'When I play live, the people *like* me, they like my songs, so what more could I want? It's given me a social life, and it's given me appreciation – which means I've finally found the love I never got as a kid.' The maternal love so cruelly denied him, 'I've found instead from the good people of the UK. How wonderful is that? These days, I can go into any pub in the country, and someone will buy me a pint, and we'll have a chat together.'

In the immediate aftermath of Tenpole Tudor's split, the singer wanted to kill himself. 'Because that was it, all my dreams since the age of nine, shot down in flames. You know, a lot of my life has been hell and torture' – and this he says with a laugh that's hard to parse – 'and I've spent much of my time trying to anaesthetise myself from the pain of my existence. But look at me now. I've never been happier. I walk down the street, and I burst into a smile. I know *everyone*. People say good morning to me, all the crackheads and the drunks, and I just feel a part of the very fabric of the land, and the people. My companions in life are what you might call the People, and I love them, I do. They've given me a job, and they've saved my bacon.

'You know, I think there's a fascinating arc to life, and to music as well,' he continues. 'You start with complete, awful hell, then you go through an ordeal, and you become stronger for it. Take the Rolling Stones' arc, for example. I've always found that to be incredibly interesting, and all the more so as they've got older. It's fascinating to me to see how they've coped with the whole ageing thing.'

This former actor, who so very nearly was once Withnail, a role which would surely have led him to an entirely *other* destiny had he nabbed it, likens the journey we endure through life to swimming across a vast stretch of water. We may not be able to see the other side, but we start out strong and hopeful, arms cleaving the waves with a muscular effortlessness and unstinting focus. But then the waves get choppier and we struggle, and still we can't see the other side, and it feels deep now, really deep, so we tire and we flounder, and we start to wonder: how much further? And we wonder: what's the point?

'The middle is the worst bit,' he says, 'because where do you go from there? You either drown, or you keep going. That's the real test of character. And I think this is why so many people who are pop stars choose to keep going. If you've made it to the middle, then there's no real going back from that, at least in your own mind. That's the part of your life that stays with you; it's who you are. And so you keep going.

'You keep going.'

NINE

THE LEGENDS' SLOT

28

'Do you really think you would like any Beatles songs *less* if you didn't happen to know everything about Paul McCartney?'

Precisely *what* qualifies an artist as a legend is open to interpretation and, if the mood suits, argument. According to Glastonbury's requirements midway through Sunday afternoon, a legend is anyone who has been around for long enough that their unfashionable old hits have become fashionable once more, now graciously embraced for their unambiguously unifying properties. It's as good a measure as any, and probably more accurate than most. In an industry systematically destroyed by its own fickle nature – nothing quite bites the hand that feeds with greater appetite – endurance is easily mistaken for quality, but in many cases these artists would never have endured in the first place were they not quite so thrillingly good at what they do.

Some legends live ably up to their billing, reminding you of their white rhino status with the manner in which they conduct themselves: by becoming recluses, refusing to interact with the hoi polloi, and by repeatedly ignoring the polite requests of earnest writers who might just want to base chapters around their achievements. You can clock a music legend, too, by how they walk into a crowded room: how they both draw the gaze and deflect all eye contact, and how they maintain an aura so palpable it might as well be radioactive. Some are undoubtedly cuckoo, while others have for so long been the recipients of rumour and hype that they've long since left the field of gravity by which the rest of us remain tethered. They are used to being listened to, obeyed, and they talk in commanding tones, living by their own means and rules. They marry and divorce at will, live in mansions and on islands and with pet monkeys, and conduct themselves like captains of industry to whom we'd do well to kowtow. Taylor Swift does not breathe the same air that we do; Justin Bieber's off in orbit somewhere.

Many, it's true, have long since gone off the boil, but during their respective purple patches, their imperial phases, they achieved more than anybody else, and they frankly did it better. For this reason, their legendary status is forever preserved, and so of course they behave like Orson Welles in *Citizen Kane* and Marlon Brando in *Apocalypse Now*; they've earned the right – which, if true, must suggest that Joan Armatrading is the exception that proves the rule. She's a legendary British singer-songwriter of the seventies and eighties who appears to have made her way through her musical life by adopting the same approach a bus driver does to the steering wheel: it's there, so steer it. There are no delusions of grandeur here; in fact, there is no admittance of grandeur in the first place.

The first communication that comes back from Armatrading's camp after requesting an interview is: 'She might not be able to give you the answers she thinks you might be looking for,' which is another way of saying, *Why me?*

There are plenty of reasons 'why' her, but Joan Armatrading has spent a lifetime deflecting the praise of her songs, and interest in the woman behind those songs. Now into her seventies, she's not about to change her stance. Nevertheless, she's a musical titan by any measure, a songwriter who, four decades ago, overcame barriers of gender, race and, possibly (because she wasn't saying) sexuality, to break through and clear a way for generations to follow in her wake. By her own estimation, however, she was doing no such thing. She simply had a bunch of songs that she wanted to play, and so she played them. As luck would have it, people listened.

'I can't take any credit for my songs,' Armatrading says. 'Because I had nothing to do with them.'

Her ability to write them came to her unbidden, from elsewhere certainly, and from God, perhaps. Born on the Caribbean island of St Kitts, she moved to the UK, specifically Birmingham, at the age of seven, and was thirteen when she realised that a musical ability, something she'd never previously sought, was alive in her fingertips. This discovery was prompted following her parents' purchase of a piano, which they'd installed in their small living room. 'I started writing songs, and I didn't stop.'

This surprised her. She'd never been much of a music fan, and far preferred listening to comedy on the radio, choosing the Goons over the Beatles every time. She also bristled at the idea that these God-given songs, which were clearly good, might bring her a level of attention. The last thing she wanted was to be noticed.

'I've always been a quite quiet person, and private, but I've also been confident, perhaps even over-confident, in my ability to do what I do. But,' she says, 'I never needed other people to tell me that. I'm not particularly gregarious, not an extrovert.'

For a non-extrovert, the fact that she took part in a repertory production of the famed seventies musical *Hair* might surprise many – the play includes nudity – but it was here that she met a lyricist, Pam Nestor, with whom she formed a professional partnership, resulting in Armatrading's debut album in 1972, *Whatever's For Us*. By 1975, she was working alone, signed to A&M, and being so ardently supported by John Peel that her singles were becoming hits. And there were many hits – 'Love and Affection', 'Down to Zero', 'Show Some Emotion', 'Me Myself I', 'All the Way from America', 'I'm Lucky', 'Drop the Pilot' – a run that lasted almost a full decade. Her 1983 greatest hits collection, *Track Record*, established her as a singer-songwriter without parallel. People kept telling her that she was a trailblazer, kept hurling praise her way, and becoming increasingly fascinated and intrigued by her because she was an enigma, a closed book.

Armatrading was all too firmly explaining nothing to no one.

'Who cares what I'm about? Who cares who I am? Do you really think you would like any Beatles songs *less* if you didn't happen to know everything about Paul McCartney?' she wonders.

She refused to talk about the lyrical themes of her songs – her 1983 single '(I Love It When You) Call Me Names' appeared to deal with domestic violence – and she refused, too, to dignify the rumours about her sexuality with anything like a response. She just kept writing songs and having hits.

But then even here, with an artist as popular as she, the hits did eventually cease, rather abruptly, too, as hits have a tendency to do. *Track Record*, surely inadvertently, called time on her run of chart success, and forever thereafter she found herself out of the spotlight. Armatrading, of course, barely noticed, and wasn't much fussed. She knew that this was what happened to every artist, of every merit. Her no longer being quite as popular today as she was yesterday was never going to change the simple fact of why she was here: to write songs every day, so long as they kept coming to her, which they did.

'Every artist finds that they are no longer fashionable at some point. There are no exceptions, none. And so all you do is you keep going, and you try to keep writing a better song than the last one. It's what I've always done. In 1976, I was trying to write a better song than I'd written in 1975. I'm still doing that today.'

On every tour she has played since, she has performed 'Love and Affection', a song written back in 1976, and her biggest hit. She doesn't resent it, but she doesn't consider herself defined by it, either. Little in her world has changed over time. Now into old age, she remains loyal to the craft, and is still a firmly closed book. When asked where she lives today, her reply is: 'England.' Whether or not she is a legend, what such a complimentary reference does for her, or how she behaves as a result, is something she doesn't much care to consider, at least publicly, and she rather wonders – aloud – why anyone would bother asking her in the first place.

'I have no control over that, so I don't know what to tell you, really,' she says.

There is a trick that interviewers like to pull in certain awkward situations in pursuit of teasing out greater insight. The trick is silence: say nothing, and let them fill it. Often it works, but not always. In this case, the silence extends until the one feeling awkward is not her.

'Goodbye,' says Joan Armatrading, closing the metaphorical door behind her with such emphasis you almost hear it click shut.

In January 2011, Adam Ant gave an interview to a newspaper to mark what may, or may not, have been his comeback. The feature revealed a legendary singer still going strong, albeit in fits and starts, three full decades after he'd first been hailed the most exciting pop star of his generation. He was living these days in a house at the end of a mews full of undulating cobblestones and tended pot plants, in an exclusive part of London, a home that was smaller than might have been expected of a pop colossus who'd sold many millions of records. The kitchen was tiny, the living room similarly cramped, and both were filled with an enthusiastic, even vigorous, mess of art spilling from shelves and scaling the walls, including endless visuals of Ant as a young man, radiant and beautiful, back when it seemed as if he held the entire nation's desires in the palm of his plump hand. Though age had since left its mark, he still looked comparably striking, a fixty-six-year-old dressed in a manner untypical of men in midlife, in a chunky skull-and-crossbones jumper and army trousers, with a purple bandanna on his head and a complicated goatee on his chin, the design of which surely required a steady hand. You couldn't easily imagine him doing anything quite so humdrum as standing in a post office queue for stamps. He was bigger than that, somehow, of higher standing: a pop star still.

He offered tea, and sat on the living-room couch, to the left of his sleeping dogs, Billy and Elvis, who over the next hour and a half snored and silently farted in approximately equal measure. Ant was keen to talk, not something you could say of all pop stars, and keener still not only to rake over the supposed good old days but also to focus on just how profusely creative he still was, and how his about-to-be-released seventeen-track album, *Adam Ant is the Blueblack Hussar in Marrying the Gunner's Daughter*, would offer ample proof of that.

The house, which he had only recently moved in to, was something of a living museum, given over to just one exhibit: The Life and Times of Adam Ant. In every corner, there seemed to be another visual reminder of who he was and who he'd been, every nook filled with framed posters, ticket stubs and gold, silver and platinum discs. In the kitchen was a leaning tower of books, copies of his 2007 autobiography *Stand and Deliver*, the name taken from his biggest hit. From his bedroom downstairs could be heard *Goody Two Shoes*, his flamboyantly camp solo hit from 1982, and this was either a curious coincidence – the radio playing an Adam Ant song at the precise moment he was giving a press interview – or else it was a CD of Ant's hits, playing on a loop.

Everywhere you looked, and everything you heard, was a reminder of all he'd achieved over the years. In this way, perhaps, Ant could live in a perpetual present tense when, for everyone else, Adam and the Ants were a largely historical concept.

By 1980, at the age of twenty-six, Ant was already iconic, an artist who'd straddled the punk that had informed him and a New

Romantic movement he would go on to help define. He dressed like a nineteenth-century naval officer gone rogue, and painted a white stripe across his impeccable cheekbones and aquiline nose. He had a habit of posing for photographs with his arms raised aloft, wrists kissing a few inches above his head. This was not how ordinary folk looked or behaved, but then Adam Ant was not ordinary, no longer the Stuart Goddard of his birth certificate, but a star for whom everything was writ large, at once faintly ludicrous and utterly compelling.

There were, of course, other memorable songs of 1980 that left a lasting impact, but none quite raised the hairs on the back of the neck like 'Kings of the Wild Frontier', 'Dog Eat Dog' or, a year later, 'Stand and Deliver' and 'Prince Charming', by which time Ant was applying lipstick to his face, missing his mouth completely and daubing it instead on his cheek. Subtlety was not part of the equation here, but then that was the whole point. This was pop music as fever dream, and its architect was the hot mercury in the phallic thermometer.

When it was suggested to Ant in 2011 that his new album, with its unwieldy title, was a comeback, his answer was withering. 'Comeback?' he repeated, shaking his head. 'I never went away.'

Not true, as it happened. *Adam Ant is the Blueblack Hussar . . .* was his first album in well over a decade (and, as it would transpire, his last, at least at the time of writing), and his reintroduction to the scene was already problematic, chiefly because he seemed so very combative. He'd recently been in the news for saying that he wanted to fight Liam Gallagher, by all accounts unhappy at the younger man's arrogance. But he was also disgruntled with fans for not being appreciative enough. A few weeks earlier, he'd played one of his not-comeback shows in a small venue in north London. The place was barely half full, and his show was a punishing two and a half hours long. He was good enough to perform the hits, which still sounded brilliant, but the hits only went so far, and so the bulk of the setlist was padded out with some of his lesser-known compositions, among them innuendo-ridden curios like 'Why Do Girls Like Horses?' and a cover of Iggy and the Stooges' 'Cock in My Pocket'. At one point, he launched into a strutting reimagining of Bruce Springsteen's 'Born in the USA', retitled 'Born in the UK', which featured a line Springsteen hadn't written: 'Oasis were a bunch of cunts with no style'. It was a strange version, not necessarily a good one, and the performance turned the atmosphere in the room to ice. Whatever was he doing? At its conclusion, the singer spat in the direction of the audience, who by this late stage had already moved towards either the bar or the exit. Ant then stormed off-stage.

Several in the thinning crowd thought that perhaps this was all part of the off-kilter performance, but when he didn't come back, they had to consider otherwise.

Adam Ant was diagnosed with bipolar disorder at the age of twenty-one, for which he was prescribed antidepressants. These, he believed, came to restrict his creative flow, and it was only when he finally weaned himself off them years later that he found the songs came easily once more. He would have several mental-health-driven episodes over the years, sudden sparks of anger that required an outlet. There were public altercations, and once he wielded a fake gun in a pub after an argument got out of hand. Police were called, and he was charged with affray and criminal damage. Other times, he was sectioned. The tabloid media coverage was as cruel and callous as it was ignorant and unhelpful, prompting Ant to campaign for better understanding for, and more empathy towards, those with mental health problems.

He said that he wanted to discuss the issue on television, in pursuit of maximum exposure. Ideally, he'd talk to the then-Prime Minister, David Cameron, on prime-time.

'He seems like an open-minded guy,' Ant mused back in 2011. 'David Dimbleby could chair it.'

He insisted that he, and people like him, were repeatedly stifled, misunderstood. Life is hard for everyone, but for those in the public eye, he argued, and those battling with their mental health, it can feel harder still.

'If you look throughout history, anybody who was really creative in life suffered in a similar way,' he suggested. 'Coleridge, Oscar Wilde, Kurt Cobain, even Winston Churchill. My problem was that I was always terribly competitive, obsessively so.'

He explained that those of a creative bent require an outlet for their work; they need to be heard. When Ant was at the height of his fame, being fawned over by fans, appearing onstage and on TV and articulating himself via vinyl and cassette, he had that outlet, and his mental health was kept in check. He felt well. But it was when the door closed on all that, and he was left with Stuart Goddard, that the problems swelled. He still had all this creativity firing around inside his head that had nowhere to go. This made him sad, angry, confused and fearful. What on earth was he to do now? When you've been that successful in life, that stimulated and sated, and when it all so abruptly goes, or gets taken away, how do you replace it? And with what?

Hardly surprising, then, that he chose to surround himself with visual and aural reminders of that time in life when, albeit viewed through rose-tinted spectacles, he felt well in himself, he felt understood, and he felt heard. The reminders allowed him a safe space within which to exist, a protective womb. It was when he stepped out of that safe space and into the unforgiving outside world that problems could, and sometimes did, occur.

Roland Orzabal was facing a member of the press in an opulent hotel suite in Los Angeles at the turn of the twenty-first century, being asked what many artists of his vintage are asked from time to time: Why keep going? What's left to prove? His band, Tears for Fears, were by now something of a heritage act, though they still seemed distanced from, and at odds with, the names they'd originally come up alongside. They'd never been poppy enough to be filed alongside ABC, and were hardly a seductive proposition in the mould of, say, Terence Trent D'Arby. They'd taken their name from Arthur Janov's 'primal scream' philosophy, and an early song was entitled 'Ideas as Opiates'; various other songs seemed to take depression as their starting point.

Despite all this, they'd been a hugely successful singles and albums act, with a canon of timeless songs, but over two decades into their career, there were no more hit singles, no Lifetime Achievement awards, and no full-throttled renaissance of the kind you sensed they craved and felt they deserved.

While his bandmate Curt Smith sat beside him frowning – Smith spent a lot of the interview frowning at Orzabal's rather ponderous monologues – Orzabal chose to answer the question of what motivated the band today by quoting a musician he greatly admired.

'Like Sting says—' he began, before being abruptly cut short.

'Oh, for fuck's sake, don't start quoting Sting,' said Smith.

Orzabal remained unrepentant, as was his way. 'As Sting says, music is its own reward.'

He's right – it is, and everything else is stuffing – but that can still be difficult to accept when your time has passed, especially when you'd once made such an impact on your chosen field. When Orzabal published a novel in 2014 entitled *Sex, Drugs & Opera*, its subheading – *There's Life After Rock 'n' Roll* – read suspiciously like a note to self.

When Annie Lennox and Dave Stewart called time on Eurythmics, one of the biggest and most fondly remembered acts of the 1980s, the former promptly went on to become a hugely successful solo star whose sudden absence the latter must have felt all too sharply. It's almost always easier for the singer. Dave Stewart had been something of a workaholic, that band's co-songwriter, guitarist and producer, and someone who, like Prince, considered every half-thought a potential idea that required capturing, nurturing and polishing, just in case.

There was a presumed effortless elegance to much of Annie Lennox's subsequent career – she had hit singles and hit albums, and then became an activist – but it was Stewart who was more swanlike in the most literal sense: gliding up top, pedalling frantically beneath the surface. It wasn't money or the continued pursuit of fame that kept him at it, but simply a need for all that creativity to find its outlet. He'd suffered with depression in the past, and one way to ameliorate it was, as Adam Ant had, to stay busy. He'd already worked with Tom Petty, Feargal Sharkey and Bob Geldof; then he worked with Siobhan Fahey and Marcella Detroit on their band Shakespears Sister (Fahey was his wife), and later with Jon Bon Jovi, Bryan Ferry, Ringo Starr, Stevie Nicks and Joss Stone. He wrote music for TV and film, shot his own films and took up photography. He discovered new musical talent and also, on the side, set up private members' clubs and various apps.

'A lot of the things I've done outside music [have] been a pain in the arse to do,' Stewart says, 'so what I'd do all the time was musical collaboration. If you look at [my career] from the outside, you'd go: "Dave has done all these kinds of things!", but it's usually to do with why, and how, music works.' What he means is, music was his first language, and he'd converse with as many people as he could. Over the years, he plucked several unknowns to work with: a young saxophonist from Denmark; a Welshman living in a disused post office; a powerhouse soul singer from the American south. Some collaborations worked better than others, but all he saw to fruition. When other business ventures failed – like a TV channel for the internet when the internet still existed on dial-up – it was because, he believes, 'I've always had that slight problem of being ahead [of my time].'

Dave Stewart never left music, and Roland Orzabal returned to it after writing his novel. Adam Ant continues to tour. But each knew enough not to let anything else too compulsively extra-curricular get in the way. If it does, the music suffers – and wherever possible that's something to be avoided, because, as Roland Orzabal said that Sting says, 'music is its own reward.' Isn't it?

29

'That didn't make me want to kill him any less'

Imagine what it must have been like to have been young and blond and handsome, often naked from the waist up, and an integral part of the world's biggest rock group, and then to up sticks – in this case, literally – and walk away from it all. Stewart Copeland, the hyperactive drummer with the Police, did just that, and did so because he fancied 'a change'.

'We also broke up,' Copeland says, 'because we didn't want to be [stuck] within the narrow constraints of a pop group any more.'

It was 1986, and the Police had just redefined what stadium bands could do. But they'd had enough. Bands bowing out on top is a mostly unheard of occurrence, and rock's well-thumbed script dictates that Copeland must have regretted his impetuous decision ever since. But no, he will tell you. No. Walking away from the Police brought him a sense of relief when he'd needed it most. Immediately, there were no more daily fistfights to be had, largely because he was no longer within arm's reach of the band's singer, Sting, and because now he finally had more of what he'd really wanted all along: autonomy, to play the king, and not the lowly prince.

'Yes, yes, life was intolerable in the band for all the reasons that we now understand,' he concedes, referring to the much-discussed enmity that had built up between him, Sting and guitarist Andy Summers, but especially between Copeland and the frontman. Their verbal sparring frequently spilled into the physical, 'but that's another conversation, a long conversation' – for another time, he means. 'There was tension all the time, but that's really not why we broke up. We just wanted to do something differently, apart.'

Nevertheless, it can hardly have been the easiest decision. Individual band members tend not to recover form when they branch out elsewhere. Many legendary singers tucked inside legendary groups never really managed it, and there is good reason why Bono, for one, has never even tried.

Two years previously, in 1984, the Police were very much on top. They'd released five albums of conspicuously strange music that would make them huge but not particularly influential, their music taut as a tightrope and built around something that sounded, or wanted to sound, like reggae – never an easy trick to pull off when your singer was born in Northumberland. Their most famous song was misconstrued as a tender love ballad when really it was about stalking, 'Every Breath You Take' an ode to romance in the same way that Mötley Crüe's 'Girls Girls Girls' was a sisterly cry for greater appreciation of women's contribution to society. They excelled in irritating album titles: *Outlandos D'Amour*, *Regatta de Blanc*, *Zenyatta Mondatta*. Their 1983 album *Synchronicity* invoked both Mephistopheles and unhealthy maternal fetishes ('Every girl I go out with / Becomes my mother in the end', from the track 'Mother'). And in their singer, they boasted an enthusiast of the lute, a stringed instrument that probably originated from ancient Mesopotamia. Sting also enjoyed a macrobiotic diet, and practised Tantra yoga.

If any band should never have made it out of the planning stages, it was them. But chemistry is a confusing science at the best of times, and the Police made thrilling rock music that translated well. But, in Copeland's estimation, they'd quickly become 'a corporation, a golden cage that required three blond heads to keep producing. We tried to dabble, and do other things, but those projects ultimately shrivelled up because we were surrounded by the corporate world that did not want any distractions, or diversions.'

But those distractions kept coming, ever more temptingly so, side projects for each of them that could only really flourish independently of the band. And the only way they could pursue them was to step outside, to kill the golden goose 'and melt down the golden cage'. Were they ready to do such a thing? By 1986, they were. 'Which was funny,' Copeland notes, 'as it actually happened at a time when we were getting along very well.'

By this point in his career, Copeland, who'd previously served time in another band, the progressive rock outfit Curved Air, was already the world's most enthusiastic drummer and, according to *Rolling Stone* magazine, the tenth most proficient. Outside the realm of heavy metal, you don't always notice the drummer. But Copeland was a propulsive windmill, six arms, eight arms, *so* many arms, each full of sinew and bicep, constantly moving – and in the middle of all that, a grinning, gurning face. You tended to notice him, and sometimes more so than you did Sting, which might just have been part of their intermittent intra-band problems. Who knows? Copeland's father had helped found the CIA; his brother Miles was the band's manager. This particular drummer, perhaps inescapably, was born to be noticed.

Back in 1984, Francis Ford Coppola noticed him. The director had made a film, *Rumble Fish*, which was arty, black-and-white and furiously atmospheric, and was looking for someone to do the soundtrack when Coppola's son, Roman, a fan of the Police, recommended Copeland.

'At the time, we were recording in Montserrat, and mixing in Montréal, but I went straight from there to California to work on this movie for Francis. And, oh my God, the bliss, the ecstasy of it! This was a creative exercise that did not involve any negotiations!'

Copeland had not been used to this. He was used to negotiations, heartache, battles, tension, and eventual capitulation to
Sting.

But Sting wasn't here.

'And so this was just a beautiful world where I was the only
person in that world, and I could do whatever the hell I wanted
to do because everybody else was engaged in their own creative
enterprise within the making of the movie. But they were not
musicians; *I* was the musician. The director left all the music to
me, and because I didn't have to negotiate, I could follow my own
creative instinct to wherever it might lead. And if I hit a blind
alley? Hey, no problem! I'd just try something else. I didn't have
to fight every inch of every creative battle, and that, to me, was
just so, so beautiful.'

They say that once you've tried Japanese Wagyu beef, you'll
never buy cow from a tin again. After *Rumble Fish*, Copeland
found it increasingly difficult to exist within a hydra-headed outfit
where you had to shout to be heard – and even then there were
no guarantees you'd be listened to. Francis Ford Coppola had
shown him there were other options open to him. It was only a
matter of time.

The soundtrack, he says, 'was a real invitation for me to find a
life for myself outside the group. And I'll tell you something else:
I'd be lying if I said that another element wasn't this feeling of
invincibility, that we, as the Police, had conquered the world, and
to be honest with you we'd found that easy, so I just figured that
anything else I wanted to do must be easy as well; that every other
mountain was going to be just as easy to climb.'

A slightly simplistic reading, of course, because the Police
conquering the world hadn't been easy so much as the result of
the perfect synergy between three gifted individuals. Few people,
for example, could name anything by Copeland's earlier band,
Curved Air, and if you can: well done. But the former drummer

had enjoyed the process, and wanted to rise to a new challenge. And to do so alone.

'See, the thing is, Sting was just not cut out to be a band member, particularly with his . . . his creative *completeness*. He doesn't much need a guitarist to come up with something for the track that he wrote, because he already figured that out himself. The same with drums. He's actually really good at arranging drums, by the way, although of course that didn't make me want to kill him any less. In fact, it increased the homicidal urgency . . .

'But, you know, all three of us were feeling this. We had other adventures we wanted to have. I wanted to enjoy the bounty that our work had brought us. And Sting, in the same way that I was frustrated in having to deal with this implacable citadel of his endless musical creations . . . Sting had the same problem with us. He was like: *Look, I write the songs, I know exactly how they go, but now I have to negotiate with these other two guys who may have their own fucking ideas?* He didn't care whether our fucking ideas were any good or not, because Sting already knew what he wanted to do, and that was fair enough.'

When he left, there were no fears, no doubts. 'I was arrogant to such fears. I thought that arrogance might even serve me well.'

Stewart Copeland has a joke. All drummers have jokes. His goes like this.

'What was the drummer's last words before he got fired from the band? *Hey guys, I've got a song.*'

When the Police split, Copeland's entire life changed overnight. Most immediately, it became quieter. 'I just thought to myself: *Wait a minute! I don't actually need to be wearing leather pants any more!* It was no longer a requirement, because I was no longer a product. I didn't need to dress up for the cameras to look the part because, now, there *was* no part. And let me tell you, that was wonderful. As a film composer, I was basically just an employee of the director; I was a craftsman. When you're a rock star, you have to serve up an artistic vision, but I no longer had to do that. After dropping my kids off at school, I became a suburban dad, styled by Gap. No longer was I a walking neon sign. Did I like being absolutely anonymous? You bet!'

Ever since, Copeland has been a jobbing, working musician. He has written film soundtracks, and music for computer games. There have been orchestral suites, and he's staged operas. He remains hungry. 'I'd kill to get a Spielberg movie, but on the other hand, there's always a second division director who'd kill to have *me* score their movie. There are always people above you, and below you, always people, so no matter where you're coming from with your aspirations, whatever level you're on is fine.'

In 2007, the band did fulfil rock's abiding cliché by getting back together, and did so in style, with an enormous world tour that would net over $800 million in profit. Either everyone has their price, or nostalgia is a fever we must all succumb to.

'No,' he says. 'I don't think nostalgia's the right word here.' (Sting would think otherwise. In an interview thirteen years after their reunion, he said that he regretted reforming the band, labelling it an 'exercise in nostalgia'.)

'It may be an important element for the fans,' Copeland allows, 'because I guess that's how music works, and we knew that if we played a new song, even if it was the best song we ever wrote, it wouldn't have anywhere near as much impact as, say, "Message in a Bottle", a song that has thirty years' worth of life experiences wrapped up in it, whether they happened to like that song at the time or not. That's what songs have: an emotional impact, and nostalgia is a big part of that, sure, but it's certainly not why we came back together. We came back together because the world was ready for us again, because I hadn't played a stadium in a real long time, and I guess because we liked the idea of burning down the world again, so we did.'

The tour proved harmonious, mostly. They played off one another brilliantly. But backstage, old issues quickly resurfaced. Copeland says: 'We were at loggerheads during rehearsals, but by the time we got to the first show, and saw the audience, that explained it all to us: *this* is what we're here for.'

But there were lots of rehearsals, and so plenty of testing times. 'By the end of the tour, we were all absolutely ready to leave, and were counting down the hours: only twelve more hours to go, only ten more hours . . . It was only when the actual end was in sight, that final hour, that we realised just what a great time we'd had, and were still having.' This might just be the perfect explanation for dysfunction: unable to fully enjoy the enjoyable thing because they'd all grown so accustomed to *not* enjoying it.

When in 2008 they walked away again, this time for the final time, without having written any new music, it was a relief. A relief, Copeland says, to firmly close the book. This was it, over. Back to the day job.

'A rock star is ultimately just a human being. You are the person that still has that avatar, and it's a picture of *you*, and the avatar is built up around you, and fans put all their hopes and desires on to it . . . But it's not you, it's really not. You're still just a skinny kid, the same kid you always were. Your words may ring louder, you may seem more hilarious to people, more popular, and you might be driving a truck rather than a car, but it's important to never forget that it's an illusion; it's all just a big illusion.'

30

**'I was making more money in a single night than my father
would make in a year'**

It might be said with confidence, perhaps even argued with solid
certainty, that at the age of seventy-five Don McLean is living his
best life. It's been several decades since his songs – particularly
'American Pie' and 'Vincent' – lifted him towards legendary status,
but the way he tells it, he is, right now, fully reaping the spoils of
that success, and all that hard work, without having to do anything else but soak it all up.

'My girlfriend,' he says, 'is a bikini model, and I love it.'

McLean has been married twice before, and has children
from his second marriage. But that was then. His current girlfriend, Paris Dylan, is a former Playboy bunny, and is almost half
a century his junior. They met in 2016 when Dylan was hired to
manage the singer's social media accounts. They quickly became a
couple. According to tabloid reports – which, whenever in doubt,
tend to err towards reliable misogyny – she has been busy helping
him 'blow his $200 million fortune on hotels, jets and Louboutin
shoes.'

McLean will suggest otherwise. Having been fortunate enough
to earn good money throughout his career, and having reached
an age where saving for your future is no longer the pressing
need it perhaps once was, he and his partner are simply enjoying
themselves while he still has time to do so. His argument: who
wouldn't?

·

Don McLean was the writer of some of the most beautiful love songs of the 1970s, sung with such purity they resembled hymns. Even when he sang other people's compositions, as he did in 1980 with Roy Orbison's 'Crying', he invested so much grace and pain into every syllable you felt it must have cost him dearly to sing it.

He cut an unlikely figure, a hirsute farm boy who probably hailed from a small town where the barber was permanently closed. He was shy, too, awkward in his bearing, and he found being suddenly adored, when at last it came, a complicated, fractious business; he'd lose sleep over it.

He'd started out on the folk circuit in the America of the late 1960s, inspired in part by Frank Sinatra and Buddy Holly. But his songs back then failed to impress, and he was turned down over seventy times by record labels before finally securing a deal. His first album, *Tapestry*, was a minor hit only, but it was his second, 1971's *American Pie*, that allowed him to break through into the big time.

'Most of the time, I was fighting against popular people like Cat Stevens, or Bob Dylan, or the Beatles, or whatever the latest thing was, and I was never in that group [of people]. No, I was on the edges. To me,' he says, 'fame and success in the music business was very much like popularity at high school. You know: "What's he wearing? Who's he dating? And that hairstyle . . . what the hell is all that about!" I had no idea that fashion was even a component to major success; I never even thought about what I was wearing . . .'

It showed, but such was his magnetism and homespun appeal that people started dressing like him, in cowboy-style shirts, and tight-fitting trousers that flared slightly at the boot. Whenever he went clothes shopping for himself, now as a famous singer, he found himself presented with racks of clothes that might help him dress more like 'Don McLean'. This troubled him, made him doubt his integrity. How to keep his own voice? How to remain true unto only himself?

'I was very much a contrarian, and I still am. Everybody back then wanted to sound like Dylan, everybody had that raw whisper; I was the opposite, I wanted to sing like an opera, in that bel canto style. I was a loner, and so when I got famous, I did what I always did, which was to close the front door, and not answer the phone.'

In the meantime, the people closest to him changed, friends and family starting to behave differently, 'because I was too famous.' Initially, he suggests, they'd rejected him because he wasn't famous *enough*, just another failed folkie. His own sense of self-worth had been similarly inclined. 'I hadn't gone to college; I had no idea who I was supposed to be. Who was I to think I could be a singer? Nobody [in his family] was a singer; they went to work in New York. So when I tried to become one, they rejected me when I failed, but when I succeeded, they rejected me because now I was too successful. For them to be around me after I'd had a hit would make them feel small and unimportant.'

If this seems a curious reaction – because if you can't trust your friends, your family, etc. – he's adamant that this was the case. 'By the time they were twenty-seven or twenty-eight, they were not a millionaire as I was. They were not known all over the world. They were still hanging out with the same people they'd always hung out with.'

The spurning hurt him, and while he may well have been able to channel some of that pain into his songwriting, it didn't make the business of life any easier to negotiate. 'I was too big a presence. If I walked into a room of strangers, everybody knew who I was, everybody had their eyes on me, everybody started asking questions, and suddenly I'm holding court, and I don't like that.'

He didn't seem to like much of anything, and was increasingly defined by his anger. The man who sang with such tenderness was, in person, due to intense provocation, a grump. 'I was like

John Lennon, you know: very negative, angry, mad. Even though [Lennon] had everything, he was always bitching about something or other. McCartney seemed much better adjusted, enjoying his life; whatever came his way, he handled it with grace. But me, I had that Lennon thing: I was pissed off.'

In the early days, pre-fame, he'd been angry because he didn't like being just another workaday musician pursuing foolish dreams. After success, he became angry because the workaday musicians he'd come up alongside competitively suddenly wanted to know him. 'These assholes didn't know what the fuck they were doing, and when my dream came true, they started jumping on my train, and that just pissed me off even more. I was like: "Where were you when I needed a friend?"'

The years of mass approval, resounding applause, and endless riches took their toll. 'All of it, day in, day out – it was a very high-caloric existence. But I tried to understand people better, to give more, and be less competitive, be more Christian. That's one thing I've really tried to learn [ever since].'

A lot of heavy weather here, success and wealth bringing him nothing but conflict and misery. By the following decade, he was old hat and over the hill, and nobody was sporting the 'Don McLean' look any more. However, McLean himself felt his own previously robust competitive streak slide into slight abeyance, and there must have been a certain relief to this. He knew that he'd done enough, that the loyal fanbase he'd built up would remain for the rest of his life. People would always want to hear 'American Pie', and each time they did, interest in his back catalogue would return. In 2000, Madonna reimagined the song as a jerky disco anthem. McLean called her version 'sensual and mystical', and you get the sense that he was grateful to her for it.

He may have rested on his laurels, then, but not entirely. The studio albums still sporadically and diligently came, alongside endlessly repackaged but otherwise identical greatest hits, as well

as that regrettable necessity for all American artists of a certain
stature: the Christmas album. He was an elder statesman now,
and would live fittingly as such. His legend would linger.

Over the years, there has been an accumulation of stories about
the man, some good, some bad, 'and so when a person now
says "Don McLean", it means five different things to them, and
not [just] one. But that's fifty years. In the beginning, I would
always tell myself that I was making thousands and thousands of
dollars a night, no matter where I was, making more money in a
single night than my father [who died when McLean was fifteen]
would make in a year. And then, later, I may be in, I may be out,
people might talk about me a lot or they might not talk about me
at all, but I'm still making more than my father did in a year, in
one night.'

So McLean would judge his continued popularity by how
much he was earning, and from this he was able to reassure himself. 'I never quit,' he says. 'You have to have a philosophy about
how you see yourself, and how you want to go about your career.'

With a sense of righteousness that rises the more he speaks,
he explains how a career starts out small, like the making of a
fire. You put a few sticks together, set it alight, and watch as the
smoke comes. Then you put on more sticks. The fire doesn't go
out, but gets bigger and bigger, 'and pretty soon it's a huge bonfire,
a beacon of light, the people come and see it in the night, and they
relate to it, and sometimes they guide their lives around that fire.
But it's a slow process, and you cannot be in a hurry, and you have
to have other interests.'

His? Well, he says, he likes reading biographies, not simply
to compare and contrast but to see what other people, from all
sorts of backgrounds and in all sorts of lives, do with their time
on earth. 'I would say to myself: "Well, you know, I went through
a very bad divorce, and a lot of things were said about me by my

ex-wife, but you just put one foot in front of the other, you work your way out of it, you move on.'"

His second marriage, to Patrisha Shnier, ended in divorce after the singer was arrested and charged with a 'misdemeanour crime of domestic violence' for which he was fined but not jailed. 'He was scaring me with the intensity of his rage and the craziness in his eyes,' Shnier was reported to have said in a news story picked up by the *Daily Mail*. In a later interview with that newspaper, McLean tried to explain himself: 'There are no winners or losers, but I am not a villain.'

'Time makes everything smaller,' he says now. 'It moves things into the past, and it may become an interesting moment of one sort or another, but it doesn't define you; other things will happen. There have been times when I was not thought of very much, or not thought of highly, and other times when I've been up there with the greatest ever.'

Many times over the years he has wanted to quit. He decided that the best years of his life were not the successful ones, but the ones immediately before, back in the 1960s, at the very beginning of his career, when all was still before him, and nothing had yet been tainted. The moment he put his first album out was when the fun stopped.

'Suddenly I was being played all over the radio, people had all these opinions, I was filling out theatres, and I had responsibility, which is something I did not want. And it's been that way ever since. I got more famous, and the weight became heavier.'

Be careful what you wish for, is what he seems to be saying here.

And then, at the age of seventy-one, having laid at least some of his more persistent demons to rest, he met Dylan Paris, as glaring a mismatch as, to him, it was glorious. Fifty years between them! People would gossip; they'd mock and taunt; his children might raise more than an eyebrow. But McLean was – and this is presumably the most important factor here – happy.

Don McLean may be many things, but he isn't stupid. Having lived a clearly complicated life riven with both internal and external conflict, the man with the purest singing voice of his generation now simply wants – as he enters autumn, with winter encroaching – a little uncomplicated fun. His relationship has had a glaring impact on his profile: more column inches in the last couple of years than he has had in the last few decades. Naturally all of these revolve around his May to December fling, in his case the *next* December. He appears to quite like it. If the paparazzi aren't trailing them, then his girlfriend's Instagram account does their work for them, littered as it is with filtered photographs of the couple all over the world, the majority of them featuring an old man in comfortable shoes posing next to a woman in a swimsuit.

But people can laugh and judge as much as they want, because McLean really doesn't care. He's in clover. 'My girlfriend, who's twenty-six and who is the greatest girl I have ever known – I mean, she's Mexican, and she really loves me – she wants to be with me everywhere we go, which is,' he points out, 'quite different from what I was used to. We were probably in 230 cities in four and a half years, and she's made every one of the shows I played.' He was quite ill a few times during their trek, he admits, but, 'she was there all the way, so I'm very lucky. And I do like [to do] things, you know, to make her happy, to see a smile on her face.'

The elephant that now shuffles from the corner of the room and into the centre is here mostly to state the obvious, that McLean is surely being taken advantage of, and that Paris's main intent is to bleed the poor man dry. She couldn't possibly love him, could she? His response: 'Believe me, I've made money on all those shows, so I'm not *wasting* money on her. I love spending money on her, but it's money I might not have earned otherwise because, personally, I might have been too lazy to go to Berlin, or someplace.' He elected to go on such an extensive tour so comparatively late in life because Paris had wanted to see Berlin, and Milan, and London; she wanted to see Paris, too. By playing concerts each night, McLean got to be reminded of his standing on the world's stage, and you can never be too old for that.

During and after lockdown, they stayed home in Los Angeles, where McLean has learned, years too late, to fully relax. He feels that his work here, in a very genuine sense, is done, and so no longer bothers trying to write songs. He has already said it all. What's left to say?

'I don't know, is the honest answer. After "American Pie", I thought maybe I had a year to enjoy this, but fifty years later, I'm still here, still doing it, and talking to you. My life has been a complete surprise, and one of the things I've learned from it is how strong I am. When I was younger, I was fearful. I was afraid to get up on stage in front of people because I thought I might bomb, that they might not like me, but I got up there and did it anyway. A lot of the old-timers like me come from working three shows a night, not just from having some lucky something on the internet. It's hard physical work, year in, year out, all right?'

McLean read an interview with the great American actor Jack Nicholson recently. Nicholson, who is in his eighties, said that he was convinced people no longer want to be moved any more. They don't want to be touched by art, they don't want to be prompted into crying. This felt like a significant realisation for the man who, as an actor, had worked hard to touch people, and manipulate their emotions, to make a lasting impression. But he felt that the world had changed, had moved on without him, and this left him confused, and a little sad.

The words resonated with McLean. 'Absolutely. I think that, on a certain level, my reluctance to write more music is the fact that I'm not sure the audience is there any more to hear it.' He says this less with sadness than a certain resignation. Life moves on, times change, and at some point we will get left behind in the way things used to be, not they way things currently are.

Jack Nicholson hasn't made a film since 2010.

In an Instagram post from October 2019, Paris Dylan wishes a 'happy birthday to the most beautiful, perfect, funniest, sweetest angel in the world. I love you more than words can ever describe. #donmclean #happybirthdaybaby.'

In the accompanying photo, the couple are locked in a tight embrace, both beaming bright teeth, with what looks like, for that captured moment at least, not a care in the world.

31

'One doctor thought it was hysteria'

In 1978, Shirley Collins, a folk singer who'd regularly been described as England's finest, abruptly retired from music. This was not so much out of want, as need: she woke up one morning to find her voice gone. She was forty-three years old.

'I just couldn't sing any more,' she says. She quickly sourced vocal tutors for help and guidance, 'but that was a disaster, because singing teachers' idea of singing just wasn't what *I* did. I think they thought I was a bit of a joke, because I never did sing properly, I didn't breathe properly, didn't use the, oh I don't know, the *cavities* in my forehead properly, or something. I think I must have had other things to think about when I was singing my songs . . .'

This mystery ailment hadn't exactly come out of nowhere, and so perhaps wasn't entirely mysterious. Stress can have a profound effect on both mental and physical health, and there was much stress in her life. Collins' second marriage had recently come to a particularly unhappy end. It left her traumatised, and doctors thought that this trauma was now manifesting itself physiologically. The worse she felt, the less enthusiasm she had for anything outside of her most pressing concerns, which was raising her two children, now as a single parent. And so, just like that, her career was over.

A diagnosis did follow: dysphonia, essentially 'an abnormal voice'. Hers wasn't working properly, but who knew why? She could talk but couldn't sing. There was no cure, no immediately effective treatment. Doctors shrugged their shoulders, and it's never nice to see doctors shrugging their shoulders. Dysphonia in itself is pretty rare; when presented with a patient showing symptoms, one can only recommend rest, sleep, and a dose of good luck.

'One doctor did use a rather Freudian word. He said he thought it was *hysteria*. That offended me so much, because I didn't think I was the sort of person to be a hysteric, or to have a hysteric condition. And so the humiliations just piled on. Every time I tried to sing, I couldn't. It was so frustrating, and strange, and it was just humiliation, embarrassment, humiliation, embarrassment, and on and on and on.'

On the quiet, she experimented with transcendental meditation, but that didn't help. Intermittently, she'd seek other potential salves, 'but however much I trusted the person I was seeing, it was always the same: "Oh, you're imagining it, you can do it if you really tried." But the thing is, I couldn't, and so eventually I accepted it for what it was. I stopped, and I just got on with life.'

There is little to suggest that a life without music in it has to be an entirely empty and barren existence, and Collins did go on to live a full and fulfilling life without it. Her children took up all of her time, and with little or no financial support from her ex-husband ('which was down partly to me, because I just didn't want anything to do with him at all') she worked hard to provide. She found work at the bookshop in the British Museum, and later worked for a literary agent in London. She got a job in public relations for the English Folk Dance and Song Society, which she thought, and partly hoped, might offer a re-entry back into music at some level, 'but when I arrived there, I found that I was just a secretary to the accountant, who was the most miserable person you've ever met in your life. I stuck it out for six months. Actually, after my first week there, I did try to get my job back at the British Museum, but I was told that they tended not to employ people once they'd left . . .'

She maintained an avid interest in folk music, albeit now at one remove. Meantime, 'being forced into early retirement is never pleasant, and I tried hard to sort of try and enjoy a different life. It's not as if I'd ever been famous in the first place, although, that said, I did occasionally get recognised. I felt rather sanguine about the whole thing. I just planned my life day by day, week by week, month by month, and that worked for me. And after a while, I just abandoned the idea of being able to sing ever again.'

A new obsession was required, though, and duly found: walking. At some point, she met a young actor, much younger than her ('it sounds trite, I know'), who lived not too far from where she and her family were, in Bexhill. They hit it off, and bonded in walking boots on rural pathways that hugged the country's southern perimeter. 'How many thousands of miles we must have walked over the years I don't know, but it brought me incredible happiness, just the physical outlet of it, the beauty of the Downs, and being with a companion you could talk to, and have a conversation with – about art, and music. What a stroke of luck that was for me.'

The years passed as she walked herself into her middle years, and then on into pensionable age. Her children grew up and left home. Collins had made peace with her fate, such as it was. She was content.

In 2004, after a clean-up at home, her very elderly mother asked Collins whether she would like her correspondence back, the letters Collins had sent her back in 1959 while on a recording trip in the US's deep south, where she and the American ethnomusicologist Alan Lomax had been tracking down examples of traditional American folk music and recording them. She'd quite forgotten about the letters. When they arrived, she laid them out in front of her, and was confronted not just by her own past but also a rich musical history. The more letters she read, the more connected she became with the music they discussed, the music she had once been so knowledgeable about. She came to realise that what she was witness to here might just be the early stages of a book, one she herself could write – because, she told herself, why not?

'Suddenly, I felt very inspired again, excited even.'

One doesn't have to sing in order to write a book. And so, on the eve of her seventieth birthday, Shirley Collins began to write.

In 1959, she had been at the very beginning of her career. Alan Lomax was her boyfriend, and together they travelled from Virginia down through Kentucky, Alabama, Mississippi and Arkansas, on the hunt for those traditional folk songs that had been sung by ordinary people as a way of documenting everyday life. These songs told the story of an entire country, and Lomax and Collins would bring them to a wider audience for the first time. The experience would go on to help determine her own path as a singer of traditional English folk songs.

Decades later, Alan Lomax would write a book about his trip, in which he cast himself as the lead, reducing Collins to a bit-part player at best when, in fact, she points out, 'I was actually a key part of the entire process.'

And so, in 2004, she worked to redress the imbalance of his book with her own: *America Over the Water*. Upon publication, it generated much interest, and its success brought her back to the forefront of the scene she had exited four decades previously. She was invited to give lectures around the country, and she did not have to be asked twice.

'Oh, it was lovely, so wonderful to be in front of an audience again, talking to them about the people I'd met, and playing them [recordings of] the music we'd found during our travels.'

A decade later, by now working in a job centre in Brighton, she received an invitation to come to a folk performance at a small

London venue, where, it was vaguely suggested, she might be persuaded to sing a couple of songs.

'I was so fed up of saying no, so I simply said: "Yes, why not?"' She sang the songs, and was rewarded with such a positive reception, she says, that, 'it gave me a jolt of hope.'

But wait. Something curious had occurred here, something remarkable, even though, the way Collins tells it, she hadn't stopped to consider it until just now. At this show, she had been invited to *sing*. She hadn't sung in forty years because she couldn't. So what happened? Where did her dysphonia go? How was she suddenly able to do it?

'Oh!' she says, and then again: 'Oh! Well . . . well, I've no idea. I never thought of that actually . . .' She falls silent. 'Do you know, I never thought about why my voice came back until you mentioned it just now. Isn't that strange?'

Trying in real time to process it, she concedes, very belatedly, that the doctors might have been right in 1978, that it might have been a stress reaction to something profoundly upsetting: the end of her marriage, this thing that had happened to her 'so completely out of the blue.'

Though she might not have dwelt too closely on the source of her miraculous recovery, she did think it wise to capitalise on it. She got busy, with much ground to make up. By now in her eighties, she signed to Domino, the record label that was home to Arctic Monkeys and Beth Gibbons, and in 2016 released her first album in thirty-eight years, *Lodestar*. As if proving the oft-repeated theory that, if a musician hangs around long enough they are rewarded with blanket praise, Shirley Collins was promptly hailed a folk legend, a national treasure. She became the subject of a documentary film and, in 2018, wrote her memoir, *All in the Downs*, which won the Penderyn Music Book Prize. In 2020, by now eighty-five, she released another album, *Heart's Ease*, which the *Observer* praised for its 'unerring brilliance'.

This is not the way most comebacks play out, and of this Collins is acutely aware.

'If you wrote my life story as a piece of fiction, I don't think you'd really believe it. I have no idea how responsible I am for it.'

She refuses to mourn the lost years, because they weren't lost at all, not in the greater sense. There was life, and she lived it.

'You can't mourn, because you're wasting too much emotional time. Also, when I did write about all that in my book, perhaps I got it out of my system, I wasn't bottling it up any more, and pretending that things weren't happening. Mostly, I'm just relieved that things worked out the way they did. Everything that happens in life brings you forward to the place you find yourself in now, and right now I'm in a really nice place, and I feel really grateful for it.

'I just hope I hold on long enough,' she continues, 'because now I really, really, *really* want to sing. Of course, I've accomplished enough to know that I won't leave this world thinking I owe any more to anybody, but I do just want to do . . . *more!* I ought to be satisfied by this stage, but somehow I'm not. Which seems a bit greedy of me, doesn't it?'

32

Bob Geldof had a cunning plan, the last-gasp attempt of a desperate man who didn't know when to quit. The frown between his unplucked eyebrows was becoming a permanent tattoo, his mood increasingly irascible. His back hurt.

He'd always known, and had accepted, that pop was a lethal game – 'when you're dead, you're dead' – but when he found his own band suddenly on their uppers when, just yesterday, they'd been superstar-bound, he thought it too fast, too abrupt, too soon. They had unfinished business.

The very existence of Geldof had long offered proof that rock stars tend to be cut from different cloth: tunnel-visioned obsessives in possession of discombobulating levels of self-belief and a silly swagger. This six-foot beanpole had grown up in Ireland convinced the place was too small to ever contain someone as combustible as he, so moved to London with his band the Boomtown Rats, and had his first number-one single in 1978 – the barnstorming 'Rat Trap' – and another a year later with 'I Don't Like Mondays', one of those rare era-defining songs whose power would probably live on for ever.

But by the early 1980s, they were drowning. Their fifth album, 1982's *V Deep*, tanked, the Rats now a pair of arthritic knees in some increasingly threadbare skinny jeans. Geldof convinced himself that this was an aberration, a blip, and something they could rectify with their sixth, which they would call *In the Long Grass*. They got an old friend, Bob Clearmountain, to mix it, and the results convinced the singer this was their best yet. 'We'd been playing together for a dozen years, we knew what we were doing, we were at the top of our game.' They would rise again.

And they would do so via its lead single, 'Dave', a rather understated rumination about a heroin overdose, of which Geldof was particularly proud; the Who's Pete Townsend called it the best thing he'd heard all year. The record company, meanwhile, were 'relatively enthusiastic', halfway hopeful it had a shot of being a hit. And the Boomtown Rats needed a hit.

'Dave' came out at a time of early Wham!, Spandau Ballet and Duran Duran. 'Everything was very glamorous,' Geldof says. 'If punk was all about the beauty of ugliness, the next generation was the ugliness of beauty; these were the children of Margaret Thatcher, so what were we doing there? Because I guess by this stage we'd usurped our initial reason for our existence. All those bands of my generation, the Jam, the Stranglers, the Pistols . . . the purpose for our [continued] existence in the early 1980s had come and gone. Some of us had become artists, we'd become songwriters – Elvis Costello is a good example – but now we were being pushed out by a generation with something different to say, and something other to offer, something that more exemplified *them*. But of course we were not aware of that. We were listening to what they were doing, and intrigued by it, and they looked fabulous, but we weren't trying to compete.'

All of which played into his deepest, most brooding fears. If the Rats really were being pushed out now, they could hardly complain. They'd done the same thing themselves almost a decade earlier. 'When we'd first come along in 1976, Cliff Richard, Status Quo, we destroyed those people overnight – forget it, goodbye – the Rolling Stones, too. And we'd done that with intent! The charts had been constipated, and we were part of that necessary laxative. This racket that people were calling punk suddenly became the pop music du jour. And so, ten years later, that happened to us. We were largely irrelevant.'

But he wasn't going to go down without a fight, and so the success of 'Dave', by any means necessary, was vital.

'In desperation, because we had a bit of money left, I gave a grand to [band members] Simon and Garry [Crowe and Roberts, drummer and guitarist respectively] to go to chart return shops around the country to buy ten copies of it here, ten copies of it there.'

He thought that bulk-buying would force the song into the charts, and get them back onto television and into people's faces. Geldof had always been good value on TV. One appearance on *Top of the Pops*, he decided, would be enough to get them, in italics, *back*.

A nice idea, albeit illegal, but it didn't work. It wasn't enough. The song failed to chart.

It was over.

On the day he drew a defeated line under 'Dave', and by extension on the beginning of the end of the band, a thoroughly disconsolate Geldof found himself, on a weekday evening in early October, back home in time for dinner. Pop stars are *never* home in time for dinner.

'I'd just had my first baby, I was thirty years old, and I thought: *That's it? What a brutal business pop music is, just completely brutal.* Had the best years of my life really already passed? It didn't feel like it. I had a house in Chelsea, a house in the country, both paid for, but I was worried sick, because what would I do now?'

Being in such a domestic setting unmoored him. He wasn't used to it. He should have been in a recording studio, on the road, in an aeroplane, talking to the press. But the consequences of steering your career into the ground is that nobody really wants you any more. Your time is yours again. Geldof turned the TV on and switched over to the news, watching BBC's Michael Buerk reporting from Ethiopia about a famine on a biblical scale.

As he watched, he felt his own suffering recede in comparison. He was appalled by the images, and profoundly saddened by them. 'Whatever my personal whingeing was, this was another order.'

He felt he had to do something, but what? Charity singles hadn't been invented yet, and so Geldof found himself in the process of doing just that. Perhaps he could write and record a song, the profits from which he could send to Africa, somehow? Then he remembered the still-stinging fate of 'Dave'. Nothing Geldof did alone would help. He needed more people, friends – and musicians, the popular ones. He phoned a friend, Midge Ure from Ultravox, and together they knocked up a song. Over the next few weeks, he approached as many pop stars as possible to take part. Those that were available said yes, while those who were far too busy found Geldof difficult to say no to. And so they said yes, too.

They called themselves Band Aid, and they titled the song 'Do They Know It's Christmas?'

Everybody knows what happened next: good things, record-breaking things, some backlash, plenty of criticism, and, inevitable in pop music, much sneering, but generally an overwhelming sense of people power and, with it, the emergence of a different Bob Geldof entirely: a former pop star now promoted to living saint who, later, would be knighted for his philanthropic efforts. The subsequent concert, Live Aid, boasted only the biggest acts around, but the Boomtown Rats sneaked onto the line-up regardless (it would have been cruel to deny Geldof that). While many bands, most notably Queen and U2, enjoyed renewed popularity in the months ahead as a result of that day, the Rats did not. So emphatically had the singer re-cast himself that no one could view him as anything *but* the man who'd fed the world. A double-edged sword, this: unwanted baggage.

'I'd be walking down the street, and people would just come up to me, giving me money, and I was like: FUCK OFF!'

Becoming the most famous person on the planet had never been his intent. 'I was now this peculiarly unique dynamic force. Nobody wanted me as a musician, they wanted me to be Saint Bob, and I *couldn't stand it*. I mean, I really couldn't stand it. It was so limiting, so imprisoning. Old ladies would approach me the way fifteen-year-olds had at the height of our pop fame, and just reach out to touch me, and then burst into tears. FUCK OFF! My pop fame had fallen off a cliff, and had been superseded by a whole different level of recognition.'

Previously, he continues, 'I'd been famous for having a talent, and whether people liked my songs or not, many had recognised them as good and decent, and I'd been garlanded and silvered, and platinumed and goldened, and then lifetime-achievemented, and all that shit. But it was for that other thing [his charitable endeavours] that I got knighted.'

All Geldof wanted was to return to music. True, he still wanted to 'stop this obscenity that's happening in Africa', and still does, every day, as chairman of Band Aid, but he wanted his band revived. He wasn't finished with the pop-star stuff, not yet. If he'd previously convinced himself that a single reappearance on *Top of the Pops* might revive his fortunes, then surely, post-Live Aid, he was a bankable entity once more?

Discussions ensued. The record company now saw mileage only in Geldof alone, but he counter-argued for two new contracts: one for a new Rats album, another for a solo record. The label capitulated, but problems soon piled up: the band wanted to record first, but the label wanted the solo album first. Geldof compromised by recording both *at once*, a lunatic idea in theory, and an insane one in practice. His bandmates became increasingly irritated, and Geldof grew increasingly exhausted. His bad back, which had been killing him for many months, now seemed intent on making metaphor literal. Inevitably, the band broke up.

Geldof would go on to release six solo albums over the years, but he found himself moving increasingly into business, which was where he could really make the most of his organisational genius, his ability to get things done. In the early 1990s, he co-founded a television production company, Planet 24, which would produce some of the decade's most successful shows, among them *The Word* and *The Big Breakfast*. He was its very public figurehead, and so remained very famous indeed, simply for being who he was: Bob Geldof.

'I was never good-looking, so I always wanted to get rich, famous and laid,' he says. 'I wanted to use the platform fame gives you, and I've done that.'

He sold his shares in Planet 24, and started other companies. His private life became, and remained, complicated. He continued to work with, and for, Africa. And he got very rich. In 2002, he became one of the founding partners of Groupcall, a company that provides data extraction to track the whereabouts of school-age children via their phones. Early in the twenty-first century, such tech was in its infancy, and Geldof was no expert, but he liked the name, and the fact that it concerned children's safety. Groupcall grew as the technology around it did. In 2020, they sold their shares to a giant US company. 'That makes it sound like it was for billions,' he says. 'It wasn't, but my partner got very wealthy . . . and I got wealth*ier*.'

All this extra-curricular activity suggests that, if music no longer needed Bob Geldof, then Bob Geldof no longer needed music, either. Thing is, he did. He couldn't let it lie, and kept returning, and not just with the sporadic solo albums, which, he points out, did well in Europe and Australia. The Rats reformed in 2013 ('the time was right'), and then came back again in 2020 to coincide with a major documentary about them in which the likes of Bono and Sinead O'Connor gushed over their cultural significance, an obituary Geldof lived to see. The band released an album, played live with a furious sense of purpose, and Geldof, who was sixty-eight at the time, felt reborn. Being in the Boomtown Rats allowed him to become a rock 'n' roll star again: 'Bobby Boomtown', as he'd styled himself.

'I hadn't understood that before. I hadn't realised the disconnect between me – this sensible, articulate person who popped up on television occasionally – and this lairy lout who fronted the band. It's a completely different character, I realise that now, and Bobby Boomtown *could not give a fuck*. Up there on stage, I sing whatever I like, and I look like a fucking idiot, and I jump all over the place. I never behaved like that as a solo performer, and I'm somebody else again in my other concerns.' Being back with the Rats allowed him to step back to a time when things had been more straightforward, less ambiguous; *free*. Music, for him, had always been elemental.

On his passport, Bob Geldof's profession is listed as 'musician', and that is how he continues to define himself. Not 'saint'. All he ever wanted was to get out of Ireland, be in a rock group, get famous, be happy, stay sated. He's managed varying levels and stages of each, and much more besides, not all of which he bargained for.

But all of it was ultimately facilitated by his being a singer in a band. Early on, he took a chance, faked a feeling of self-belief until he believed it himself, then ran with it, loudly. It worked.

TEN

THE MAVERICKS

Maverick: /ˈmav(ə)rɪk/, noun
1. An unorthodox or independent-minded person.
2. A singer unlikely to write a hit single to order, and a genial Christmas song? *Never*.
Similar: individualist, non-conformist, free spirit.
Consequential side effect: vexingly difficult to work with, a right ball-ache.

33

'Over the course of my career,' says Rufus Wainwright, 'I've had eleven managers.' He makes this point with a smile, and then a propulsive laugh: he's *boasting* here. 'The general consensus, I think, is that people don't know *how* to manage me. On the one hand, I have a lot of notoriety, I can tour the world, but then I can also disappear and try to conquer this whole other realm, the classical world, which requires me to disappear for months on end into this black hole. And pop managers, well, they couldn't really . . .' They couldn't really *manage* him, is what he's trying to say. And this is perfectly fine for Wainwright, one of the more outré performers of his generation. He wouldn't have it any other way.

'Sometimes I'll think: Did I really walk away from all this just to write an opera? And if I did, is that either incredibly brilliant of me, or incredibly stupid? Because right now, I can't tell.'

Wainwright has always thought that the trick to, as he puts it, 'all this', is to branch out, spread your wings, harness the creativity that elevated you into this position in the first place, and then use it to reach for the stars, the glittering, sparkling stars. Of course, it helps if you happen to be the progeny of musical legends as he is, which should mean, genetically speaking, that reaching for stars is something woven so tightly into your DNA that it resembles a nice crochet pattern. He's been singing since the early 1990s, and continues to do so today, but he peaked – certainly commercially and arguably creatively – back in 2003.

'It's all a matter of perspective,' he says, correctly.

His father was Loudon Wainwright III, his mother Kate McGarrigle. The former was a famously louche singer-songwriter of the 1970s, who was so jealous of his new son taking up the lion's share of his wife's attention that he wrote a song about it, 'Rufus is a Tit Man'; the latter was a folk artist much revered in her native Canada. The couple divorced when Rufus was three years old, and you do not grow up in such an environment, he suggests, surrounded by harmonious music and marital strife, without inhaling it and having it define you.

'There have always been two forces that have driven me in my career, in terms of making it both interesting for myself, and for the world. One is the conscious, the other, the subconscious.'

Here was an opera fanatic who craved the adulation of pop stardom, and a pop star desperate to write librettos. Both, in his estimation, were as theatrical as the other, and both well within his grasp. He set his heart on becoming a pop star first, because pop stars tend to be young and wild, and Wainwright, in his twenties, was certainly that. The opera could come later, when his hair turned grey.

His pursuit was studious. He'd learned that to become a pop star, you had to lead a certain kind of life, and for this he was entirely prepared. Pop stars, in the main, are not wallflowers. 'I was like: "At all costs, I must conquer this territory! I will do anything in order to break through those palace walls!" If that meant doing drugs with whoever, sleeping with whoever, fine. I mean, within reason, of course, but I was getting to all the right parties, the parties you had to be seen at, so I was really grasping that mantle. I'm talking here about something you'd enjoy, incidentally; it wasn't, like, a Harvey Weinstein situation. No, this was something I *wanted* to do. I wanted to live this crazy rock 'n' roll life and become a star, so I did.'

As estate agents are fond of saying, location is everything. Wainwright knew that Montréal, where he'd grown up, was too sleepy, nice and convivial for the pursuit of carnage, and so he decamped to Los Angeles, where all new residents are required to sell their souls. The drugs were readily available here, and they were good. It was amid this climate, in 1998, that he recorded his self-titled debut. It got good notices and the nodding appreciation of his peers, where he'd been expecting garlands. For his next album, he needed to turn up the dial.

'For a lot of people, the seminal work is the second album, and so I remember being incredibly cognisant of that jump, and just how important it was likely to be for me. I remembered how important my mother's second album was, and artists like the Eurythmics. The "sophomore album": that's the hallmark. If it doesn't match up to the debut, and beat it, then you're kind of doomed.'

Sick of the sunshine, he decided a certain seediness was now required. He switched coasts and moved to New York, specifically Chelsea, because Chelsea was where, in the sixties and seventies, rock stars came to take overdoses and die. What's more romantic than that? Here, he became enthusiastically vampiric, would sleep during the day and rise at dusk to sink his fangs into the twilight world around him. Every night another party, so much sex on offer, and he did so many drugs – crystal meth, in particular, but also ecstasy and ketamine – that he went temporarily blind. The overdose he was so earnestly pursuing remained tantalisingly out of reach, but only just – perfect for the myth he was busy constructing. This was life lived at the extreme, and from which great songs are born.

'I loved it, I really did. There were some difficult moments, sure, and some challenging periods, but, look, I wanted to be there. I had songs to peddle, and so this was my repertoire.'

With 2001's *Poses*, a beautifully ripe album that offered everything that would go on to prove his hallmarks – cherry red melodies, lush arrangements, and a vocal style that contained all the collapsing drama of the final fifteen minutes of *Swan Lake* – Wainwright found himself on the cusp of the big time, almost there. In his avid pursuit of hedonism, he'd been proved right: so long as he didn't actually die, this was a win–win situation. This was how you became infamous.

'I remember one moment in particular, incredibly inebriated in the back of a taxi, it was summer, and very hot, and we were just rushing down Sixth Avenue, and I knew that this was maybe the happiest I'd ever been in my life. It was like I just clocked the moment, you know, that this was *my* moment, that I'd never get any better than this. Why? Because I'd made it in New York!'

But the hedonist, like Oliver Twist, always craves more, and Rufus Wainwright wanted more. You don't burn the candle at both ends without something melting in the middle. He could boast proper demons now, tempestuous mood swings, increasingly dark thoughts, broken love affairs, broken hearts, and a drug habit bordering on addiction. The warrior-like pose he'd affected throughout the recording of his second album was now spent. Also, he still wasn't successful enough. All very well that a hip corner of downtown New York was at last affording him its respect before finding something else to fawn over, but he wanted a bigger scale: he wanted curtain calls, the entire world on its feet.

His third album, *Want One*, arrived in the summer of 2003. Its opening track, 'Oh What a World', brazenly sampled Ravel's *Bolero*, and it ended with 'Dinner at Eight', a spectacular lyrical takedown of his father's myriad paternal failings amid rococo flourishes of baroque melodic splendour. If Wainwright was trying to announce his masterpiece here, then job done. The world did swoon, this time. In fact, for a time, it was impossible to speak to any musician who *didn't* proclaim: 'Have you heard the new Rufus Wainwright?' He was among the most celebrated songwriters of his generation now, more fêted than either of his parents, more celebrated than his singer-songwriter sister, Martha.

This was very much *it*.

But now that he'd done it, he could only try to repeat it with successive albums that were good but not quite as good, even if they were occasionally better. With his growing fanbase satisfied, he could only continue to please them. Surprising them would be conspicuously harder.

'Oh, I was old news by the time I was thirty,' he says. 'And I knew it. I knew, very fundamentally, that that was the case, that that was how the industry was viewing me, especially in America. They were already on to their next young slaughterhouse victim.'

Time, then, for Act II.

Wainwright wrote his first opera, possibly with a quill in the cramped garret of his imagination, in 2009. He was thirty-six, still precociously young for opera, which of course pleased him no end. *Prima Donna* recounted the story of Régine, a soprano who hadn't sung in public for six years, and who fell for the journalist sent to find out why she'd withdrawn from the spotlight. It was originally commissioned by the Metropolitan Opera in New York but ultimately never staged there, for reasons lost to the small print of bureaucracy. Or maybe they just didn't like it? *Prima Donna* eventually got its debut at the Manchester International Festival, Wainwright electing to dress for the opening night as Verdi.

In the same way Verdi wasn't always appreciated in his lifetime, neither was Wainwright's first effort. '[A] flimsy plot, spun out into a cheesy piece of full-length musical theatre,' wrote the *Independent*. 'Musically, [it] is at best banal, at worst boring.'

Wainwright was philosophical. 'You don't hit your stride [in opera] until your forties.'

Nevertheless, he was on a different path now, and saw little point in just cranking out more studio albums for the sake of it. To further flummox certain critics – and fans – he recorded an album of Judy Garland songs with a flamboyance that made his operatic effort seem as sombre as a funeral – the accompanying DVD was entitled *Rufus! Rufus! Rufus! Does Judy! Judy! Judy!* – and he later added music to the sonnets of William Shakespeare for the album *Take All My Loves,* adamant with each new project that in order to keep his creative hunger alive, he had to stretch all the way to the tips of his toes. No wonder he went through quite so many managers. In tearing up the script, he was becoming increasingly difficult to read.

'Look, I don't pretend in any way to be an innovator,' he says, 'and I've never tried to reinvent the wheel. I am not in any way avant-garde. Instead, I've simply always had this searing need to do *exactly* what I'm feeling in the moment, and so that's where I put my eggs, how I play my cards. And I think that, at the end of the day, my fans, the listeners, can hear that. They can hear that whatever I do, there is a sincerity to it.

'The singer in me,' he continues, 'has an appetite, this strange animalistic quality that lives inside my singing voice, and needs to be fed. So that's why I'm always pushing myself. I push myself melodically, with my own songs, but I also want to sing other people's songs. So I will sing Judy, I'll sing Joni Mitchell, and if I get a crazy need to suddenly sing a bunch of Canadian folk songs, or maybe my mother's old songs, or to collaborate with someone else, like Robbie Williams, or my sister, then you know what? I'll do that. To be a great singer, I feel, is all about being a great survivor, and that's what I'm trying to do in this crazy industry: survive.'

The very fact of his surviving-not-dying has brought him much fulfilment in life. He remained close to his mother until her death from clear cell sarcoma in 2010, and has reconciled with his father. In 2012, he married Jörn Weisbrodt, an artistic director, and a year later Wainwright and Leonard Cohen's daughter Lorca collaborated on a strictly biological project and had a child together, Viva Katherine; Weisbrodt, Wainwright explains, is 'Deputy Dad'.

Like many pop stars of his vintage – he is almost fifty – he has taken up painting in recent years, an empty canvas as inviting to him as the piano in his front room, and he remains fuelled by an ambition that will see him create until the day he does at last die – of natural causes, he hopes. His inspiration in this pursuit is Ludwig van Beethoven. It was hardly going to be Axl Rose, was it?

'They say that as Beethoven was dying, he heard some lightning, or maybe thunder, or something – and if it was thunder, it must have been pretty loud, as he was deaf – and that he stood up and tried to conduct the lightning, and then he died. I find that rather enthralling, don't you?'

34

'Look at my performances, look at the videos, look at what I'm *doing!*'

Most mavericks, by their very nature, are fated to exist on the very edges of popular culture, miles from Kylie, nowhere near Coldplay. But this is fine: it's their natural setting, and it feeds them; there is cachet to being misunderstood in your own lifetime.

When Björk Guðmundsdóttir quit the Icelandic band the Sugarcubes in 1992 to become the most wilfully maverick pop star of the age, each of her six bandmates were required to seek other gigs, new lives. One of them, Einar Örn, became a bartender.

'I just fell back to being drunk in Reykjavík,' Örn says happily, 'and being part of the local scene again.'

Örn had just become a father, and so the solidity of a nine-to-five, even one that stretched to the frigid post-midnight hours of closing time, suited him. He hadn't left the music industry completely; he had simply diversified while considering his next move. The Sugarcubes, emanating from an island of just 250,000 people, had had little idea that they'd ever go on to find success all over the world with glorious oddities like 'Birthday' and 'Deus', or that their debut album, *Life's Too Good*, would be among the most celebrated records of 1987, but then this was down almost exclusively, if not *quite* entirely, to Björk, a singer of rare elfin charm, and someone whose evident sense of artistic abandon was never going to be contained within one unit for very long.

Watching his former co-singer blossom was, Örn says, 'fantastic, absolutely fantastic. I was joyous for her, on her behalf, that she was able to do what she'd always wanted to do. There was never any envy or any regrets regarding the Sugarcubes. It was good while it lasted, and then, you know, you move on.'

And so he did. Alongside the bartending, he worked for various internet companies. For four years, he was a city councillor, promoting arts and culture in his hometown, and put on gigs for Blur and the Prodigy. He became an artist, his paintings reminiscent of the New York pop artist Keith Haring: an endless parade of skeletal images that resemble monsters. 'I draw what I see,' he says.

If the Sugarcubes had always been a wilfully perverse kind of pop band, their warped lullabies dipped in absinthe and sung in hiccups, Örn was its maverick extreme. Like Bez in the Happy Mondays, he was an addendum to the main focal point, and a seemingly deranged one at that: his style of dancing gave the impression of being beaten senseless by invisible adversaries. Unlike Bez, he was permitted a microphone, which might not initially have been the wisest idea. Unsure of what to do with it, he simply shouted into it.

'I was just going to bring noise into the fold,' he says, 'because that was an obvious choice for me: noise. They [his fellow band members] knew how to play their instruments; I knew how to make noise. It was only when the drummer said, "You sing," that I started to sing, too.'

But what to sing? He'd never considered songwriting before. On pieces of scrap paper, he now gave it a go, writing three words per line, then three more, until he had something that was, in his estimation, 'poem-related. And that was the key for me, that I could express myself. I liked that.'

This was how Örn came to invoke his inner shaman, previously dormant but now rudely alive. And so he and Björk began to *duet*, though not in any way comparable to, say, Sonny and Cher, or Peaches and Herb, or Hoddle and Waddle. They jarred. 'In my mind, I was always doing pure pop music, but people always say to me I'm too avant-garde. I'm like: "Really?"'

Örn enjoyed himself in the Sugarcubes, and had uncorked something that would not now go back into its bottle simply because his singing partner had gone out into the world. He started another band, Ghostigital, which exists intermittently, on an ethos of *no compromise*. They are not overly concerned with recording albums so much as they are live performances that purportedly benefit from no rehearsals, just improvisation: a series of electronically enhanced soundscapes over which Örn screams his insides out and throws himself across the stage, impervious to the threat of injury.

'It's art,' he says, 'and it's addressing my shaman, releasing unknown powers, unknown forces, to see what shape they take. It's very loud.'

It sounds dreadful.

'It's great,' he counters. 'Some people, they've puked when we play, because it's so extreme.'

Like Einar Örn's former bandmate Björk, Róisín Murphy was possessed of too singular a vision to simply spend her career in one band, singing one kind of song. She had too many ideas and concepts, where the brilliant and the hare-brained entwined to create something off-kilter, and occasionally divine. She'd see songs visually, as three-dimensional renderings of her peculiar imagination; she'd see how they'd look in video, and the clothes she'd have to wear in order to fully render them as three-dimensional depictions, and how dazzling it would be. But only Murphy could see it; to everyone else, it was a blur.

'You have to pull people along with you,' is how Murphy describes this singular pursuit, and her necessary fight to conjure it. 'You know, I've never worked with the same [video] crew twice. I always try to lay it out to them as clearly as possible, but then to them I'm just a not very famous middle-aged singer trying to tell them what to do, trying to tell them my ideas, and that it'll be okay in the end, it'll work out . . . But I still have to win them over, and that is so incredibly hard, so incredibly frustrating.' She laughs out loud, a dog barking in the distance. 'But I don't let go, and I pull it off eventually.'

For Murphy, the maverick requires tenacity. She has to show teeth. 'See, the whole point of creativity is to finish things, to see it through. I've seen so many creative people, really brilliant people, simply too afraid to let others hear their music, to see it, experience it.' With this, she empathises. She feels it, too. 'I've got to be careful I don't let myself get like that. But it's frustrating; it's frustrating when you're misunderstood.'

She wants to convey just how important it is that she defines herself in this way, and that all artists do: with this attention to detail, this bloody-mindedness, and an unswerving need to bring such visions off, in sound and colour. The music will benefit from it.

Or will it? Occasionally she'll wonder: *Yes, but what's the point of all this*? 'Because,' she says, 'I'm just a fucking girl doing some tunes at the end of the day, aren't I? I need to remind myself of that sometimes.'

Róisín Murphy joined her first band out of love. Born in Ireland and raised in Manchester, she was nineteen when she met, and fell for, a guitarist and songwriter named Mark Brydon. It was the mid-nineties. Brydon was older than her, taciturn in a way that made him enigmatic. Emboldened by drink, although Murphy doesn't particularly need to drink to feel emboldened, she approached him, asking if he liked her tight sweater. Lo, Moloko was born.

The more dance music bled into the mainstream during that decade, the more Moloko made sense. They blended electronic with funk, elements of trip hop and the cartoon caricatures of pure pop, then launched the entire confection into the air and watched confetti rain down. Several of their songs would later be hailed Ibiza classics – 'Sing It Back', 'The Time Is Now' – while others threw deliberately more oblique shapes that made them less easy to pigeonhole, and consequently more fascinating. You were increasingly interested to hear what they might come up with next.

As ABBA can attest, it's rarely a good idea to mix the personal with the professional, even if in the short-term it does add emotional heft to your songwriting. Murphy's relationship with Brydon was an intense one, fuelled by alcohol and drugs. Murphy chose not to hide this, and in fact tended to play it out, irrespective of who came into her orbit. Visiting press were often coerced into bearing uncomfortable witness to another of their spats, which often reached their climax on tour, post-show, euphoria loosening lips and confirming not only that the course of true love rarely runs smooth, but that only a fool would cross someone as formidable as Murphy.

By March 2003, the pair had split, but were contractually obliged to promote and tour their latest, and last, album, *Statues*. By now, Murphy was a rare kind of star: unpredictable, dominant, inspired. Murphy herself, however, was less convinced of her worth.

'I didn't know if I could do all this without my boyfriend. I was coming up to thirty, and I didn't know whether the whole thing had come to an end for me. The band had only broken up because *we* [she and Brydon] had broken up. We were still very much a romantic couple when we'd started *Statues*, but after that it was just palaver. We'd broken up, got back together for a couple of nights, then a few months went by, you can't stop calling each other, but it was really just the trail-off, a long letting go.' The tour itself was a success. 'Oh, we had a fucking ball. Well, *I* did, anyway.

I don't know about Brydon. He might have been quietly seething the whole time . . .'

Home, alone, no bandmates around her because she no longer had bandmates, and no longer in love, she panicked. How quiet everything had suddenly become.

'I was shitting myself. I never felt like I'd really hit my stride, and I certainly didn't feel that I was now running off into some great career without him. It just felt that my entire career was in the balance.'

In time, she began working with somebody new, the producer Matthew Herbert. Together they made her first solo album, *Ruby Blue*, 'and everything just came, it felt natural. Matthew would record me moving, dancing, shouting, screaming, banging things around the house. It was like the whole album was just made out of *me*, and that was perfect, in retrospect. For him, I couldn't make a bad sound, I could only make interesting ones. With him, I really started owning my own shit, much more than I ever did in Moloko. Now, as a solo artist, with Matthew producing, I could work quicker, was more focused, and it was all so much more enjoyable. I found that the enjoyment is not [comprised of] the awful bits *before* you make something, but when you've actually *made* it.'

The success of that album led to her signing to EMI for her next record, *Overpowered*. 'For the first time – and in fact, the *only* time – I didn't have to worry how much everything was costing; I could do whatever I wanted. I could talk about *vision*.'

Full artistic control is rarely offered to artists, but for *Overpowered*, Murphy got it, and she used it. She started dressing like the kind of clown Salvador Dalí might have created. If she wanted a string section to be recorded in, say, Philadelphia, 'I got it, because I was boss. I was flown all around the world, business class, first class, Miami to Philadelphia to Barcelona, then back to Miami, then Las Vegas, then New York for the mixing. It was,' she says, '*amazing*.'

It was also to be short-lived. Artistic control is only re-awarded if it pays off. On this occasion, it didn't. The album reached number twenty in the charts, nineteen places lower than everyone had hoped, meaning the record company didn't see a return on its investment. Her contract came to an abrupt end during her first pregnancy. Then her relationship with her unborn baby's father ended. She went back home to Ireland, where she lived with her mother, and didn't make a peep for the next eight years. She routinely fretted, but she needn't have: everyone that has a period of great productivity will, at some point, fall silent for a while, and Murphy had good reason to. She tried writing songs, but nothing came. No matter – at least, not for the time being.

'But I tell you what,' she says. 'I made a lot of money during that period, *a lot*.'

While her creativity remained a fallow field, her back catalogue was busy working for her. Invitations came to DJ at clubs and private events, the currency of her name alone enough to draw crowds. She'd once been a singer whose best songs had become club anthems; it made sense, then, that she who makes them can spin them, too. But Murphy was never a fan of DJing. 'Always hated it, if I'm honest, but I did respect it, and I'd always known that DJs had been so important to my life. Without a handful of them, I wouldn't be doing what I'm doing today; they were my educators, and they'd certainly taught me more than school ever had.'

So she said yes to the invites. She DJed – at private parties, for brand launches, and occasionally for friends' weddings. Her favourites were the Russian oligarchs.

'I was in Mykonos one time, took my mum and the baby, and we were guests of some very rich Russian people, really nice people, playing for their kid's twenty-first birthday. [We were] staying in this amazing villa, swimming in the pool every day, my mum saying to me: "If you'd asked me as a young woman if I was ever going to end up here, in this amazing villa in Greece, and all of it paid for by a Russian, I'd have told you you're a fucking madwoman!"

'So it was kind of an interesting time for me. I wasn't highly visible, from the public's point of view, but I made loads of money, and I didn't have to work too hard for it.'

When she returned to recording music in 2015, she did so with habitually wilful intent. The album that, at least at first, was hailed her comeback wasn't actually an album at all, but rather an EP, *Mi Senti*, which comprised cover versions of six purportedly classic Italian pop songs that nobody outside of Italy had ever heard (her DJ/producer boyfriend, and father to her second child, is Italian), sung convincingly in their original language. This was no cunning ploy, clearly, to wheedle her way back into the charts. Instead, it was a statement of singular intent: *I'll do as I please*. 'I liked the songs,' she says, 'so I sang them.'

Subsequent releases – full albums, this time, labouring under deliberately ominous titles like *Hairless Toys* and *Take Her Up to Monto* – would follow a comparably idiosyncratic path, strange and curious things, thrumming fabulously to their own beat, each sounding nothing like Moloko, nothing like her earlier solo work, but instead entirely their own thing, and entirely Róisín Murphy.

This, you might think, is a good thing: to be an outlier, master of your own destiny, beholden to nothing but the peculiar colours that blossom in your mind whenever the lights are out. Murphy is the recipient of the kind of praise most artists would kill for. Critics hail her singular vision, and that she does what she does so very well. They wonder why she doesn't connect with a wider audience too blinkered to notice the real thing when they see it, and they mean this as a compliment. But Murphy reads this differently. She considers it a criticism and a slight; it makes her clench her fists, thin her lips and snarl. The maverick in excelsis: underappreciated by cloth ears.

'Every time they come to write about me,' she says, 'the first fucking, *fucking*, FUCKING paragraph is: "Why is Róisín Murphy not more popular?" So the first thing they say is negative, never: "Well, she's amazing, great"; no, the first line is: "She's not a pop star." But I deserve to have respect! To have the slate wiped clean every time they come to look at a new record I've made. Look at my performances, look at the videos, look at what I'm *doing*!"'

There's a reason why so many pop stars tend to conform, to rein in any rampancy, to tone down the vibrancy, and to not dress all the time like a surrealist's nightmare. It's so much *easier*, it exacts far less of a toll, and it stops the vein that runs from the forehead into the hairline from throbbing quite so much.

She must suffer terribly from headaches.

'I do like boats in the Mediterranean,' she muses, 'and sometimes I think I'd just like to do that instead, a happy retirement on me boat, in the Med, and just fucking relax, you know?'

35

'In some ways, I think I really wasn't suited to music at all'

The dress might have been a mistake, in retrospect. And if not the dress, then the way it hung down, beneath the nipples, while being raised at its hem to reveal tight black underwear, a posing pouch. The stockings were an elegant touch. But what was most confounding about this ensemble, displayed on the cover of the album *My Beauty*, was that it was modelled by Kevin Rowland, formerly of Dexys Midnight Runners, a man whose most enduring fashion statement to date had been a pair of dungarees and a donkey jacket. There was nothing wrong with him wearing a dress now – he'd always had an eye for fashion, and it did look good on him; David Beckham, who would be photographed wearing a sarong two years later, presumably took note – but the intent behind it was never made clear, and the reaction it prompted back in 1999, from both his fans and even his own record label, undermined the record it represented, a collection of lovingly rendered cover versions of his favourite songs. *My Beauty* was supposed to herald the comeback of one of the UK's most celebrated songwriters, his first album in eleven years. Over twenty years later it would be hailed, by some at least, as a minor masterpiece, but back then it conspired to bury him.

'I found that very disappointing,' Rowland says. 'It took me a while to come back from that.'

By this point in his long and disjointed career, Kevin Rowland was used to being misunderstood, a singer almost continually at loggerheads: with himself, his band members, his ever-changing sense of style, his core fanbase. In 1982, then the frontman of Dexys, he wrote 'Come On Eileen', a barrel-chested declaration of defiant love packed with a visceral potency, and whose appearance at every wedding disco ever since – a legal requirement on mainland Britain since 1983 – has somehow not dimmed its celebratory power so much as perpetually enhanced it.

But 'Come On Eileen' hints at a picture of freewheeling joy that was otherwise largely absent from the band's day-to-day existence. Things were, in fact, always complicated. There's a story dating from two years before in which Rowland felt compelled to steal the master tapes of his band's debut album and hold them to ransom, belatedly furious that the royalty rate EMI had offered wasn't sufficient. Unless they improved the offer – on a contract already signed by the band – they wouldn't see the tapes again. Rowland was the son of a burly builder, and was burly himself; he was good at threatening behaviour, and seemed unconcerned that it may not necessarily endear him to his paymasters. Later in their career, upon the receiving end of less-than-favourable reviews in the music press, he'd articulate his displeasure to the journalists that wrote them with a swift punch to the face.

Dexys' music had always been a brilliantly idiosyncratic act, coupling the propulsive momentum of Van Morrison circa 1964 with funk and soul and saxophone parps, Rowland's voice like whiskey dipped in beef stock, raising both the hairs and the hackles. They looked less like a band than they did a gang when they formed in Birmingham in 1978, and their first number one – 1980's 'Geno', a raucous tribute to the soul singer Geno Washington – came comparatively quickly. This, and 'Come On Eileen', constituted a gathering momentum from which more, surely, was to come – so long as Rowland was willing. Turns out he wasn't.

By 1985, Dexys were a very different band, and their third album, *Don't Stand Me Down*, proved it. Gone were the dungarees and donkey jackets, and in came sober suits, the four remaining members – there had been seven at one point – now more resembling a legal team that specialised in divorce. The music was more thoughtful, more ruminative; it had a whiff of melancholy and introspection to it. The album was only seven tracks long, and none sounded like singles. The critics, unwittingly asking for a punch from its author, admitted to not liking it very much, but, as they would later do with Rowland's solo album, subsequently decided it might have been a masterpiece after all. Too late; the damage was done. And there was damage: Rowland, once so cocksure and full of swagger, had lost his confidence. When they played live now, he found himself drenched in fear, a worrying new development.

'Between songs, I was just thinking to myself: *Oh boy, I'd better not leave any space between these songs, because they're going to heckle me, they're going to shout things, unpleasant things.*'

Three years previously, they'd been hailed the best band in Britain. What, he wondered, had gone so very wrong? Awful thought: was it *his* fault? Even today, he's not sure. 'I don't know, I don't know. I just knew that I couldn't write the same old songs again, and so I never even tried. I wanted to do something different. But people didn't want anything different from us, that was the problem.'

Don't Stand Me Down, living up to its immediate critical reception, flopped, and Rowland, so recently such a thrilling creative talent, became the man who fell to earth.

The first thing he felt when he landed was relief. 'Now I could get off this merry-go-round at last, because I'd been feeling the pressure. But I was also disappointed, definitely. I'd been too confident, too arrogant; I'd thought that everyone would just hear our new album and go "Wow".' When that didn't happen, he became, he thinks, 'probably quite depressed.' He didn't leave the house, and started taking drugs. It would be six months before anything tangible happened, his record company extending an olive branch in the form of a 'debriefing session'. They suggested that he re-record his vocal for one of the album's tracks, 'Listen to This', only this time with a little more intent, perhaps more energy. This was progress, of sorts, the label showing willing. Rowland refused. The original vocal, he told them, was good enough.

'Looking back, it probably wouldn't have been the end of the world if I *had* re-recorded it. I *might* have got a better vocal for it. I don't know, I don't know. But if it had been a hit, and made the album more successful, that . . . well, it would have been a good thing.'

But, he says, 'I just felt I had too much of the weight of the world on my shoulders with that album, and I felt *so* misunder-stood. When people are telling you that you've fucked up, you kind of start to believe it. I started to believe it.'

He went back to his drugs as a counterbalance to feeling 'like a loser, a fuck-up. I was pissed off. At what? At it all! It'd all been very intense, an endless merry-go-round, no holidays, working all the time, all just about the music, and I was exhausted. Music had been an obsession, and it had taken a lot of brainpower, not just for me, but for all the band. I needed a break, really. And in those days, I wasn't rational – not like I am now. I'm much more rational now. Not completely, not *that* rational, perhaps' – he smiles – 'but I can understand the value of it. But I didn't know how to do that shit in those days. I was just not conscious, really. We'd just done the best thing we'd ever done, and it hadn't worked, so what were we supposed to do next?'

Precisely what he was supposed to do, in a professional sense, was to simply go away. And for three years, he did. Nothing was heard from him until 1988, when, at the age of thirty-three, he released his first solo album, *The Wanderer*. Its songs had been dashed off quickly, 'in half an hour, an hour tops', an exercise in going through the motions. This would prove a waste of time – for him, for those who worked on it with him, and for his label, whose patience was being sorely tested.

'You walk into the record label, and they just weren't as friendly as they used to be. It's funny,' he says, 'nobody ever says to you: "Kevin, you know what? We're not sure what we're going to do next with you." Instead, they just blame you when it all fails. When the record's not a success, it's *your* fault, and so you take on all those feelings. The label doesn't sit you down and talk to you. And they don't drop you either, because they don't want to lose you to the competition – just in case you *do* come up with something good next. And so they just remain sort of not as friendly, no more: "Hey, Kevin! How're you?" It's a head-fuck, and you just have to work it out yourself.'

Obsessives tend to struggle at reinvention. When he was eventually dropped, Rowland discovered he had no other interests outside of music. He simply didn't know how to function as someone not entirely consumed by his work. If cocaine numbed him, it also drained his finances. Signing on quickly sobered him up. At the dole office, he was asked whether he could see himself as a waiter, a carpenter, a builder. He had to fill out forms in waiting rooms sitting on hard plastic chairs beneath unflattering lighting. Some of his fellow unemployed recognised him. They'd sing 'Come On Eileen' out loud, as if half-expecting him to sing along. 'I could have done without that,' he says.

Any money he did make, he spent on more drugs. His life became 'chaotic', and by 1991 he was declared bankrupt. Next came rehab, living in close confines with twenty-six other men, 'and I'd never felt so alone in my life.'

One afternoon while at rehab, he heard the radio playing 'The Greatest Love of All', a soppy but heartfelt croon written by George

Benson but later made globally famous by Whitney Houston. He found the song overwhelming, felt that it spoke directly to him, and came to feel that its message, its spirit, did nothing less than save his life, in the way that songs sometimes do. Its power never entirely left him. By 1999, at last feeling re-energised towards his erstwhile profession, he knew what he had to do: record an album of covers, not necessarily of his all-time favourites, but rather comprised of those that had spoken to him most at key moments in his life: the Beatles' 'The Long and Winding Road', the Monkees' 'Daydream Believer', 'You'll Never Walk Alone' by Rogers and Hammerstein, and 'The Greatest Love of All'. He would sing them with an earnestness so conspicuously free of flare or showmanship that they sounded more like confessionals. He'd call the album *My Beauty*, and for its sleeve he would wear a dress, because, he says, 'I thought it looked good.'

This was music as purging, made in gratitude, delivered with a devout respect.

It would not find an audience – not yet.

'I've done a lot of work on myself over the years, and at my age now, sixty-six, I've had a lot of experience,' he says. 'No offence to my family, but I had no tools for living, for growing up. I used to believe that if I got successful, all my problems would be over. But they weren't. The insecurities came out double. The very worst thing is when everyone thinks you're having a great time. It's hard to say to them: "You know what? I'm really struggling here." If you haven't got it going on inside you, then whatever else you do doesn't really mean very much.'

Since quitting drugs, he has given traditional therapy a wide berth, seeking instead a different kind of enlightenment, much of it spiritual: Buddhism, Taoism, 'some Indian stuff, Chinese stuff, just anything, really. A bit of meditation. And I've also learned how to admit when I'm wrong. I'm a better person for it now, definitely.'

In 2002, he fell in love, and was set to marry. His bride-to-be had a daughter, he was living in Brighton, and together they wanted to buy a house, but he couldn't afford it, so he got the band back together. This was supposed to be a stopgap with one directive in mind: the musician's equivalent of popping to the cash machine. But being back with the band re-energised him. Music! He realised just how much he'd missed it, and the obsession took over again, music all he could think about.

The marriage didn't happen.

Kevin Rowland eventually paid off all his debts in 2004, finally entering into a space of comparative financial security with 'Come On Eileen' paying him a living wage. In 2020 he oversaw the re-release of the much-beleaguered *My Beauty*, this time to rapturous critical acclaim. If musical mavericks are destined to rarely be appreciated in their time, Rowland was forced to concede that later was better than never. But he also had to admit, to himself, that this abiding preoccupation in life had been his undoing, an endless trial by fire. Music had used him up; he was worn out.

And now, he's had enough.

'I'm trying not to do this any more, actually. I really don't want to do it any more. It's funny,' he suggests, 'I've got the best manager now that I've ever had [Tim Vigon], and I'm not making him any money! But he's such a great help to me, in so many ways. I mean, look, there might be a time when I do want to do it again, if I managed to get some songs together, but these days, I'm wiser, more sensible, and the fact is I'm interested in other things.'

He attempted to start his own fashion line in 2019, but that didn't work out. 'There's a couple of other things, which I'm not going to tell you about, but I do want to do them, and it won't be music.

'I wish I'd been able to enjoy it more, to have been able to relax and just enjoy it. But I wasn't. There's a lot of things I wish I'd done differently, but I do feel at peace now, and I want to be more present in my life, to enjoy it more. If I was able to do music in a balanced way where I wasn't so fucking passionate about it, and where it didn't just burn me out completely, I would, but I can't, and I don't want to go through that again.

'You know, I could have ended up on a building site. My dad wanted me to do that with him, but I didn't. I did actually like hairdressing, though, and I was good at that. I liked cutting hair. In some ways,' he says, 'I think I really wasn't suited to music at all . . .'

But Rowland would ultimately have a change of heart. Going back on all he said here, he later - though not too much later – decided to return to music after all. He announced that the band was getting back together, having reworked their album *Too-Rye-Ay* to mark its 40th anniversary. They even toured.

Clearly, music had him by the scruff of his neck, and wasn't going to let go.

36

'I wanted adulation and got it, but I had to die to survive it'

On the 2017 album *Prometheus & Pandora* by Sananda Maitreya, there are no fewer than fifty-three songs, a triple album that is long even by the standards of triple albums. All sorts of things are going on within it, all sorts of styles and arresting vocal lines, longueurs and flashes of inspiration, but one track stands out for the title alone: 'Limp Dick Blues'. 'I'm a fellow who likes to drink and smoke,' Maitreya sings with the mournful intonation of a lovelorn balladeer. 'It used to once hang down to the tops of my shoes / Now all I've got is these limp dick blues.'

This, it hardly needs pointing out, is unusually intimate territory for even the most confessional singer-songwriter, at once a cocky boast *and* a morose admission of midlife malfunction. Any artist's manager, you fancy, might advise caution, a rethink even; lyrics about lovers leaving home make for a much more palatable lingua franca. But when you are a fifty-seven-year-old lone gun, beholden to no one but yourself, gloriously untied to market forces – and, it must be said, no longer stifled by the expectation of a braying global audience – you can do whatever the hell you please.

Prometheus & Pandora was, as its sleeve notes make clear, 'written, arranged, produced, performed & conceived by Sananda Maitreya', which is another way of saying: *mine, all mine*. When you find you can no longer exist within the recording industry, you simply continue to do so *outside* it. And this is, Maitreya seems to be suggesting, both eminently possible *and* creatively fulfilling.

Long before he became a man with a mysterious name of Buddhist extraction, and a settled father of two, happily married and living in one of Europe's more elegant cities, Maitreya was somebody else entirely. Specifically, he was Terence Trent D'Arby, perhaps the most virile pop star of the 1980s if we do him the courtesy of overlooking Prince. D'Arby arrived on the international music scene like few others before him, blazing so very brightly and then either abruptly crumbling in the face of impossible pressure (and an over-inflated arrogance) or, in his own view, having his career deliberately scuppered by dark forces. Whichever is truer, one thing is certain: his global popularity withdrew with a breathtaking alacrity. One moment he was here, the next – whoosh, gone.

There are, as we have seen, all sorts of rituals that can be fulfilled when this happens to the waning artist: a bout of debilitating depression; drugs; rehab. But D'Arby would elect to act with the flourish for which he had been so recently celebrated. In 1994, his career having passed the point of no return, 'Terence Trent D'Arby' committed artistic suicide and was swiftly buried; in his place rose 'Sananda Maitreya'.

Anyone who would confuse the two in future, who assumed that they were still fundamentally the same person, would find themselves the prompt recipient of his withering disdain.

Seven years previously, Terence Trent D'Arby was a most startling individual, a heady brew of Michael Jackson, James Brown and Sam Cooke – hips, voice, looks – and he had the braggadocio of an undefeated Muhammad Ali. It seemed unreasonable that one human being could have been endowed with such gifts, but this twenty-five-year-old American of Scots/Irish descent, with a bit of Native American in him, carried it off with such aplomb you might have imagined him concocted by scientists; the first test-tube pop star, perhaps. To hear him sing was to be willingly corrupted by his licentiousness: the hit singles he racked up in quick succession

– 'If You Let Me Stay', 'Sign Your Name', 'Wishing Well' – had emphatically nothing to do with either limp dicks or blues. He was beautiful and knew it, and *humble* was not in his arsenal. His debut album, *The Hardline According to . . .* sold a million copies in three days, and would go on to sell eight million more.

He talked a good fight, too – Muhammad Ali is no accidental reference point – and if ever his nascent genius was in doubt, he'd remind you of it. He once said: 'I am a holographic representation in the third dimension of what was requested by your souls that one of your favourite artists [should] be.' Not the most flowing of sentences, true, but its intent was clear: all thrust and puffed chest. He also said: 'I can only say this with all relative humility: I saw myself as a Beatle.' In other words, the chosen one. For one magazine cover, he posed naked but for a fig leaf.

If all this was too good to be true, then thank heavens for the fly in the ointment. D'Arby's talent was of the compulsive kind. Like Prince, he wanted to indulge his artistry, to stretch and flex and show what else he could do. And after such stratospheric early success, he was never going to be tamed or restrained, much less open to suggestion. When his second album, 1989's *Neither Fish Nor Flesh*, boasted nothing as radio-friendly-feverish as 'If You Let Me Stay', public interest was withdrawn, requiring D'Arby to doubt his talent, which was not his default setting.

It couldn't be over, he reasoned, because what he was doing here was simply following his fate. The man had been born to sing.

'I was two years old when I first heard the Beatles, and I knew right away that it awoke in me my destiny,' he says. 'It was the moment Arthur pulled his sword from the stone. In my tender young heart, I somehow knew that I was also meant to be a Beatle somewhere in time.'

He began his musical education in earnest, not just the Beatles, but the Rolling Stones, Jimi Hendrix, Stevie Wonder, Sly and the Family Stone and Duke Ellington, David Bowie and the Jackson 5,

Led Zeppelin, Aretha Franklin, Rod Stewart and Frank Sinatra. He chose to idolise only those worthy of it, showing little interest in those he considered 'false gods'.

'To be an idol is to know what it is to idolise. I learned projection from my heroes, who gave up what was needed.'

The night John Lennon was killed, D'Arby, then eighteen, had a dream that Lennon walked into his body. After that, it was only a matter of time. 'I wanted adulation and got it. But,' he adds, 'I had to die to survive it.'

If his introduction to the world stage had happened to him just like the manifestation of all those childhood dreams, then what came next resembled nightmares. Following the failure of *Neither Fish Nor Flesh*, he moved to Los Angeles, where he grew increasingly convinced that there were certain individuals within the record industry unhappy that the presiding superstars of the day – Michael Jackson, Prince – were being effortlessly usurped by this hip young gunslinger, and that the upstart had to be stifled. The counter – and perhaps more sensible – argument that he'd stifled his own career with, as one newspaper review put it, his 'artistic overreach', and that the new material was simply not as good as what came before it, was something he would not, and could not, countenance. Instead, he believed that a shadowy cabal of tastemakers, whose job it was to take care of, and mollify, those established stars, had conspired successfully to silence him.

Maitreya, who you will have noticed doesn't always employ the most direct language when there is access to more serpentine vocabulary instead, now conjures up an image of suppression communist regimes might recognise.

'All nightmares,' he says, 'begin as a dream. In order to lure you deeper into the forest, the dream has to offer sweet enticements. But once lost deep inside the forest, real fireworks begin, and the nightmare portion sets up shop and runs the business for a while.

If you survive it, the tales at your disposal will be impressive, but most of us don't survive it.'

This forest began to close around him, he suggests, 'when the powers that be begin to understand that your nature is not to use your power to subdue people into submission but rather to liberate. Once this is seen by the governors of the State apparatus, the tendency is for them to suppress this power, not to promote it. The laws of the State are clear: who promotes the State, and its prerogatives, gets promoted by the State. But I disagreed where the State wanted to keep the consciousness of the people, so me and the State got a divorce.'

Meantime, a slightly more malleable and agreeable Black superstar was incoming: Lenny Kravitz. He'd do.

Two more D'Arby albums followed, to little effect. There was talk of him 'living the life of a tormented recluse' in a mansion on Sunset Boulevard, and a confusing story of the mansion going up in flames while he was in it.

But seclusion was necessary for Maitreya to come through.

'That time worked well [for me, but] I was grateful to move on from such excess and artifice. I didn't give a fuck about it then, and even less about it now that memory has been kind enough to allow me to forget most of it.'

To help deal with the PTSD he endured at the truncation of his career, he duly performed his ritualistic suicide of Terence Trent D'Arby. Sananda Maitreya would be a different entity altogether, fresh canvas, new paint. It would take a while for him to return to making music, perhaps because the longer you don't do it, the harder it is to resume. Even idols get stage fright.

'What hinders creativity most is not paying attention to your flame, and I faced the sort of life and pressures that all pioneers face. Our lives are difficult [but] artists are bound by Providence to be true if they wish to be blessed to carry some of Prometheus' flame [Prometheus being the Greek god of fire]. Were our lives not difficult,' he suggests, clarifying somewhat, 'we wouldn't be able to reach as many people. So "difficult" comes in handy.'

The artist must suffer, then.

By the turn of the next century, he began recording again. By now, he was living in Milan, married to an architect and former TV presenter, and was father to two small children. He has written nine albums as Sananda Maitreya, released on his own label, each unwieldy but fascinating, proof of a still rampant creativity. If he is no longer the Adonis he once was, then no matter, he says. We're all human; we wither and age. And though there is a pertinent question to address, of whether anyone is listening any more – Sananda Maitreya has fewer than 5,000 Spotify listeners a month at the time of writing, while Terence Trent D'Arby has close to a million – this, he will insist, is beside the point.

But then, several months after our interview, he takes the decision to subsume Terence Trent D'Arby's catalogue on Spotify into Sananda Maitreya's, at once absorbing his former self into the artist he has become and, perhaps most importantly, bolstering his current numbers. In the streaming world, evidently, it's all about the numbers.

'In truth,' he says, 'I am only just now beginning to allow myself to feel some small sense of wonderment at the works I've been inspired to write. The music industry [remains] the beast that she is. That will never change. Her *shape* may change, but her nature remains the same, and the point is that I took from her what I could. And so it goes. What drives me is that there is still creative life in me pushing to get out. I am still driven by the work, but just as much by the need to stay sane. Music is given to us,' he suggests, 'to help us stay a bit closer to our right minds.'

When asked whether he misses the old days, and what, if anything, he hankers for from the time in which he was seemingly omnipotent, the time when the world was listening, he chooses to answer like this: 'I miss the unbridled bold naked stupidity of youth's vibrant electric hubris.'

But otherwise, he's happy to be free of it and, ultimately, at peace. Five decades since he first started making music, he has got the balance right, and found his level. The forest didn't swallow him up; those dark forces allowed him a pass. Prince died; Michael Jackson died. *He* lived. The relief, the sheer blessed relief he must feel at having come out the other side intact.

The satisfaction, too.

37

'Egoic'

In 2010, Stoke-on-Trent's most successful celebrity export elected to take a pay cut and went back to his old job. Within concerned circles, the move surprised as many as it titillated: his last tour had been his most profitable yet, and so the precise reasons for Robbie Williams rejoining Take That, the boy band he'd quit amid tabloid-tickling acrimony back in 1995 when he was just twenty-one years old, wasn't immediately clear. He did endeavour to explain himself to the fourth estate, but explanation and fact rarely count for much when rumour and conjecture prove *much* more fun.

'In the Twittersphere at the time,' Williams says now, 'it was deemed that Rob's career was going down the pan and he needed to join Take That [again]. But the previous tour I'd done had broke all records. If I'd gone on by myself, I would still have sold more tickets worldwide [than the band] because I'm more famous worldwide.'

His decision, he explains, was prompted more by personal reasons. 'I genuinely needed to do it because at the time I was going through one of my many mental breakdowns.'

There had been a long period of agoraphobia, and suggestions that he hadn't left his house much at all for three full years. To then start another solo album and arrange an accompanying world tour felt far too exposing for him, too frightening, and so becoming part of the gang again, one of five, appealed in ways it hadn't before. It offered him protection, and friends – not necessarily to hide behind, but rather to stand alongside.

Another reason was to build bridges, and lay to rest any lingering resentment he might have felt towards them, particularly frontman Gary Barlow.

'There were some demons from the past, yeah,' he concedes, 'a rucksack full of rocks that I needed to get rid of.' And there was a final reason, too: 'I'd watched their *Circus* tour that they did [in 2009] and thought it was the best thing I'd seen, possibly ever, and I wanted to be a part of it.'

So, while he would be taking a pay cut ('I made less than a quarter of what I'd normally make alone'), his intentions were good, he says. 'They were what you'd hope they would be if you'd been a Take That fan.'

He'd returned at what was probably the optimum time to do so. Take That had originally split a year after Williams left, boy bands being notoriously delicate edifices that are quick to crumble once a key part of the scaffolding has been removed. But when they reformed ten years later, in 2005 – without Williams, who was by then one of the world's biggest pop stars – they achieved something vanishingly rare in their field: not only were they a better band second time around, but they appealed to a wider audience too, including the more precious music fan who, previously, might have crossed the road to avoid them.

By 2010, then, they were on a critical and commercial high, the *Circus* tour Williams so admired having been one of the most successful ever staged in the UK. The album they then made together, *Progress* – a collaborative project where previously Barlow had done most of the grunt work – was widely hailed their masterpiece. It sounded nothing like the act they'd been before.

Reunions are not supposed to proceed this seamlessly, and mostly they don't. Williams knew this, of course, and so was perhaps wise not to hang around for too long afterwards, electing to bail out of Take That once again – in friendlier circumstances this time around – while they were still cresting the wave of blanket adulation. Demons had been vanquished, there was nothing left to prove, and they got to write the happy ending they'd denied themselves previously.

They've co-existed in parallel ever since, all earlier enmity replaced by that precious thing most bands crave in one way or another: harmony.

Robbie Williams had first quit the band in the mid-nineties because he'd grown tired of their teen appeal, their ruthless hit-making efficiency, and the earnest smiles they were contractually obliged to deliver on Saturday morning kids' TV. He wanted now to run in the opposite direction, and embrace debauchery and oblivion, become a different kind of pop star. He drank, took drugs, dyed his hair peroxide blond. He didn't want to be Gary Barlow, he wanted to be Liam Gallagher: two fingers and Tennent's lager. He'd long felt stifled by the straight-laced Barlow, ostensibly Take That's benign dictator, and needed to prove to the watching world that there was more to him than choreographed limbs and a cheeky grin. He wanted to make mistakes – and make his own great pop songs – and this was something he could only ever do away from the established hierarchy, and alone.

Musically, he got off to a faulty start in mid-1996, by releasing an entirely straightforward cover of George Michael's 'Freedom!', the message conveyed here that the only way he could possibly show what he was capable of was by singing someone else's song. But 'Freedom!' was merely a stopgap while he got on with the business, between pub breaks and an underlying self-doubt, of writing his first album, 1997's *Life Thru a Lens*. He had hooked up with Guy Chambers by now, and 'Angels' was waiting in the wings. By the time he'd won over the crowd at Glastonbury in 1997, he was on his way.

Over the next few years, eleven of his twelve albums would go to number one; he would win a record-breaking eighteen Brit Awards, and would enter the Guinness Book of World Records in 2006 for selling 1.6 million gig tickets in a single day. His combination of earnest balladry, effusive pop theatrics and performative chops made him one of the great entertainers of his era. Marmite for many, perhaps, but superstardom always did divide taste. Alongside Elvis Presley, he is the biggest-selling solo artist in UK chart history.

He insists today that he never saw it coming, none of it.

'You can only ever see in front of your nose, really, can't you?' Joining a boy band that had a half chance of success was as big as the teenage Robbie's dreams got. 'You have no idea what's going to be at the end of that journey,' he says. 'Back then, I didn't look past, "I'm going to buy a white Porsche, and pick me mate up in it". That really was the entirety of my ambition back then: be on *Top of the Pops*, buy a Porsche, pick my mate up, and buy some trainers.'

The Porsche would have to remain a fantasy. He never passed his driving test.

Williams' lingering imposter syndrome would not be assuaged by his great success, but rather compounded; the more hits he had, the stronger the conviction that beneath him lay thin ice. Whenever anyone criticised him, and routinely they did, it stung. And yet he couldn't help but bait them. In many ways, Williams behaved unlike so many pop stars, uninterested in being brooding and enigmatic, but rather laying out his flamboyantly dysfunctional personality traits like a market stallholder arranging his wares for public perusal. Few singers with his level of success, for example, would go on to TV chat shows and discuss their mental health – long before mental health became the mainstream topic it is today – but Robbie did. It ultimately worked in his favour, making him eminently relatable – he was fallible too, he was just like us – but it also left him exposed, with nowhere to hide. Meanwhile, he wanted desperately to be liked, and loved, and so he cracked jokes, and did funny dances, and never sat still. For Robbie, the world was a stage, with everyone gazing up at him. He liked to convince himself he was developing thicker skin, but on many mornings he struggled to get out of bed. He was popular with women, but could string together longer sentences than he could a lasting relationship. His celebrity soon became the gilded cage of cliché.

'I felt very driven in the early days, and I felt in competition with the world, and with myself. But then I was living through a mental illness,' he says, 'and that mental illness was called depression. I had my life, which was Knebworth, and quadruple-platinum-selling albums, and nothing could touch the sides. I hate the term *suffering from depression*, and I wish there was another way to describe it, but nothing that was coming into my life could crowd it out or stop it. I remember my dad coming over to Los Angeles and looking around my house, and just saying: "When you get down, just take a look at all this . . ." And I was like: "Dad, that's like saying to somebody with cancer: *You've got a nice garden . . .*" That's just how it was for me. I suppose I got fast-tracked to the zenith of my discomfort because of the job I'd picked, but I would have got there anyway, even if I'd been a dustman.'

In October 2002, Williams signed his multi-million pound deal with EMI. 'I'm rich beyond my wildest dreams!' he told the press conference. By this point, he was successful in most of the world's major record-buying territories, with the glaring exception of America. America, he was repeatedly told, didn't 'get' him. He was too eager to please, and cracked too many jokes – and most of those were very British in flavour. He was Norman Wisdom in a world of Foo Fighters.

But this actually suited him rather well. He was famous enough as it was, and struggling to cope: a certain anonymity, then, was a balm. He subsequently emigrated to the country that loved him least, where he could live, if not quite a normal life – normal lives do not unfold within mansions – then at least a quiet one. The house he bought was situated within a gated community; the Beach Boys' Brian Wilson was a neighbour; Tom Jones lived just down the road. It was huge, and boasted winding staircases you half expected Greta Garbo to descend. There was an undulating garden out back, a pool, a view, staff, personal assistants, a live-in chef. The mammoth dog he owned that looked more like a wolf was actually part-wolf. The sun shone through every dustless window, and there were always houseguests milling about the place, keeping it – and him – occupied.

By this time, he'd weaned himself off drink and drugs, but was taking *a lot* of prescription medication, and had developed a caffeine addiction. Several times a day, his security man would drive him down to the nearest Starbucks or the Coffee Bean & Tea Leaf for a triple espresso, which he downed like a shot. When he wasn't writing or recording, his free time taunted him. There were just so many hours that needed filling; the milling houseguests offered a crucial diversion. He bought another, smaller property, further up the Hollywood Hills. It had its own five-a-side football pitch, and it was to here he retreated most afternoons for a kickabout with friends and visiting dignitaries from the UK. Gordon Ramsay was a regular guest, as was the Sex Pistols' Steve Jones, alongside various British bands and actors whose promotional tours and junkets included a West Coast stopover. If he ever needed to make up numbers, he'd head to a nearby shopping mall searching for British tourists. To these people, he'd introduce himself and say: 'Fancy a game?'

Evenings could be harder to fill, but not impossible. Then single, he'd meet women in bars, Americans who had no idea who he was, then bring them back home and put on a DVD of his record-breaking 2003 Knebworth shows, one man playing to 125,000 fans a night for a record-breaking three nights. As a seduction technique, it proved reliably successful.

You can pass a lot of time in this way. He did.

In 2006, Williams made the most impetuous record of his career. *Rudebox* was, ostensibly, him having a lark. It contained songs as far in style from signature tracks like 'Angels' and 'Feel' as it was possible to get. Instead, he played with form and content (and expectation), indulged in some Stoke-on-Trent-accented rapping, impersonated Serge Gainsbourg (badly), and finished the album with a song called 'Dickhead' that contained the lines, 'I got a bucket of shit, ohh yeah . . . Not dog shit, cow shit, horse shit, real shit.'

'What a bizarre, baffling and downright strange album this is,' one review went, while the *Guardian* concluded, 'If nothing else, *Rudebox* is a sharp reminder that Robbie Williams is unique.'

If the faithful had been expecting another 'Rock DJ', another 'Millennium', they were to be disappointed. *Rudebox*'s lack of critical appeal was compounded by its comparative commercial failure. It ended his imperial phase.

'I really enjoyed making that record, and I thought everyone else would enjoy it as well, because that's what had happened with all the other albums,' he says. In its defence, he adds, 'it felt more authentically Rob-from-Stoke than anything I'd done before. I'm not saying everything else I'd done was inauthentic, but when I started making these bleeps and blobs, and interesting noises, I was like: *Oh, this is me*.

'But, yeah, the ensuing killing of the album [critically, he means] really affected me. It was the first time I'd gone to the table and missed the ball; I'd missed the white, whereas for six or seven albums before that, I was winning every frame. It caused a chink in my armour, and I think I'm still affected by that today. Not neurotically affected,' he stresses, 'but it has made me second-think myself. You know, the worst thing a band or artist can do is to try to recreate what they had before, but I found myself both trying to carry on in the same vein, while also giving the fans – or whoever – what they want, and what the industry wants from me.'

The age-old problem, then: who to make music for, and how much of a sacrifice will that require from the artist? He began checking now whether what he was writing was good enough to be successful, and whether he still even craved that success. Part of him wanted to admit that he no longer cared but the entertainer in him suggested otherwise.

The entertainer won.

'Do I want everybody to stick with me? Do I unashamedly want to still be one of the biggest artists in the world?' he says. 'Yeah, yes I do. And so, how am I going to achieve that?'

At the time of writing, Williams had a stash of seventy new songs ready to go. Some, he knew, or thought he knew, had the potential to be big hit singles, 'songs that in any other decade I've existed in would have been big hits.' Others were more experimental, songs in which he sounded like Lou Reed or David Bowie. 'They sound odd, but I've always liked odd.'

So, which to go with: those that might reveal him as avant-garde, and weird, and interestingly 'odd', or the tried-and-tested big pop anthems that people still notionally expect from him, and will get him played on the radio, and interviewed on the television, and keep him satisfyingly famous?

'I'm forty-seven years old, and my fans don't necessarily stream songs, which means it's incredibly difficult to get into the Top 40 for me these days. So what do I do? Do I put out what makes me happy? Or do I put out those I deem to be big hits? And if they're *not* big hits, simply because the oxygen isn't quite there for me any more, does that mean I forego putting out something that I think might be more . . . *worthy*? It's difficult. Do you see what I'm saying?'

In 2016, Williams released his eleventh album, *The Heavy Entertainment Show*, in which old Robbie met new Robbie and perhaps ushered forth a viable future for him, packed as it was with cinematic pop songs, the obligatory impish asides, and a more reflective, intimate aspect.

By now, he was married to the American actress Ayda Field and had two children (two more would swiftly follow), and several songs on the album revealed a ripe love for them all. If 'Motherfucker' was an unusual love letter to his son – the singer explaining that, while his son might occasionally struggle in life, just like his father, he was ultimately made of strong stuff, so don't fret too much – the ballad 'When You Know' was redolent of one who at last had found his soulmate. 'She hates the same people as . . . me,' he sang in a romantic croon.

Williams had never previously sounded quite as content, or whole, as this.

'That's because now I fucking *love* my job,' he says, 'and it is a job. Before the kids arrived, nothing kind of made sense to me. Was this a vocation, a vacation? Who was this morphing blob who kept going forwards, kept writing lyrics, kept getting up on stage . . . and all the money, and all the, the *things*? There wasn't a shape that completely made sense in front of me, of why I was doing this, who I was, what I was all about. But then the kids came, and everything *did* make sense: *Daddy goes to work*. Once I've got that – in my soul, in my system – and once [I accepted that] the incredible spotlight that once was on me had moved on to other people, I just got to enjoy the level of fame and success that most people would enjoy. And I'm happy about that, I love it.'

The album was significant for another reason. Its launch single, 'Party Like a Russian', a propulsive foot-stomp seemingly designed for stadium singalongs, flopped – but properly flopped, barely scraping the Top 100. That had never happened to him before.

'That thing I'd been trying to stave off for at least three albums,' he says, 'actually finally happened.' The single's midweek chart position offered an early, bowel-loosening indication of its scant sales, and by Sunday's confirmation, it was nowhere to be seen. The end of an era.

'But,' Williams says, 'on Monday the world carried on spinning, and I . . . I was all right. I was. I wasn't depressed.' He slips into present tense now. 'My ego is dented a fraction, of course, but that can be banged out in the garage, and isn't a total write-off.' What he's trying to say, he adds, 'is that I survived. I survived what I was most scared of. Everything was okay.'

He'd been seeing the incremental shift for several years, no longer courted quite so vociferously by the more commercial radio stations, but rather by those whose playlists primarily featured legacy acts. 'I was now being played alongside Phil Collins and ABBA on Smooth Radio, but that's okay, because I like Phil Collins and ABBA, and I've no problem being a legacy act, because maybe, maybe, I'll get to be Rod Stewart in years to come. Rod Stewart is still Rod Stewart, and Tom Jones is still Tom Jones, whether either of them last had a hit thirty-five years ago or five years ago. Is it egoic to compare myself to those legends?' He shrugs. 'I am the next one in that field, I think. Aren't I?'

The last time he took a career break was in the mid-2000s, when he felt depressed and lost and alone. He grew the hermit's beard, reanimated an interest in UFOs, and watched a lot of television. His more recent career break has been a far healthier one, and has allowed him to stealthily branch out and extend the brand. The way he sees it, he has at last successfully extricated himself from the album/tour/album cycle, and can now diversify, mix things up a little.

'I had a great time turning everything down in my pomp,' he says, 'and there was a lot of power in saying no, because I could, because everything was coming my way back then, and everything I was doing was working. But now's the time in my life to start saying yes to things.'

Having already dabbled in the role of TV talent show judge – he was on *The X Factor* in 2018 – he wants to do more prime-time television, delving further into the bottomless pit of the Saturday night TV that everybody seems to hate except those who actually watch it, in their very many millions. He wants to act, too, on both the small screen and the big, and even to play himself in the inevitable biopic of his life. If Elton John and Queen can have feature films made of their life and times, why not Robbie Williams? He also paints these days, and plans to exhibit his art around the world.

There is, too, a continued desire to write more music, music that he hopes will please both his fans and himself. His experimental segues have found their way onto compilation albums he releases only on his website to completists; the others he still polishes until they shine like smash hits, in the hope that they will become smash hits, because, well . . . because old habits are old habits. It's what he does.

'There are different levels of fame, and I've moved down a few gears, but I'm really, really happy here. I understand that new opportunities only come by still being relevant, and that's still important to me – it's part of the competitive spirit, the ego, and the necessity of being a human being living in a capitalist society – but where I am, right now? It's fucking great.'

Most surprising is that he has found a kind of personal equilibrium, a steadiness of mood that had previously been denied him. Depression doesn't just vanish, of course, because this isn't how mental health works. But he has a structure in place to keep it at least at arm's length. To fully function, to remain *up*, he stays active and engaged. Being a workaholic, it turns out, was good for him all along.

'Left to my own devices, if I don't get up and create, then the demons return. So all this,' he says, referencing his family, the various homes he maintains around the world, the music, the art, the sheer bloody performance of it all, 'it's meditative for me. When I go to bed now, I don't have to take sleeping tablets because Radio Rob won't stop being neurotic. No, instead I go to bed thinking about ideas. There's no room for any more demons if I just carry on creating. And I'm in a position now where I can enjoy the spoils of my labours.'

Robbie Williams is the pop star who had his cake and ate it, and who now wants, as perhaps all pop stars ultimately do, more cake. Who's ever truly satisfied with the crumbs?

'I've had a very interesting first half of my life,' he says. 'I'd like a very interesting second half, too.'

FADE OUT

After the KLF were finished treating the music industry like a precious applecart that needed upending, they famously deleted their back catalogue, determined, where others lacked the guts, to self-guillotine. They died young in order to leave behind them perfectly preserved memories, permitting nothing to turn sour and curdle. No comeback, no diminishing returns, no, 'Oh God, not *them* again?' Just – *gone*. Of all the grand artistic statements of an act that once persuaded country legend Tammy Wynette to sing the line, 'They're justified, and they're ancient / And they drive an ice cream van', this was surely their most compelling.

However.

Six months after I spoke with Bill Drummond, the band suddenly uploaded their music to a streaming service for the first time, to coincide with the release of a new documentary film about them. Proof, then, that even those that do dare to leave it all behind don't ever really leave it *all* behind.

Musicians continue to play, and strive to have their music played, for themselves as much as for anyone else, because it's what they do, it's what they're here for, and because it gives the rest of us something to cling on to on a Saturday night, or while we walk the dog, when we fall in love or are dumped, or when someone close to us dies, or simply when we want something other than silence in our lives. Mostly, we don't want silence. We want a soundtrack, and we want our favourites, and so the band plays on. The band always plays on.

And who can blame them? When you've had the thrill of being cheered, adored and applauded for something you created in the privacy of your own head, and have the world chant it back to you, can anything else come quite as close? If you try to walk away from it, it calls you back. And so the pop stars and the troubadours, the legends and the mavericks, *all* of them, they keep coming back. It's a compulsion and a yearning, a yearning shared by anyone who ever straddled a microphone stand, and opened their mouths to sing.

ACKNOWLEDGEMENTS

Pop stars are used to answering all manner of questions, but the probing tends mostly to focus on their new music, their often extravagant lifestyles, and what fun it is to receive awards. They don't often have to face, or are expected to actually answer, questions about career dips and fallibility, necessary resilience and dogged self-belief.

So I'm really very grateful to all the artists who took the time to talk to me with such candour, honesty and insight. Thank you to Billy Bragg, Bob Geldof, Róisín Murphy, Joan Armatrading, Alex Kapranos, Gary Lightbody, Eddie Chacon, Tjinder Singh, Peter Perrett, Sananda Maitreya, Lloyd Cole, Justin Currie, Suzanne Vega, Wendy James, Tim Burgess, Shirley Collins, Don McLean, Donny Tourette, Shaun Ryder, Tony James, Lisa Maffia, Kevin Rowland, Andrez Harriott, Wayne Hussey, Ed Tudor-Pole, CeeLo Green, Tim Booth, Rob Birch, Robert Howard, Dave Balfe, Dennis Seaton, Simon Rowbottom, Natalie Merchant, Paul Cattermole, Stewart Copeland, Sonya Madan, Einar Örn, Peter Cunnah, Dave Stewart, David Gray, Rufus Wainwright, Guy Chambers, Justin Hawkins, Brian Nash, Martin Carr, Joe Jackson, Tanya Donelly, Boff Whalley, Liam Ó Maonlaí, Leo Sayer, Bill Drummond and Robbie Williams.

I'm also grateful to those who facilitated many of these conversations: Ted Cummings for getting the ball rolling and keeping it rolling, Michael Loney, Tim Vigon, Aoife Kitt, Tarquin Gotch, Lou Goodliffe, Barbara Charone, Susie Ember, Matthew Rankin, Sam Maffia, Francesca Francone, Debra Geddes, Steve Phillips, Fran DeFeo, Andy Prevezer, Mark Spector, Victoria Bastable, David

Sullivan, David Whitehead, Anita Heryet, Mark Sydow, Duncan Jordan, Tracy Bufferd, Rhianna Kenny, and anyone I may have inadvertently forgotten.

Thanks to Dan Keeling and Dr Alan Redman, and to Shaggy and Beth Gibbons, for background, overview and context; also to Katy Guest at Boundless for first allowing me to write on this subject at length – a version of my Sananda Maitreya interview first appeared on Boundless in 2019.

Extra special thanks to my brilliant editor Richard Roper, for his belief, enthusiasm and wise counsel, to Katie Green and Feyi Oyesanya for such sensitive copy-editing, Rosie Margesson for publicity, and all the team at Headline.

I'd like to thank Steve Price for his sterling suggestions and his infectious encouragement, which came at just the right time. And at home – the kitchen, mostly – I'd like to thank Elena, Amaya and Evie, for always being there, for being such able and welcome diversions, and for reminding me that there is more to life than music, so long as there is music playing quietly somewhere in the background.

INDEX

10,000 Maniacs 228–9

ABBA 15, 175, 330
Ace of Base 90
Adele 14, 55, 61, 183
Akon 159
Albarn, Damon 80, 84
All Saints 261
Ant, Adam 69, 279–83, 285, 286
Aphex Twin 89
Apple, Fiona 247
Appleton, Nicole 101
Archer, Al 52
Arctic Monkeys 307
Aristotle 191
Armatrading, Joan 276–9
Asher D 153, 154
Atlanta 238, 239
Atomic Kitten 153
Australia 233, 236

Babyshambles 26
Badalamenti, Angelo 199
Balfe, Dave 83–5, 87
Balfe, David 5
Band Aid 312, 313
Barbados 38–9
Barking 69
Barkley, Gnarls 239, 240
Barlow, Gary 351, 352
Barrett, Tina 131
Bassey, Shirley 52
Battersea 153
Beach Boys, the 89
Beatles, the 15, 83, 89, 102, 162, 183,
    277, 295, 345
Beckham, David 335
Bee Gees 236

Beethoven, Ludwig van 325
Belly 226–7
Benson, George 339–40
Bexhill 305
Beyoncé 61, 65–6, 183, 208
Bez 36, 37, 38–40, 41, 43–4, 45, 327
Bhosle, Asha 253
Birch, Rob 56–9
Birmingham 105, 107, 277, 336
Björk 326–7, 327–8
Black Flag 184
Black Grape 40, 41–2, 45
Blair, Tony 256, 262
Blink-182 27
Blondie 80
Blow Monkeys, the 215, 216
Blunkett, David 154
Blunt, James 62, 63
Blunt, Martin 48
Blur 51, 80, 83, 83–4, 256
Bon Jovi, Jon 285
Bonehead 51
Bono 144, 180, 181, 186, 288, 315
Boo Radleys, the 87, 89–92, 103–4
Boomtown Rats, the 309–11, 312,
    313–14, 314–15
Booth, Tim 196–203
Bowie, David 174, 175, 214, 224, 345
Boy George 69
Boyz II Men 120
Bradford 130–1
Bragg, Billy 27, 68–76, 215, 258
Brazil 212
Breeders, the 226
Brighton 306–7
Brixton 57, 153, 155
Brookes, Jon 48
Brown, James 105

Brydon, Mark 329–31
Buck, Peter 71
Buerk, Michael 311
Bukowski, Charles 171
Burgess, Tim 47–52, 75
Butler, Bernard 199
Butlin's Minehead 29–31
Buxton 212

California 22, 23, 49, 212
Cameron, David 282
Cardiff 93, 94
Carey, Mariah 84, 159
Carr, Martin 86–95, 99
Cash, Johnny 174
Catatonia 80
Cattermole, Paul 122–32
Cauty, Jimmy 5, 6
Celine 158
Chacon, Eddie 252–3
Chadwick, Guy 103
Chambers, Guy 101–3, 352
Chapman, Tracy 228, 246
Charlatans, the 47, 48–9, 51
Charles and Eddie 252
Chumbawamba 258–64
Church, the 61
Clash, the 89, 143, 148, 163
Clearmountain, Bob 309
Cobain, Kurt 15
Cocker, Jarvis 84–5
Cohen, Leonard 144, 174, 224–5, 325
Cohen, Lorca 325
Coldplay 65, 182, 185, 194
Cole, Lloyd 210–11, 212–15, 223, 224–5
Cole, Paula 247
Collins, Phil 359
Collins, Rob 48
Collins, Shirley 303–8
Coltrane, John 90, 91
Connecticut 245
Cook, Paul 143
Copeland, Miles 289
Copeland, Stewart 287–93
Coppola, Francis Ford 289–90
Cornershop 251, 253–5
Costello, Elvis 150, 310
Cowell, Simon 84, 120, 220, 263
Cox, Courteney 185
Craven, Beverley 5–6
Crazyhead 83

Crowe, Simon 311
Culture Beat 90
Culture Club 106
Cunnah, Peter 255–7
Cure, the 27
Currie, Justin 217–19, 223–4
Curved Air 289, 290
Cyprus 155

Daltrey, Roger 236
Damage 120–1
Dammers, Jerry 69
Danger Mouse 239
Daphne & Celeste 52
D'Arby, Terence Trent 284, 343–9
Darkness, the 187–9, 190–1, 194
Deal, Kim 226
Decker, Carol 4
Del Amitri 217–19
Del Rey, Lana 103
Delhi 80
Denmark 142
Detroit, Marcella 285
Dexys Midnight Runners 51, 52, 335–7
DJ Meck (Craig Dimech) 233
Dr Robert 69
Doherty, Pete 26
Donelly, Tanya 226–7
Drummond, Bill 3–14, 55, 83, 365–6
Duran Duran 4, 68, 157, 310
Dylan, Bob 14, 69, 72, 73, 214, 224,
    225, 231, 234, 237, 295, 296
Dylan, Paris 294, 299–301, 302

E Street Band, the 198, 200
Eagles 218
Echobelly 79–83
Eilish, Billie 208–9
Elastica 80
Eldritch, Andrew 142
Ellington, Duke 345
Ellis, Warren 29
Ethiopia 311–12
Eurythmics 284

Fahey, Siobhan 285
Fatboy Slim 251, 253–4
Ferry, Bryan 285
Field, Ayda 358
Flaming Lips 89, 180
Flowered Up 83

Food Records 83, 84
Foo Fighters 65
Frankie Goes to Hollywood 112–16, 135
Franklin, Aretha 346
Frantz, Chris 38, 39, 148
Franz Ferdinand 51, 171–7
Frischmann, Justine 80
Fuller, Simon 122, 125

Gainsbourg, Serge 356
Gallagher, Liam 80, 281, 352
Gallagher, Noel 162
Gay Dad 83
Geldof, Bob 163, 285, 309–15
Geldof, Peaches 163
Generation X 139, 144
Ghostigital 328
Gibb, Barry 52
Gibbons, Beth 307
Gill, Peter 115, 118
Gillespie, Bobby 144
Glastonbury 100–1, 275, 352
G-Man 153, 154, 155
Goodie Mob 239
Gorillaz 43, 144
Grant, Eddy 39
Grant, Kelvin 107
Grant, Michael 109
Grant, Richard E. 268
Gray, David 59–67
Green, CeeLo 238–43
Greenbaum, Norman 267
Grundy, Bill 136–7
Guns N' Roses 187
Guthrie, Nora 73
Guthrie, Woody 72–4

Happy Mondays 35, 36–40, 45, 83, 198, 327
Harriott, Andrez 120–2
Harrison, George 268
Harry, Debbie 147, 151
Hawkins, Justin 188–95
Hendrix, Jimi 15, 345
Herbert, Matthew 331
Hersh, Kristin 226
Hewlett, Jamie 144
High, the 83
Hockney, David 237
Hook, Peter 52
Horn, Trevor 112, 114, 115, 116

Hot Leg 191
Hothouse Flowers 220–3
Houston, Whitney 340
Howard, Robert 215–16
Howells, Kim 154
Hoxton 166
Hussey, Wayne 211–12

Iceland 326
Idol, Billy 139, 142, 143
Iggy and the Stooges 282
Indigo Girls 228
Ireland 309, 315, 329, 332

Jackson, Joe 233–4
Jackson, Michael 105, 207, 236, 346, 349
Jackson 5, the 345
Jagger, Mick 136, 266
Jam, the 310
James 196, 197–9, 200–1
James, Penelope 144
James, Tony 138–45, 159
James, Wendy 146–52
Janov, Arthur 284
Jesus Jones 83
Jewel 247
Joel, Billy 14
John, Elton 61, 360
Johnson, Holly 5, 112–16, 118
Jones, Mick 143, 148, 150
Jones, Steve 136–7, 143, 355
Jones, Tom 224–5, 355, 359
Joplin, Janis 15
Joy Division 51, 52

Kajagoogoo 68, 112
Kapranos, Alex 51, 171–7, 178, 186
Kathmandu 79, 81
Kaufman, James 191–2
Kellie, Mike 25
Kermit 41, 42
Kershaw, Nik 12
Khan, Chaka 103
King, Mark 69
Kinnock, Neil 69
KLF, the 5, 6, 13, 365–6
Knebworth 354, 356
Kooks, the 159
Kosovo 62
Kravitz, Lenny 347

Kubrick, Stanley 141
Kuenssberg, Laura 9

Lady Gaga 180
Le Bon, Simon 70
Led Zeppelin 346
Lee, Jacknife 180–1
Leeds 258
Lennon, John 297, 346
Lennox, Annie 103, 284–5
Lightbody, Gary 178–86
Lilith Fair 247
Little Mix 219–20
Liverpool 111–12, 119, 261
Lomax, Alan 305, 306
Los Angeles 49–50, 107, 108, 162,
　　178–80, 184, 184–6, 199–200,
　　283–4, 321, 346
Love, Courtney 163
Love Minus Zero 30
Lowestoft 187
Luton 154
Lynch, David 50

MC Harvey 153, 154
MC Romeo 153
McCarthy, Nick 173, 174
McCartney, Linda 105
McCartney, Paul 4, 13, 94–5, 105, 231,
　　236, 297
MacColl, Kirsty 70, 71
McDaid, Johnny 185
MacGowan, Shane 36
McGregor, Conor 182
McIntosh, Bradley 130–1
McKenzie, Al 255
McLachlan, Sarah 247
McLaren, Malcolm 138
McLean, Bitty 90
McLean, Don 294–302
Madan, Sonya 80–2
Madchester 37, 47, 83, 198
Madonna 80–1, 146, 151, 297
Mael, Ron 176
Mael, Russell 176
Maffia, Lisa 153–8
Mair, Alan 24, 25
Maitreya, Sananda 343–4, 346–7,
　　347–8, 348
Major, John 70, 256
Manchester 36, 37, 43, 91, 196, 329

Manson, Marilyn 144
Margate 58, 158
Marley, Bob 60
Maroon 5 194
Marr, Johnny 71
Martika 246
Martin, George 103
Massachusetts 223
Megaman 153, 154, 156
Melanie C 103
Menand, Louis 3
Menswear 83
Merchant, Natalie 226, 227–31
Merchant, Stephen 179–80
Mercury, Freddie 61, 188
Mercury Rev 180
Milan 348
Minehead 29–31
Minogue, Kylie 103
Mission, the 211–12
Moloko 329–31, 331
Montréal 320–1
Morissette, Alanis 247
Morley, Paul 112
Morris, Stephen 52
Morrison, Jim 15
Morrissey 80, 213
Mötley Crüe 288
Murphy, Róisín 328–34
Musical Youth 105–7, 109, 161
My Bloody Valentine 61
Mykonos 332–3
My Life Story 83

Nash, Brian 111–19
Nepal 79
Nestor, Pam 277
Neutrino 153, 156
New Order 51
New York 24, 72, 151, 163, 213–14, 223,
　　321–2
Newcastle 143
Nicholson, Jack 301–2
Nicks, Stevie 228, 285
Norfolk 51, 66
Northside 83
Nottingham 56
Nutter, Alice 263

Ó Maonlaí, Liam 220–3, 229
Oakenfold, Paul 38

Oasis 51, 80, 91, 162, 256, 282
Ocean, Frank 252
O'Connor, Sinead 246, 315
Only Ones, the 21–4, 25, 29–31, 33, 180
Orbison, Roy 295
Örn, Einar 326–8
Orzabal, Roland 283–4, 286
O'Toole, Mark 115, 118
Oxide 153, 156

Paris 151–2
Paris Angels 83
Parsons, Dave 149
Peckham 153
Peel, John 277
Perrett, Peter 22–34, 35, 180
Perrett, Zena 24, 26, 28, 32
Perry, Jon 25
Perry, Lee 'Scratch' 45
Pettigrew, Charles 252
Petty, Tom 285
Pink Fairies 138
Pink Floyd 48, 57
Police, the 287–91, 292–3
Portishead 60
Poullain, Frankie 190
Prefab Sprout 51
Prescott, John 261
Presley, Elvis 14, 135–6, 352
Primal Scream 56, 144
Prince 11–12, 105, 214, 285, 345, 346, 349
Pulp 80, 84–5, 180
Pussycat Dolls, the 239, 240

Queen 312, 360

Ramones 163
Ramsay, Gordon 355
Read, Mike 113
R.E.M. 27, 81, 228
Reynolds, Simon 115
Rice, Damien 219–20
Richard, Cliff 68, 310
Richards, Keith 36
Rihanna 207–8
Roberts, Garry 311
Rogers, Tony 48
Rolling Stones, the 83, 102, 183, 186, 266, 271, 310, 345
Rollins, Henry 184

Ronson, Mark 130–1
Rose, Axl 162
Rowbottom, Simon 87, 89, 92, 99–100, 103–4
Rowland, Kevin 52, 335–42
Rowntree, Dave 51
Rutherford, Paul 112
Ruthless Rap Assassins 41
Ryder, Joanne, 46
Ryder, Paul, 36, 40
Ryder, Shaun 35–46, 47, 75, 198

S Club 3 130–1
S Club 7 122, 125–7, 130–1
Salford 48, 50
Sayer, Leo 164, 233–7
Scotland 87
Seaton, Dennis 104–10
Seger, Bob 218
Sex Pistols 136–7, 137, 147, 163, 266, 310
Shakespears Sister 285
Sharkey, Feargal 285
Sheeran, Ed 63, 65, 185
Shnier, Patrisha 299
Shoreditch 92
Showbiz, Grant 71
Sigue Sigue Sputnik 137–42, 144
Sinatra, Frank 346
Singh, Tjinder 251, 253–5
Siouxsie Sioux 136
Sisters of Mercy, the 142
Skat D 153, 154
Skua 127–8
Slayer, Christian 148, 149
Sleeper 80
Sly and the Family Stone 345
Smith, Curt 284
Smith, Wendy 51
Smiths, the 80, 198
Snow Patrol 179, 180–4, 186
So Solid Crew 153–7
Soho 210, 214
Solange 252
Somerville, Jimmy 69
Spain 216
Spandau Ballet 52, 310
Sparks 176
Spearritt, Hannah 125–6
Springsteen, Bruce 114, 180, 198, 200, 209–10, 282

Starr, Ringo 285
Status Quo 310
Stereo MC's 56–8
Stevens, Cat 295
Stewart, Dave 61, 108, 284–6, 346
Stewart, Rod 13, 359
Sting 284, 286, 287–8, 288, 289, 290, 291, 292
Stipe, Michael 71, 81
Stoke-on-Trent 350
Stone, Joss 285
Stone Roses, the 37
Stranglers, the 310
Strawberry Switchblade 9, 10–11
Suede 89
Sugarcubes, the 326, 327–8
Summer, Donna 105, 107
Summers, Andy 287
Sunderland 268
Supernaturals, the 83
Switzerland 189–90, 193

Take That 126, 350–2
Talking Heads 38, 148, 171
Teardrop Explodes, the 83
Tears for Fears 284
Techniques, the 106
Tenpole Tudor 251–2, 266, 267–8, 270
Thatcher, Margaret 68, 72, 215, 258
Three Lads, the 118
Throwing Muses 226
Tikaram, Tanita 246
Tin Machine 224
Topanga Canyon 196, 200
Tourette, Dirk 160, 162
Tourette, Donny (Patrick Brannan) 160–7
Towers of London 160–5, 166, 167
Townsend, Pete 310
Transvision Vamp 146, 147–9
Tudor-Pole, Ed 265–71
Tyler, Bonnie 52
Tyler, Steven 193

U2 14, 65, 182, 183, 186, 312

Ultravox 312
Ure, Midge 312

Vega, Suzanne 228, 244–8
Venice 6
Verve, the 89
Voice of the Beehive 83

Wainwright, Loudon III 320
Wainwright, Martha 322
Wainwright, Rufus 103, 319–25
Waite, Freddie 106
Waite, Patrick 107
Ward, Shayne 159
Warhol, Andy 263
Warwick, Dionne 68, 114
Washington, Geno 336
Washington DC 106
Weinstein, Harvey 320
Weisbrodt, Jörn 324–5
Weller, Paul 68–9, 215
Wener, Louise 80
Westlife 121
Weymouth, Tina 38, 39
Whalley, Allan 258–64
Wham! 310
Whiteread, Rachel 6
Who, the 21, 23
Wilco 74
Williams, Robbie 45, 100–3, 126, 128, 350–61
Wills, Juliet 73, 75
Wilson, Brian 87, 355
Winehouse, Amy 15
Winterbottom, Michael 44
Wirral, the 87
Wogan, Terry 140
Wonder, Stevie 105, 108, 345
Wynette, Tammy 365

Yoko Ono 49
Young, Neil 174

Zodiac Mindwarp 83
Zoo Records 5, 83